DO NOT REMOVE
CARDS FROM POCKET

ALLEN COUNTY PUBLIC LIBRARY

FORT WAYNE, INDIANA 46802

You may return this book to any agency, branch,
or bookmobile of the Allen County Public Library.

DEMCO

➤ In a Shattered Mirror

➤ In a Shattered Mirror

The Later Poetry of Anna Akhmatova

Susan Amert

Stanford University Press
Stanford, California
1992

Stanford University Press
Stanford, California
© 1992 by the Board of Trustees of the
Leland Stanford Junior University
Printed in the United States of America

CIP data are at the end of the book

To Sasha Lehrman

Preface

This book is devoted to the later, post-1935 poetry of Anna Akhmatova (1889–1966), which has received, with the exception of *Poem Without a Hero,* surprisingly little critical attention. The later poetry differs radically from the sublimely transparent lyrical miniatures of the early period, most strikingly in its manifest difficulty and complexity, in its often self-conscious opacity. The main reason for the difficulty of the later poetry is its saturation with literary quotations and allusions, and a major focus of this study is the complex role played in Akhmatova's poetics by these references. In contrast to the relative lyrical homogeneity of the early period, the later poetry is very diverse, featuring lengthy elegies and playful odes, innovative narrative poems and poetic cycles, as well as an array of disparate dictions and tones—ranging from bitter invective to a coldly distanced irony to what could be called an otherworldly lyricism. At the same time, the relatively unified image of the lyrical persona in the early verse is fragmented in the later period into a multiplicity of masks and guises.

I am mainly interested in the poetics of the later work, which I approach through close readings of major texts, and everything that bears on the creation of a given text I consider relevant to its interpretation. The poetics of Akhmatova's later work was shaped by sociopolitical, moral-philosophical, and religious concerns, no less than by aesthetic ones, and one of my aims has been to illuminate the multifaceted relations of these poems to both the sociopolitical context and the literary tradition to which they belong. A respect for the integrity of both the texts and their author has in-

spired me throughout; no modern-day sophist has persuaded me of
its irrelevance.

I am grateful to the University of Delaware for generously providing a grant to Stanford University Press to cover the costs of the
Cyrillic typesetting, and to Richard Zipser, chair of the Department
of Foreign Languages and Literatures, for his support. Many
people contributed to the writing of this book, and several of them
deserve special mention. My interest in Akhmatova stems from a
1977 Yale graduate seminar on Acmeism taught by Omry Ronen
that introduced me to what Osip Mandelstam called the "vypuk-
laia radost' uznavaniia"/"convex joy of recognition." This book is
an outgrowth of my dissertation, written under the direction of
Victor Erlich, and it still bears traces of his wise counsel. I am particularly indebted to Stephanie Sandler, who read and commented
on drafts of most of this text over the years and alerted me to several key Pushkinian references in Akhmatova; she also generously
shared with me the Akhmatova-related results of a visit to Soviet
archives.

Susanne Fusso contributed in a variety of ways to the writing of
this book, and her unflagging enthusiasm for it over the years and
her expert margaritas under the pear tree brightened many a dark
moment. Chapter 3 owes a special debt to Catherine Ciepiela of
Amherst College, as does the *Sweetbrier* chapter to Kay Amert for
her spirited response to it. Robert Jackson, a faithful supporter of
this project from its inception, read a number of drafts of the book
and gave me many helpful suggestions. My thanks are due to Tomas Venclova and Sergei Davydov for their comments on parts of
this text, and to Vladimir Alexandrov, who gave the entire manuscript a careful reading. I also benefited from the questions and
comments of the Yale graduate students who took my 1988 seminar on Akhmatova, especially John Sobolewski, Diana Senechal,
and Nancy Andersen. The Akhmatova Centennial Conference at
Bellagio, Italy, in June 1989, organized by Sonia Ketchian, gave me
the opportunity to discuss Akhmatova's work with leading specialists in the field, including Roman Timenchik, who kindly answered
for me several otherwise unanswerable questions about Akhmato-

va's life, archives, and poems. I am deeply grateful to Helen Tartar of Stanford University Press for her steadfast interest in this project over the years. Finally, my debt to Sasha Lehrman is in a category of its own: he eagerly read every draft of every part of this book, and his creative and informed responses helped in many ways to shape the book's final form.

The first portion of chapter 2 appeared in the article "Akhmatova's 'Song of the Motherland': Rereading the Opening Texts of *Rekviem*" (*Slavic Review* 49 [1990]: 374–89). Portions of chapter 3 were published in condensed form in the *Akhmatova Centennial Volume: Papers from the Akhmatova Centennial Conference Held at the Bellagio Study and Conference Center, June, 1989,* edited by Sonia I. Ketchian (Berkeley, Calif.: Berkeley Slavic Specialties, 1991).

S. A.

Contents

➤ In a Shattered Mirror

Chapter 1

Secrets of the Craft

Без тайны нет стихов.
Without mystery there is no poetry.
—Anna Akhmatova

Нет лирики без диалога.
There is no lyric poetry without dialogue.
—Osip Mandelstam

Akhmatova's 1947 essay on Alexander Pushkin's *Stone Guest* begins with a discussion of Pushkin's fall from grace with his reading public in the later years of his life. At first, she writes, Pushkin was adored by his contemporaries, but around 1830 they recoiled from him because of the profound change in his writing:

The reason for this lies above all in Pushkin himself. He had changed. Instead of *The Prisoner of the Caucasus*, he writes *The Little House in Kolomna*; instead of *The Fountain of Bakhchisarai—The Little Tragedies*, then *The Golden Cockerel, The Bronze Horseman*. His contemporaries were perplexed, his enemies and enviers exulted. His friends kept silent.[1]

She then cites Pushkin's own remarks on the subject, including an excerpt from a draft of his 1830 article on Evgenii Baratynskii, a poet who had likewise fallen into disfavor with his readers in the late 1820's:

The concepts, the feelings of an eighteen-year-old poet are near and dear to everyone, young readers understand him and ecstatically recognize in his works their own feelings and thoughts, expressed clearly, vividly, and harmoniously. But the years go by, the young poet matures, his talent grows, the concepts become more lofty, the feelings change. His songs are no longer the same. But the readers remain the same and if anything are only colder of heart and more indifferent to the poetry of life.[2]

According to Akhmatova, Pushkin is actually developing here the ideas of Baratynskii himself, ideas set forth in an 1828 letter to Pushkin. Baratynskii was writing with reference to the failure of the later chapters of *Eugene Onegin* with Pushkin's readers:

I think that here in Russia a poet can count on great success only in his first, immature experiments. All young people support him, finding in him almost their own feelings, almost their own thoughts. . . . The poet develops, writes with great thoughtfulness, with great profundity: he's boring to officers, and brigadiers won't accept him, because his poetry all the same is not prose.[3]

By revealing Pushkin's indebtedness to Baratynskii, Akhmatova implicitly demonstrates that in the essay Pushkin is actually writing as much about himself as about Baratynskii. Similarly, in exploring Pushkin's relations with his readers, Akhmatova is at the same time writing obliquely about herself—about the profound change in her poetry and the concomitant change in her relations with her readers. Her career conformed to the pattern described in her essay on Pushkin. In the later years, instead of the lyric miniatures of *Chetki* (*Beads*, 1914) and *Belaia staia* (*White Flock*, 1917), she wrote the monumental, highly opaque *Poema bez geroia* (*Poem Without a Hero*, 1940–66) and a series of large verse cycles, including *Severnye elegii* (*The Northern Elegies*) and *Shipovnik tsvetet* (*The Sweetbrier Blooms*).

Hinting at the change in her poetry's reception, toward the beginning of the *Stone Guest* essay Akhmatova quotes a passage from the eighth chapter of *Eugene Onegin* describing the change in the reception of Pushkin's work in the late 1820's:

И альманахи, и журналы,
Где поученья нам твердят,
Где нынче так меня бранят,
А где такие мадригалы
Себе встречал я иногда.[4]

both "almanacs" and magazines
where sermons into us are drummed,
where I'm today abused so much
but where *such* madrigals
to me addressed I met with now and then.[5]

Akhmatova does not comment on these lines, for it is well known that Pushkin is contrasting the ecstatic reception of his first works with the outpouring in 1829 and 1830 of negative reviews of his latest work, including *Poltava*, *Count Nulin*, and the seventh chapter of *Eugene Onegin*. Iurii Lotman has summed up the situation as follows: "The unification of such disparate, in essence mutually antagonistic critics as Bulgarin, Grech, Nadezhdin, and Polevoi, in their common condemnation of Pushkin's poetry, turned the criticism of 1829–1830 into the journalistic persecution of the poet."[6] In quoting these lines from *Eugene Onegin*, Akhmatova is indirectly alluding to her own situation in 1947: in the aftermath of the August 14, 1946, resolution of the Communist Party, she was being viciously persecuted in the Soviet press. Branding her poetry as anachronistic and ideologically harmful,[7] the resolution censured two Leningrad literary journals, *Zvezda* (Star) and *Leningrad*, for publishing her poetry in the 1940's; *Leningrad* was shut down, but *Zvezda* survived to join the chorus of abuse.

In the phrase *takie madrigaly* (such madrigals), Pushkin refers to the ecstatic reception in the early 1820's of his first narrative poems, such as *Ruslan and Liudmila* and *The Prisoner of the Caucasus*.[8] Akhmatova's early work similarly enjoyed extraordinary success. With the appearance of her first book, *Vecher* (*Evening*, 1912), she was declared a major new literary talent,[9] and the publication of her next two collections, *Beads* (1914) and *White Flock* (1917), brought her general recognition as one of Russia's leading poets. In the years immediately following the revolution, two more collections were published, *Podorozhnik* (*Plantain*, 1919) and *Anno Domini MCMXXI* (1922), but the critical reception of her work, particularly in the early 1920's, was mixed, ranging from admiring scholarly monographs to excoriating ideological attacks.[10] On the whole, the "madrigals" ended in the mid-1920's, for by then Akhmatova had effectively been dismissed by Marxist critics as a vestige of the past. Furthermore, from 1925 to 1940 none of Akhmatova's poetry was published in the Soviet Union, the result, she claimed, of a secret Communist Party Central Committee resolution banning her work from print.[11] The years from the mid-1920's to the mid-1930's have usually been called her "period of silence" because Akhmatova wrote relatively few poems during that time. The poet herself in later years publicly insisted that this was instead a period of her silencing by the authorities, and she adamantly denied that she ever quit writing poetry as, for instance, in the autobiographical sketch "Korotko o sebe"/"Briefly about Myself": "Ia ne perestavala pisat' stikhi" (*S*, 1: 47)/"I did not stop writing poems." In one of her notebooks, however, Akhmatova pinpoints 1936 as the year when she started writing again.[12] When she did, her songs, to borrow Pushkin's phrase, were no longer the same. Akhmatova described the change in her work in similar terms in one of her notebook entries: "no pocherk u menia izmenilsia, golos uzhe zvuchit po-drugomu."[13]/"but my handwriting has changed, my voice sounds different now."

In the excerpts quoted above, Pushkin and Baratynskii conceive of the change in a poet's style as a natural development. The change in Akhmatova's voice was far from natural. Marina Tsvetaeva, in an essay called "Poets with a History and Poets Without a History," identified Akhmatova as one of the latter—quintessentially lyric poets whose style is fully developed in their very first poems.[14] Such poets do not, in Tsvetaeva's view, develop or mature. Poets "with a history," by contrast, go through many phases and are typically poets of themes (Goethe and Pushkin are prime examples).[15] Akhmatova may have been born a "poet without a history," but the cataclysmic events she lived through—particularly the Russian revolution and its aftermath—transformed her into a "poet with a history." The opening of the fifth Northern Elegy expresses it well:

> Меня, как реку,
> Суровая эпоха повернула.[16]

> I, like a river,
> Have been turned by the harsh epoch.

The reference is to the postrevolutionary penchant for modifying and controlling nature, for instance, by changing the course of rivers or by altering the climate of a region. In the elegy Akhmatova is referring to her life, but the image nevertheless aptly expresses the change effected in her poetry.

A late autobiographical fragment gives Akhmatova's own account of that history, defining the change in her work from the early to the later period:

Итак поздняя А[хматова] выходит из жанра «любовного дневника» («Четки»)—жанра, в кот[ором] она не знает соперников и кот[орый] она оставила, м[ожет] б[ыть], даже с некоторым сожалением и оглядкой, и переходит на раздумья о роли и судьбе поэта, о ремесле, на легко набросанные широкие полотна. Появляется острое ощущение истории.[17]

Thus the later A[khmatova] leaves the genre of the "erotic diary" (*Beads*)—a genre in which she knows no rivals and which she left, perhaps, even with some regret and a backward glance, and switches to meditations on the role and fate of the poet, on the craft, to lightly sketched, broad canvases. A keen sense of history emerges.

The abandonment of the early manner is viewed as an egress from the confines of the early style, which is defined in terms of a single genre—the "erotic diary" [*liubovnyi dnevnik*]. Whereas the word "erotic" bespeaks the primary orientation on the sentiment of love in the early lyrics, the word "diary" reflects both their confessional tone and their formal unity and coherence—the impression that together the early poems comprise a larger whole. It was precisely in the mirror of the exquisite lyrical miniatures of Akhmatova's "erotic diary" that the young poet's contemporaries "recognize[d] . . . their own feelings and thoughts," in Pushkin's phrase.

In the later period, the "erotic diary" is given up for what are termed *razdum'ia* (meditations), implying that the early poetry's relative immediacy of lyrical expression yields to a more mediated, reflective form of expression. The word *razdum'ia* likewise suggests sustained poetic discourse, signaling Akhmatova's preoccupation in the later period with larger forms, in contrast to the small forms that dominate the early work: she composes a series of longer, meditative elegies, writes larger verse cycles, and experiments freely with the narrative poem, even inventing her own genre—the *malen'kaia poema* (little narrative poem). These formal changes are accompanied by changes in thematics, where the focus shifts from love to the "role and fate of the poet." The mention of history at the end of the fragment—"A keen sense of history emerges"— identifies another of the chief thematic concerns of the later period and effectively explains the shift from love to the role and fate of the poet: historical forces intervene, impinging on the individual; the "lyrical heroine" (Boris Eikhenbaum's term) of the early books simply happens to be a poet, but in the later work the persona is first and foremost a poet, and her experiences are defined in terms of her métier.

In Pushkin's comparison of a poet's early and later work, the feelings and ideas of the young poet are "expressed clearly, vividly, and harmoniously," implying that clarity and harmony are not typical of the mature poet's work. The implicit contrast accurately sums up the relationship between the early and the later Akhmatova: not only was her early work praised precisely for its clarity and vividness ("clarity" was a frequent refrain in proto-Acmeist and Acmeist manifestoes, where it was contrasted with the vagueness of Symbolist poetry),[18] the broad appeal of the early poems was at least in part a function of their relative simplicity. By contrast, not only is the later poetry difficult, but it thematizes its own complexity and obscurity.

The crucial role of the metapoetic in the acutely self-conscious later work is alluded to in the first prose fragment cited above, which singles out as a central theme the poet's *remeslo* (craft).[19] The second part of *Poem Without a Hero* is largely metapoetic in nature, as is *Tainy remesla* (*Secrets of the Craft*), one of the major later lyrical cycles consisting of ten poems written between 1936 and 1960.[20] The cycle's title is highly revealing, for the word *remeslo* (craft) is redolent of the poetics of the Acmeists, who conceived of the poet as craftsman, as maker of the poetic text. The word *taina*, by contrast, recalls Symbolist poetics, for it embraces the same spectrum of meanings and connotations as both "secret" and "mystery" together, ranging from that which is hidden to that which cannot be penetrated by reason but can be known through faith or by divine revelation. The religious connotations of the latter recall the Russian Symbolists' view of the poet as theurgist (*pontifex*) possessing and revealing higher knowledge. Akhmatova's secrets, however, cannot be contained in the stale, borrowed imagery of the Symbolists. She creates her own symbols afresh, out of words that often seem plain and prosaic, as if overheard from ordinary speech. Hers are "secrets," not ritual-bound "mysteries" (*tainstva*), and she flaunts them by speaking in paradoxes, teasing the reader with familiar, colloquial lines such as "doroga ne skazhu kuda" (*SP*, 251)/"the road that goes I won't say where"; "chto-to, o chem teper' ne nado vspominat'" (*SP*, 331)/"something that should not be recalled now"; "ia znaiu druguiu prichinu,/O nei my s toboi ne prochtem" (*SP*, 302)/"I know another reason,/But you and I will not read about it," all too familiar to Akhmatova's Russian readers from their own secretive lives. The Formalist notion of *obnazhenie priema* (the baring of the device)[21] aptly describes the poet's technique here: the device of concealment is oxymoronically being laid bare.[22]

Akhmatova's flaunting of her use of concealment reaches an apogee in the beginning of "Bol'shaia ispoved'" ("A Great Confession"), written in the 1960's:

Позвольте скрыть мне всё: мой пол и возраст,
Цвет кожи, веру, даже день рожденья
И вообще всё то, что можно скрыть.

(S, 3: 503)[23]

Allow me to conceal everything: my sex and age,
Skin color, faith, even day of birth,
And generally everything that can be concealed.

Confessions typically begin by professing the intention to reveal everything about the author. Akhmatova disappoints the expectations raised by the title of the text and begins her "Great Confession" with the request that she be permitted "to conceal everything" about herself. Ironically, everything that she asks to conceal is in fact universally well known. Concealment is not simply laid bare here, it serves as the basis for a spirited parody of the genre of the confession.

The title "A Great Confession" harks back to Akhmatova's early poetry, which was largely confessional in tone, but not self-consciously so—that is, the early lyrics do not thematize their confessional nature. Nevertheless, though the early poems disclose to the reader the persona's experiences and emotions, they rely to a great extent on concealing information from the reader. In his 1925 study of Akhmatova's stylistics, Viktor Vinogradov demonstrates how much the early poetry leaves unspoken: in keeping with the diary-like format, the lyrical persona refers to people, events, places, and things known only to herself and her addressee, as well as to a narrow circle of intimate friends. This creates, according to Vinogradov, an aura of mystery around individual details, intensifying for the reader their emotional charge.[24] Paradoxically, the prevailing spirit of intimacy ensures that the reader is denied apparently important information such as the identity of a given text's addressee.

The young Akhmatova also intentionally obscured the connections between her private life and her poetry. In assembling collections of poems, she would disrupt the sequence in which they were written. Instead of creating cycles of poems addressed to a single individual, she would abstain from grouping such poems together.[25] On occasion she even supplied her poems with false dedications. Lidiia Chukovskaia records a telling instance of this in her memoirs of Akhmatova: the poet told her in 1955 that she falsely dedicated the 1922 lyric "Kak mog ty, sil'nyi i svobodnyi" (*SP*, 158)/"How could you, strong and free" to Vladimir Shileiko, her second husband, to "put an end to gossip."[26] True to her penchant for mystification, Akhmatova refrained from telling Chukovskaia the name of the actual addressee, thereby creating through her confession a new mystery. Similarly, in a prose note to *Poem Without a Hero*, authorial secrets are oxymoronically equated with the author's confessions: "Thus, this sixth page . . . became the repository of these authorial secrets (confessions)."[27] With the publication in 1922 of her fifth collection of poems, *Anno Domini MCMXXI*, yet another technique for obscuring the relations between a given text and the extratextual domain emerges: Akhmatova altered the dates of some of her poems when preparing them for publication. The initial impetus for doing this was to mask the import of poems written in response to the execution of the poet Nikolai Gumilev, Akhmatova's first husband, in August 1921. Gumilev was shot for treason, along with sixty other men and women, for allegedly participating in the Tagantsev conspiracy against the Bolsheviks.[28] The poem "Ne byvat' tebe v zhivykh" ("It is not for you to remain alive") was published in *Anno Domini MCMXXI* with the date of 1914, associating the death of the addressee with the beginning of World War I. In *Beg vremeni* (*The Flight of Time*, 1965), the date was corrected to read 1921, clarifying the lyric's reference to Gumilev's death.[29]

This repertory of techniques served Akhmatova in good stead later in her career. When she emerged from her "period of silence" in the far from "vegetarian" later 1930's,[30] the entire Russian nation had been forced into silence. Lyrical poetry had been discredited and virtually forbidden, and straightforward lyrical expression would result only in arrest, imprisonment, and a journey to Siberia—as it ultimately did for Osip Mandelstam, for instance. Not only was the poet herself in danger: already in 1934, Akhmatova's only son (by Nikolai Gumilev), Lev Gumilev, and her third husband, the art historian and critic Nikolai Punin, had been arrested and incarcerated; in 1937, Lev Gumilev was rearrested and eventually sent to the camps. Writing "for the drawer" (*v stol*) was not a viable alternative, given the notorious searches carried out by Stalin's security police. One option was to commit poems to memory instead of to paper: *Rekviem* (*Requiem*) was preserved in this way for some two decades by the poet and a few trusted friends. Another option was to write, but indirectly, obliquely, hinting at what could not be stated directly, enciphering forbidden content, masking dangerous references, and concealing crucial facts. The eighth poem of *Requiem*, "Prigovor" ("The Sentence"), written in 1939 in response to the sentencing of Akhmatova's son to hard labor, is a good example. The poem was first published in the journal *Zvezda* in 1940 without its title and dated 1934, so that it would be read by the censor as a typical love poem.[31]

The lyric "Cleopatra," dated February 7, 1940, treats the same events as those that inspired "The Sentence" but disguises its reference to them in a different way, by employing the literary-historical mask of the Egyptian queen:

Клеопатра

> Александрийские чертоги
> Покрыла сладостная тень.
> —Пушкин

Уже целовала Антония мертвые губы,
Уже на коленях пред Августом слезы лила...
И предали слуги. Грохочут победные трубы
Под римским орлом, и вечерняя стелется мгла.
И входит последний плененный ее красотою,
Высокий и статный, и шепчет в смятении он:
Тебя, как рабыню, в триумфе пошлет пред собою...
Но шеи лебяжьей всё так же спокоен наклон.

А завтра детей закуют. О, как мало осталось
Ей дела на свете—еще с мужиком пошутить
И черную змейку, как будто прощальную жалость,
На смуглую грудь равнодушной рукой положить.

(SP, 194)

Cleopatra

> A sweet shadow covered
> The Alexandrian palaces.
> —Pushkin

She had already kissed the dead lips of Antony,
Already shed tears on her knees before Augustus,

And the servants betrayed her. The trumpets of victory roar
Under the Roman eagle, and the evening mist is spreading.
And the last one captivated by her beauty enters,
Tall and well-built, and he whispers in confusion:
"You, like a slave . . . he will send before himself in triumph . . ."
But the slope of her swan's neck stays just as calm.

And tomorrow the children will be put in chains. O, how little is left
For her to do on earth—to joke with this man
And with an indifferent hand to place on the swarthy breast
The black snake, as if a parting act of pity.

Along with the epigraph from Pushkin's "Egipetskie nochi" ("Egyptian Nights"), the poem was published in 1940 with a second epigraph from Shakespeare's *Antony and Cleopatra*, "I am air and fire," which was subsequently removed.[32] Together the epigraphs define the provenience of Akhmatova's "Cleopatra": the story told takes as its point of departure Cleopatra's plight in the fifth act of Shakespeare's tragedy, but it also incorporates elements of Pushkin's erotic tale, writing the end of Pushkin's fragment. In 1940, the presence of the two epigraphs proclaimed the text's literariness, as did the fact that it was a sonnet and that it was written in amphibrachic pentameter, a meter highly unusual for Akhmatova. These marks of literariness obscure the threefold relevance of Akhmatova's "Cleopatra" to the poet's own situation in 1940: first, the state of captivity—elsewhere, particularly in *Requiem*, Akhmatova portrays the whole Russian nation as enslaved by Stalin; second, the reference to the impending enchainment of Cleopatra's children alludes to the arrest and imprisonment of the poet's son Lev Gumilev; and finally, the motif of Cleopatra vainly shedding tears before Augustus alludes to Akhmatova's unsuccessful attempts to win her son's freedom by petitioning high-ranking Soviet officials. Compare this line from the fifth numbered poem of *Requiem*: "Kidalas' v nogi palacha" (*S*, 1: 364)/"I threw myself at the feet of the hangman."[33]

The later poetry abounds in the masks of literary-historical and legendary heroines,[34] most frequently as mediated through art forms such as painting and opera: for example, in a 1939 lyric Akhmatova envisions herself as akin to the protesting Old Believer Morozova as painted by Surikov—being hauled away to prison on a sledge ("Ia znaiu, s mesta ne sdvinut'sia" [*S*, 3: 49]/"I know that I cannot move from this place"); in *Putem vseia zemli* (*The Way of All the Earth*, 1940), Akhmatova aligns herself with the woman of Kitezh from Rimsky-Korsakov's 1907 opera *Skazanie o nevidimom grade Kitezhe i deve Fevronii* (*The Tale of the Invisible City of Kitezh and the Maiden Fevroniia*); the mask of Virgil's Dido, with a few touches from Purcell's *Dido and Aeneas*, dominates the cycle *The Sweetbrier Blooms*. Through the stories of these heroines, the poet images her own predicament, but in contrast to "Cleopatra," in almost every case she explicitly identifies her fate with theirs. Akhmatova's first five collections are devoid of such masks. The first one appears in the lyric "Lotova zhena" ("Lot's Wife"), written in 1924, just before Akhmatova's "period of silence" began. It was originally published with an epigraph from Genesis 19: 26, in the Russian Church Slavic: "I ozresia zhena ego vspiat', i byst' stolp slan."/"But his wife looked back from behind him, and she became a pillar of salt." The lyric treats the Genesis story of the flight of Lot and his family from Sodom immediately before its destruction, but whereas the Genesis account mentions Lot's wife only in passing, Akhmatova illuminates her experience through an interior monologue psychologically motivating the fatal backward glance.

In his 1924 essay on contemporary Russian poetry, "Promezhutok" ("The Interval"), Iurii Tynianov singled out "Lot's Wife" as emblematic of Akhmatova's recent poetry, commenting: "The Bible that was lying on the table as an accessory of the room has become a source of images."[35] The reference is to these lines from a 1915 lyric:

А в Библии красный кленовый лист
Заложен на Песни Песней.

(*SP*, 94)

And in the Bible a red maple leaf
Marks the Song of Songs.

Both the Bible and the maple leaf figure here as *realia*, symbolically conveying the persona's erotic mood. The Bible is closed, and its imagery is not treated in the lyric, recalling another closed book that functions as an accessory in the early lyrics:

> Здесь лежала его треуголка
> И растрепанный том Парни.
> <div align="center">(<i>SP</i>, 27)</div>

> Here lay his three-cornered hat
> And a well-worn volume of Parny.

In "Lot's Wife," by contrast, the Bible is the source of the story told.

The change in the status of the book from "an accessory of the room" into "a source of images" prefigures the profound transformation of Akhmatova's poetics in the later period. The book, understood as verbal art or more broadly as art in general, becomes the source of two types of images: first, the complex construct of the *dramatis persona*, as witnessed in the multiplicity of masks adopted by Akhmatova in the years after *Anno Domini MCMXXI*; and second, the *chuzhoe slovo* (someone else's word), as evidenced in the seminal role of literary quotations and references in the later poetry. The early poetry is not, to be sure, devoid of literary allusions. To give but one example, again from "Smuglyi otrok brodil po alleiam"/"The swarthy youth wandered through the alleys," in the lines:

> И столетие мы лелеем
> Еле слышный шелест шагов.
> <div align="center">(<i>SP</i>, 26)</div>

> And for a century we have been cherishing
> The barely audible rustling of his footsteps.

Akhmatova is recalling Pushkin's famous poem "Vospominaniia v Tsarskom sele" ("Memories in Tsarskoe Selo," 1814):

> Здесь каждый шаг в душе рождает
> Воспоминанья прежних лет...[36]

> Here every footstep gives birth in the soul
> To recollections of bygone years . . .

In Pushkin, the word *shag* (footstep) is used fairly abstractly, with no appeal to the senses. Akhmatova brings Pushkin's *shag* to life, informing it with a new concreteness, by describing not only the sound—*shelest* (rustling)—made by Pushkin's steps, but also the very specific quality of that sound—*ele slyshnyi* (barely audible). The poem as a whole does not, however, hinge on the recognition of the literary reference.

In the later period, the role of literary quotations and references takes on pivotal importance: the identification and interpretation of literary references becomes crucial to an understanding of Akhmatova's poetry, which speaks through such echoes and allusions. The later metapoetry foregrounds the role of references, as, for instance, in the following quatrain from 1944:

> От странной лирики, где каждый шаг—секрет,
> Где пропасти налево и направо,
> Где под ногой, как лист увядший, слава,
> По-видимому, мне спасенья нет.
>
> (SP, 295)

> From these strange lyrics, where every step is a secret,
> Where chasms are to the left and to the right,
> Where underfoot, like a faded leaf, lies glory,
> Apparently, there is no salvation for me.

The first line articulates the distinctive trait of the later work: it abounds in secrets, allusions, and hints. The second line—"Gde propasti nalevo i napravo"/"Where chasms are to the left and to the right"—contains a key to those secrets, for the word *propast'* (chasm), along with its synonym *bezdna* (abyss), is one of the tropes in the later poetry for its subtextual dimension. A look into that dimension is afforded in these lines dating from 1959:

> Стихи эти были с подтекстом
> Таким, что как в бездну глядишь.
> А бездна та манит и тянет,
> И ввек не доищешься дна,
> И ввек говорить не устанет
> Пустая ее тишина.
>
> (SP, 303)

These lines came with such subtextual depths
That it is as if you were looking into an abyss.
And that abyss draws and attracts you,
And you will never search through to the bottom,
And its empty silence will never
Tire of speaking.

In Akhmatova, *podtekst* designates anything and everything that underlies the text but is not directly expressed in it, everything that the poet does not, cannot, or must not state or refer to explicitly within the text, whether it be another literary work or series of works or some other aspect of the extratextual realm. Hence the translation of *podtekst* as "subtextual depths."[37] The dominant metaphor in the lines quoted above is of the *podtekst* as a *bezdna* (abyss), a word repeated twice in the text and alluded to for a third time in the circumlocution "I vvek ne doishchesh'sia dna"/"And you will never search through to the bottom." And the primary attribute of the *bezdna* is limitlessness, which is also suggested temporally in the repetition of the word *vvek* (forever).

Akhmatova's portrayal of the subtextual domain in this text has much in common with certain well-known passages in Osip Mandelstam's critical prose. First, from the essay "Vypad" ("The Lunge," 1924):

В отличие от грамоты музыкальной, от нотного письма, например, поэтическое письмо в значительной степени представляет большой пробел, зияющее отсутствие множества знаков, значков, указателей, подразумеваемых, единственно делающих текст понятным и закономерным.[38]

In contrast to musical writing, the writing of notes, for instance, poetic writing to a significant degree represents a large blank, a gaping absence of a multitude of signs, marks, indicators, and implied things, which alone make the text comprehensible and orderly.

Akhmatova's *bezdna* (abyss) corresponds to, and possibly derives from, Mandelstam's collocation "bol'shoi probel"/"big blank" and the synonymous "ziiaiushchee otsutstvie"/"gaping absence"; compare the fixed collocation "ziiaiushchaia bezdna"/"gaping abyss," as well as Akhmatova's use of the epithet "pustoi"/"empty." Akh-

matova's paradoxical "I vvek govorit' ne ustanet/Pustaia ee tishina"/"And its empty silence will never/Tire of speaking," by contrast, harks back to the following sentences from Mandelstam's
"Razgovor o Dante" ("Conversation about Dante"): "Tsitata ne
est' vypiska. Tsitata est' tsikada. Neumolkaemost' ei svoist-
venna." [39]/"A citation is not an excerpt. A citation is a cicada. It is
characterized by not falling silent." Whereas Mandelstam in this
instance is talking specifically about references within the literary
work to other texts, Akhmatova makes this *neumolkaemost'* (the
trait of not falling silent) an attribute of the "empty silence" of the
abyss: "I vvek govorit' ne ustanet/Pustaia ee tishina."/"And its
empty silence will never/Tire of speaking."

In her metapoetic utterances of the later period, Akhmatova constantly foregrounds this aspect of her poetics. Thus she defines poetry as "Odna velikolepnaia tsitata" (*SP*, 298)/"One magnificent
quotation," a definition that is a partial quotation: Akhmatova is
echoing a line from Gumilev's "Orel" ("The Eagle"): "Ego velikolepnaia mogila"/"His magnificent grave." [40] The First Dedication of
Poem Without a Hero is addressed to Osip Mandelstam and
abounds in allusions to his poetry. [41] The initial lines of the First
Dedication proclaim that the text is being written on the addressee's draft—that is, the text is a palimpsest:

> ...а так как мне бумаги не хватило,
> Я на твоем пишу черновике.
> И вот чужое слово проступает
> $$(S, 2: \text{101})$$

> . . . and since I didn't have enough paper,
> I am writing on your draft.
> And here someone else's word shows through

Instead of identifying the word that shows through as the addressee's, Akhmatova uses the indefinite "chuzhoe slovo"/"someone
else's word," in recognition of the crucial role of literary references
in Mandelstam's work. Elsewhere in *Poem Without a Hero*, Akhmatova underscores the presence of literary references in the work
by predicting that she will be accused of plagiarism ("Obviniat v

plagiate" [*S*, 2: 126]); compare her confession in the fourth poem of *Secrets of the Craft*, "Poet" ("The Poet," 1959): "Nalevo beru i napravo" (*SP*, 203)/"I take from the left and from the right." Akhmatova's incorporation of quotations from and allusions to other Russian and Western European writers accomplishes what Iurii Levin et al. have defined as the chief project of Akhmatova and Mandelstam after the revolution—the preservation of the cultural tradition.[42]

In large part, meaning is encoded in the later poetry through literary quotations and references. The constant emphasis on the role of concealment and secrets in the later metapoetry challenges the reader to decipher those texts, to uncover their deeper levels of meaning, to recognize literary references and come to terms with their significance. This book has been written in response to that challenge, and it reads key later texts by identifying crucial literary references, allusions, and echoes and interpreting their significance.[43] The poet's warning to her readers—"you will never search through to the bottom"—is not meant to discourage interpretation; rather, it asserts the fundamental open-endedness and infinite allusiveness of the later poetry.[44] The same notion is expressed in *Poem Without a Hero*'s "Vmesto predisloviia" ("Instead of a Fore-word"): "Nikakikh tret'ikh, sed'mykh, dvadtsat' deviatykh smyslov poema ne soderzhit" (*S*, 2: 100)/"The poem does not contain any third, seventh, or twenty-ninth meanings." Accordingly, the analyses and interpretations presented here do not presume to be exhaustive. They do, however, illuminate the pivotal role of literary reminiscences in the later poetry.

Of particular importance among these references are those to Akhmatova's own poetry, that is, her self-reminiscences. The early studies by Vinogradov, Eikhenbaum, and Viktor Zhirmunskii all emphasized the limited scope of Akhmatova's poetic lexicon. Through repetition, the elements of her vocabulary carry with them specific associations and nuances accrued through previous usage, attaining what approaches the expressiveness of symbols.[45] In the later poetry, the poet's attitude toward the elements of her vocabulary becomes bolder, more ironic and self-conscious. Particularly typical of the later poetry is the inversion, reversal, or negation of elements of the poetic lexicon, as demonstrated in these lines from a posthumously published lyric:

> Увы! лирический поэт
> Обязан быть мужчиной,
> Иначе все пойдет вверх дном
> До часа расставанья—
> И сад—не сад, и дом—не дом,
> Свиданье—не свиданье.
>
> (*SP*, 316)

> Alas! the lyric poet
> Is obliged to be a man,
> Otherwise everything turns upside down
> Until the hour of parting—
> And the garden is not a garden, the house is not a house,
> The rendezvous is not a rendezvous.

The initial lines parody Nikolai Nekrasov's prophetic dictum "Poetom mozesh' ty ne byt',/No grazhdaninom byt' obiazan."[46]/"You may not be a poet,/But you are obliged to be a citizen." The words *sad* (garden), *dom* (house), and *svidan'e* (rendezvous) are crucial elements of the early Akhmatova's lyrical lexicon, elements that define the poetic universe of the early poetry. In the text quoted above, however, they are defined through their negation, bespeaking, in the first place, estrangement and alienation, and signaling the conversion of presence into absence, of code into anticode. The final two lines above are evocative of the transmogrification of Russian life after the revolution, and each of the negated elements is associated with a major theme in the later poetry: the devastation of the house, the destruction of the garden, and the *nevstrecha* (nonmeeting), a central image in *The Sweetbrier Blooms*. The anticode is identified specifically with the female gender, with the feminine—the realm of the irrational, the opaque, the paradoxical— and Akhmatova is playfully claiming this realm as her own.

The later lyrics abound in riddles and paradoxes, and the single paradox that best captures the essence of the later work is that of the silence that speaks, as expressed in the lines already quoted: "I vvek govorit' ne ustanet/Pustaia ee tishina."/"And its empty silence will never/Tire of speaking." The prose remarks introducing the fourth chapter of *Poem Without a Hero* conclude with the oxymoronic phrase "govorit sama Tishina" (*S*, 1: 119)/"Silence herself speaks," conjuring up the image of a personified Silence who utters the lines that follow. The lyric "Poet" ("The Poet"), in a somewhat different vein, culminates in the enigmatic confession that the poet takes "vse u nochnoi tishiny" (*SP*, 203)/"everything from the still of night." As these quotations suggest, Akhmatova's later poetry mediates between silence and speech, between muteness and voice.[47] On one level, this mediation is accomplished through literary reminiscences. By weaving into her poetry abundant literary references and allusions, Akhmatova quite literally makes the silence speak: the source texts of these references and allusions reverberate in Akhmatova's texts even though they are not explicitly articulated there. What is not directly expressed in Akhmatova's text is evoked in it through a reference to another text or series of texts in which it is named.

The *Requiem* poem "Tikho l'etsia tikhii Don" ("Quiet flows the quiet Don") saliently illustrates the workings of such references in Akhmatova. The text's penultimate line reads: "Muzh v mogile, syn v t'iurme" (*S*, 1: 363)./"[My] husband is in the grave, [my] son is in prison." Commentators have repeatedly noted the affinity of "Quiet flows the quiet Don" with folk poetry,[48] but they have missed the important literary allusion in the penultimate line. Akhmatova is echoing Pushkin's *The Fountain of Bakhchisarai* (1824), specifically the line, "Otets v mogile, doch' v plenu"[49]/"The father is in the grave, the daughter is in captivity." Through this allusion, Akhmatova is metonymically referring to the lines that immediately follow in Pushkin's text[50] to comment on the plight of her native land:

Скупой наследник в замке правит
И тягостным ярмом бесславит
Опустошенную страну.[51]

A miserly heir in the castle governs
And with an onerous yoke defames
The devastated country.

These lines constitute Akhmatova's ingeniously concealed portrait of Stalin, conveying her assessment of his rule.

The theme of silence has another, more literal significance in the later poetry as well, one bound up with Akhmatova's own predicament in society—the silencing of her voice. In the decade following the Zhdanov attack in August 1946, Akhmatova effectively ceased writing poetry. During those years she published only the cycle *Slava miru* (*Glory to Peace*, 1950), written ostensibly to glorify Stalin but in fact to appease him and thereby save the life of her son, who had been rearrested in 1949 along with Nikolai Punin and sentenced to the camps. As the following chapters will demonstrate, the theme of silence in the later poetry often serves metonymically to image the suppression of speech.

In the "Tails" portion of *Poem Without a Hero*, Akhmatova recalls her early poetry, citing two of the early collections by name:

Я—тишайшая, я—простая,
«Подорожник», «Белая стая»...
Оправдаться...но как, друзья?

(*S*, 2: 126)

I am the quietest, I am simple,
Plantain, White Flock . . .
To justify myself . . . but how, my friends?

These lines emphasize how different *Poem Without a Hero* is from two of the early collections (*Plantain* was published in 1921, *White Flock* in 1917). Akhmatova's directly addressing her readers here constitutes a radical departure from the poetics of the early work, in which the addressee is usually the poet's beloved but never the reader per se. Just as Pushkin's readers were perplexed by the change in his work, Akhmatova's readers were bewildered by the change in hers. *Poem Without a Hero* inspired the most controversy and resistance. Some readers, troubled by the opacity of the work, advised the author to make it more comprehensible.[52] Others rejected it altogether, as Akhmatova writes with considerable irony in "Iz pis'ma k N" ("From a Letter to N"): "Others, especially women, considered *Poem Without a Hero* to be a betrayal of some former 'ideal,' and what is even worse, the unmasking of my pristine poems of *Chetki/Beads*, which they 'loved so much' " (*S*, 2: 98). Akhmatova then gives another description of the radical change in her relations with her readers: instead of a "stream of syrup" ("vmesto potoka patoki"), she met with "true indignation" (*S*, 2: 98) for the first time in her career. Yet the poet seems to delight in her readers' indignation, for she pointedly refuses to change what she has written, quoting Pilate's words from John 19: 22: " 'Ezhe pisakh—pisakh' " (*S*, 2: 100)/" 'What I have written I have written.' "

By explicitly incorporating into her later work the theme of its reception, of the reader's response to it,[53] Akhmatova projects a new relationship between reader and text, one that demands the reader's active involvement in deciphering the text. This is a difficult quest, but one offering incalculable rewards, as Akhmatova herself suggests in the 1959 lyric "Chitatel' " ("The Reader").[54] Standing at the very center of *Secrets of the Craft*, the poem contains the key to the later Akhmatova's conception of the relations between poet, reader, and text:

Читатель

Не должен быть очень несчастным
И, главное, скрытным. О нет!
Чтоб быть современнику ясным,
Весь настежь распахнут поэт.

И рампа торчит под ногами,
Все мертвенно, пусто, светло,
Лайм-лайта холодное пламя
Его заклеймило чело.

А каждый читатель как тайна,
Как в землю закопанный клад,

Пусть самый последний, случайный,
Всю жизнь промолчавший подряд.

Там все, что природа запрячет,
Когда ей угодно, от нас,
Там кто-то беспомощно плачет
В какой-то назначенный час.

И сколько там сумрака ночи,
И тени, и сколько прохлад,
Там те незнакомые очи,
До света со мной говорят,

За что-то меня упрекают
И в чем-то согласны со мной...
Так исповедь льется немая,
Беседы блаженнейший зной.

Наш век на земле быстротечен
И тесен назначенный круг.
А он неизменен и вечен—
Поэта неведомый друг.

(SP, 203–4)

The Reader

He shouldn't be very unhappy,
Or, most important, secretive. O no!
To be clear to his contemporary,
The poet is opened up wide.

And the footlights protrude underfoot,
All is deathly, empty, and bright,
The cold flame of the limelight
Has branded his brow.

But every reader is like a secret,
Like a treasure buried in the earth,
Even if it be the very last, accidental one,
Who was silent his whole life through.

There is everything there that nature,
When it suits her, hides from us.

There someone helplessly weeps
At some appointed hour.

And how much darkness of night is there,
And shadow, and how much coolness,
There those unfamiliar eyes
Speak with me until it is light,

Reproaching me for something,
And agreeing with me about something . . .
Thus the mute confession flows,
The most blessed heat of conversation.

Our age on earth is fleeting,
And narrow is the appointed circle,
But he is unchanging, eternal—
The poet's unknown friend.

"The Reader" unexpectedly begins with a description not of the reader but of the poet; the focus turns to the reader only in the third stanza of the text. The tone of the initial quatrain is highly ironic: the notion that the poet should conceal nothing is contradicted in all of Akhmatova's later work. The rationale given for the interdiction on secretiveness—that the poet should "be clear to his contemporary"—recalls the demands made on Russian poets throughout the modern age: nineteenth-century editors and critics demanded clarity from writers (compare Pushkin's use of the word "clear" to describe the popular style of young poets), as did their postrevolutionary counterparts, the zealous overseers of the doctrine of Socialist Realism, which requires that the writer's "message" be both ideologically correct and accessible to the broad masses. The first two lines of "The Reader" recall the beginning of Valerii Briusov's 1907 lyric "Poetu" ("To the Poet"), which lays a very different burden on the poet:[55]

Ты должен быть гордым, как знамя;
Ты должен быть острым, как меч;
Как Данту, подземное пламя
Должно тебе щеки обжечь.[56]

You must be proud, like a banner;
You must be sharp, like a sword;
The subterranean flame must burn
Your cheeks, like Dante's.

Briusov's view of the poet is antithetical to that sketched in the first stanza of "The Reader": the poet must be true to his higher calling, utterly disregarding the views of his contemporaries. For Briusov, it is the poet's lot to suffer, as underscored in lines 3–4 above, as well as in the last two lines of the poem: "I pomni: ot veka iz ternii/ Poeta zavetnyi venok." [57]/ "And remember: the cherished wreath of the poet is forever made of thorns." This is in striking contrast to Akhmatova's poet, who is not supposed to be "very unhappy." [58]

The irony subsides in the second stanza of "The Reader," which develops the notion that the poet must bare all through the metaphor of the poet as an actor standing alone upon a brightly lit stage, recalling Shakespeare's dictum "All the world's a stage" (*As You Like It*, 2.7), an image that ultimately goes back to Epictetus and the Stoics. [59] Akhmatova is specifically alluding to a well-known Russian text that takes the same metaphor as its point of departure—Boris Pasternak's "Gamlet" ("Hamlet"), one of the poems of *Doctor Zhivago*:

Гамлет

Гул затих. Я вышел на подмостки.
Прислонясь к дверному косяку,
Я ловлю в далеком отголоске
Что случится на моем веку.

На меня наставлен сумрак ночи
Тысячью биноклей на оси.
Если только можно, Авва Отче,
Чашу эту мимо пронеси.

Я люблю Твой замысел упрямый
И играть согласен эту роль.
Но сейчас идет другая драма,
И на этот раз меня уволь.

Но продуман распорядок действий,
И неотвратим конец пути.
Я—один, всё тонет в фарисействе.
Жизнь прожить—не поле перейти.⁶⁰

Hamlet

The roar died down. I stepped out onto the stage.
Leaning against the door frame,
I try to catch in the distant echo
What will happen in my age.

The darkness of night is aimed at me
Like a thousand binoculars.
If it is only possible, Abba, Father,
Carry this cup past me.

I love your stubborn conception
And agree to play this role.
But now another drama is going on,
And this time let me go.

But the order of the acts has been thought through
And the end of the road is irreversible.
I am alone, everything drowns in Pharisaism.
To live life through is not a simple thing.

From the stage of a theater, Pasternak's lyrical persona quotes Jesus' prayer in the Garden of Gethsemane. Akhmatova echoes Pasternak's conception in "Hamlet" of the poet's Christ-like role in society by mentioning the poet's "branded brow" (line 8). As retrospectively illuminated by the latter phrase, the first stanza's concluding words "raspakhnut poet"/"the poet is opened up" call to mind the phonologically similar and grammatically parallel phrase "raspiat poet"/"the poet is crucified." ⁶¹

Akhmatova's "A skol'ko tam sumraka nochi" (line 17)/"And how much darkness of night is there" contains another allusion to Pasternak's "Hamlet," namely to the lines "Na menia nastavlen sumrak nochi/Tysiach'iu binoklei na osi."/"The darkness of night is aimed at me/Like a thousand binoculars." Conjuring up the darkened theater, these lines metonymically represent the poet's spectators through the image of binoculars menacingly aimed directly at the poet. The audience in Akhmatova's "Reader" occupies the same space as Pasternak's spectators, a space filled by the "darkness of night." But while that darkness threatens Pasternak's persona, in Akhmatova it is intriguing, attractive, and highly valued, for it conceals the poet's readers, each of whom is likened to a "secret" and to buried treasure. And whereas Pasternak dispenses with the poet's spectators in just two lines, Akhmatova devotes a full four stanzas to them, describing in detail what is hidden by the "darkness of night," depicting their experience as readers. It is this that Pasternak, wholly engrossed in the poet's drama and monologue, excludes from "Hamlet."

In the darkened theater of Akhmatova's "Reader," the poet apparently speaks while the reader remains silent. The reader is, furthermore, identified with speechlessness in the line "Vsiu zhizn' promolchavshii podriad"/"Who was silent his whole life through" —an allusion to the repressive nature of Soviet society and the silencing of the Russian people through fear. Yet the silence of the audience is broken by the sound of someone "helplessly weep[ing]." And then the poet perceives in the darkened hall not a thousand binoculars but the actual eyes of the reader, a striking contrast to Pasternak's dehumanizing metonymy, particularly given the traditional symbolism of the eyes as the windows of the soul. Far from threatening the poet, the reader's eyes communicate with the poet: "Tam te neznakomye ochi/Do sveta so mnoi govoriat" (lines 19–20)/"There those unfamiliar eyes/Speak with me until it is light."

Later in the text (line 24) this exchange between poet and reader is called a *beseda* (conversation), a term recalling Osip Mandelstam's 1913 essay on the relationship between poet and reader, "O sobesednike" ("On the Interlocutor"). Criticizing the Symbolists for their neglect of the "interrelation" between speaker and addressee that "accompanies the speech act,"[62] Mandelstam argues that the essence of lyric poetry lies in its dialogic nature: "Net liriki bez dialoga"[63]/"Without dialogue there is no lyric poetry." Mandelstam asserts that the poet's addressee is not a concrete individual, but rather an "ideal'nyi drug-sobesednik"/"ideal friend-interlocutor," who is "neizvestnyi, no opredelennyi"/"unknown, but definite."[64] In Mandelstam's view, addressing such a reader will maximize the effectiveness of the speech act. In "The Reader," Akhmatova draws on the various ways Mandelstam describes his ideal reader: he twice characterizes his "addressee" and "interlocutor" as *tainstvennyi* (mysterious),[65] an epithet that is echoed in Akhmatova's simile: "A kazhdyi chitatel' kak taina" (line 9)/"But every reader is like a secret." Furthermore, Mandelstam's two collocations "ideal'nyi drug-sobesednik"/"ideal friend-interlocutor" and "neizvestnyi adresat"/"unknown addressee"[66] are merged by Akhmatova in the concluding line of "The Reader": "Poeta nevedomyi drug"/"The poet's unknown friend."

For all these parallels, Akhmatova significantly recasts Mandelstam's treatment of the poet's addressee, reinterpreting the nature of the dialogue between poet and reader that defines lyric poetry. In keeping with Baratynskii's notion of the "reader in posterity," Mandelstam repeatedly stresses the distance separating the poet from the ideal reader, through phrases such as "dalekii, neizvestnyi adresat"/"distant, unknown addressee" and "Skuchno peresheptyvat'sia s sosedom"/"It's boring to whisper back and forth with a neighbor,"[67] as well as in the following excerpt:

Расстояние разлуки стирает черты милого человека. Только тогда у меня возникает желание сказать ему то важное, что я не мог сказать, когда владел его обликом во всей реальной полноте.[68]

The distance of separation erases the features of a dear person. Only then does there arise in me the desire to say to him the important thing I could not say when I possessed his appearance in all of its real fullness.

Akhmatova diverges from Mandelstam by locating both the poet and the reader in the same theater—the theater of life. Except for the eyes, the reader's features are obscured by darkness so that the reader remains unknown, but nevertheless reader and poet communicate with each other. And far from being simply an auditor, Akhmatova's reader actively communes with the poet, responding to the poet's work: "Za chto-to menia uprekaiut,/I v chem-to soglasny so mnoi"/"Reproaching me for something,/And agreeing with me about something." Furthermore, the reader's innermost thoughts and feelings are expressed, albeit nonverbally: "Tak ispoved' l'etsia nemaia"/"Thus the mute confession flows." The latter line completely reverses the roles of poet and reader suggested in the opening stanzas of the lyric: here the confession is the reader's own. Akhmatova conceives of relations between poet and reader as a true dialogue, envisioning the reader's response to the poet's work, including the reader's own confession.

In Akhmatova's design, the obvious disparity in the situations of poet and reader, with the poet stage center, brightly illuminated and speaking, and the reader sitting silently in the theater, veiled in darkness, is offset by profound similarities revealed as the text unfolds. Both poet and reader are, first, utterly isolated: around the poet everything is *pusto* (empty), while the reader's isolation is expressed both in the buried treasure metaphor and in the adverb *bespomoshchno* (helplessly, line 15).[69] The notion of burial is especially germane to the description of the reader's realm: "I skol'ko tam sumraka nochi,/I teni, i skol'ko prokhlad" (lines 20–21)/"And how much darkness of night is there,/And shadow, and how much coolness.". The three attributes named—darkness, shadow, and coolness—are together suggestive of the grave, harking back to the description of the poet's surroundings as "mertvenno" (line 6)/ "deathly." What is more, the phrase "skol'ko prokhlad"/"how much coolness" recalls the epithet "kholodnoe"/"cold" ascribed to the flame that branded the poet's brow. Most important, the "dramas" being played out by poet and reader are one and the same: while the poet on stage is facing the hour of darkness, the reader is similarly confronting suffering and death: "Tam kto-to bespomoshchno plachet, / V kakoi-to naznachennyi chas" (lines 15–16)/ "There someone helplessly weeps/At some appointed hour."

These similarities are borne out in the final stanza, which explicitly links the poet and the reader: "Nash vek na zemle bystrotechen,/I tesen naznachennyi krug"/"Our age on earth is fleeting,/And narrow is the appointed circle." The lives of human beings— poets and readers alike—are brief, circumscribed by the "ap-

poets and readers alike—are brief, circumscribed by the "appointed circle," hence the close bond between poet and reader. The "beseda"/"conversation" between poet and reader "l'etsia"/"flows" without end, transcending the narrow limits of human life. What is more, that communion between poet and reader overcomes the isolation of both, providing true friendship. It overcomes the coldness from which both suffer by generating warmth, as emphasized in the phrase "Besedy blazhenneishii znoi"/"The blessed heat of conversation." The first and only image of warmth in the text, this "heat" is a source for both poet and reader not only of comfort but also of bliss, of supreme felicity (as expressed in the epithet *blazhenneishii*), signaling the transcendence of suffering and fear. Finally, the conversation between poet and reader continues "do sveta" (line 20)/"until it is light"—an ambiguous image that may be read both as until the lights come up in the theater and as until the coming of dawn and the end of night. There is the further implication, as well, that the conversation itself facilitates the coming of light.[70]

In the image of the "most blessed heat of conversation," Akhmatova is referring to a well-known passage in Mandelstam's essay "O prirode slova" ("On the Nature of the Word") that defines the role of Hellenism in the world as the "ochelovechenie okruzhaiush-chego mira, sogrevanie ego tonchaishim teleologicheskim teplom"/ "humanization of the surrounding world, its warming with the most subtle teleological warmth."[71] In Akhmatova's "Reader," this is precisely what poetry is shown to accomplish. Through the writing and reading of poetry, human suffering is transcended, and so is the ephemerality of human life: Akhmatova confers immortality on the poet's reader, in a twist on the maxim *ars longa, vita brevis*.[72] What is more, through a miraculous and unparalleled inclusiveness, Akhmatova confers this immortality on every reader: "A *kazhdyi chitatel'* kak taina"/"And *every reader* is like a secret" (emphasis added). When reading poetry, every reader partakes of eternity, overcoming the constraints and limitations of social life and transcending the narrow bounds of human existence.

Chapter 2

Akhmatova's Song of the Motherland: The Framing Texts of *Requiem*

Hostias et preces tibi,
Domine, laudis offerimus:
tu suscipe pro animabus illis,
quarum hodie memoriam facimus:
fac eas, Domine, de morte
transire ad vitam.
—The Requiem Mass

Покойный Алигьери создал
бы десятый круг ада.
The late Dante would have
created a tenth circle of hell.
—Anna Akhmatova

Akhmatova's *Requiem* is a deceptively simple piece. Compared to the opacity and self-conscious literariness of *Poem Without a Hero*, *Requiem* seems transparent, much like Akhmatova's early lyrics, and appears to demand little in the way of commentary or elucidation.[1] Its very form and scope, however, as well as the dates of its composition, 1935–61, identify it as a product of the "later Akhmatova"—the Akhmatova who resumed writing in the mid-1930's after a decade of relative poetic inactivity, the Akhmatova who created *Poem Without a Hero*. *Requiem* fully adheres to the poetics of the later work,[2] most strikingly in the salient role of intertextual references—allusions to Russian literature and the Western European literary tradition—a role that has only recently begun to be acknowledged.[3]

The workings of intertextuality in *Requiem* are a primary subject

of this chapter, which focuses on the first two texts of the *poema*[4]—
"Vmesto predisloviia" ("Instead of a Foreword"), the short prose
preface written in 1957, and the "Posviashchenie" ("Dedication"),
twenty-five lines of verse composed in March 1940. Although they
have as yet received little critical attention,[5] these texts are of pivotal importance in *Requiem*: together, they image the poet and her
addressees, defining their relations through references to Dante and
Pushkin, among others. By incorporating these allusions into *Requiem*, Akhmatova places herself in the tradition of Dante and
Pushkin, claiming their moral authority as her own. The opening
text, "Instead of a Foreword," tells the story of the genesis of *Requiem*, concomitantly elucidating its nature and purpose. The
"Dedication," which constitutes a brilliant recasting of the genre of
the "mass song," serves as the overture of *Requiem*, prefiguring the
tragic progression of the ten numbered texts and the restorative
impulse of the "Epilogue."

"Instead of a Foreword": The Tenth Circle

This laconic text sets the stage. Its power in large part stems from
the author's use of understatement; a strong tension exists between
the text's matter-of-fact narrative tone, recalling reportage, and its
subject matter. Understatement and restraint are, of course, distinctive features of Akhmatova's poetry, and despite its markedly unpoetic tone, "Instead of a Foreword" is couched in terms of Akhmatova's poetic idiom; it employs a number of devices central to
the early poetry and likewise recasts certain prominent images and
motifs. Here is the whole text:

> В страшные годы ежовщины я провела семнадцать месяцев в
> тюремных очередях в Ленинграде. Как-то раз кто-то «опознал»
> меня. Тогда стоящая за мной женщина с голубыми губами,
> которая, конечно, никогда не слыхала моего имени, очнулась от
> свойственного нам всем оцепенения и спросила меня на ухо (там
> все говорили шепотом):
> —А это вы можете описать?

И я сказала:
—Могу.
Тогда что-то вроде улыбки скользнуло по тому, что
некогда было ее лицом. (*S*, 1: 361)

In the terrible years of the Ezhov terror, I spent seventeen months in the prison lines in Leningrad. Once someone "identified" me. Then a blue-lipped woman standing behind me, who had, of course, never heard my name, came to from the torpor characteristic of us all and asked me in a whisper (everyone spoke in whispers there), "But can you describe this?"
And I said, "I can."
Then something like a smile slipped across what had once been her face.

This first-person narrative begins by identifying the historical context, seventeen months during the "terrible years of the Ezhov terror." [6] Declaring her presence in Leningrad's prison lines during that period, the author goes on to relate a specific incident that occurred. An estranged act of recognition initiates the episode: "Kak-to raz kto-to 'opoznal' menia."/"Once someone 'identified' me." The neutral verb *uznal* (recognized) is replaced here by the specialized *opoznal*, which literally means "identified," as in the judicial expression *opoznat' prestupnika* (to identify a criminal), suggesting the narrator's complicity in the crime of being closely related to an incarcerated "enemy of the nation"—a crime often sufficient during those years to result in imprisonment. The verb also figures in the forensic expression *opoznat' trup* (to identify a corpse), in keeping with the imagery of lifelessness that pervades "Instead of a Foreword." The woman behind the speaker is distinguished by her "golubye guby"/"blue lips" (replacing the customary alliteration "golubye glaza"/"blue eyes"), an emblem of lifelessness. [7] In the phrase "svoistvennoe nam vsem otsepenenie"/"torpor characteristic of us all," this deathlike condition is defined as the common bond uniting all those standing in line, for *otsepenenie* conjures up notions of paralysis, insensibility, and even rigor mortis.

The theme of lifelessness finds its ultimate development in the telling evocation of a gesture in the final sentence: "Togda chto-to vrode ulybki skol'znulo po tomu, chto nekogda bylo ee litsom."/

"Then something like a smile slipped across what had once been her face." The foregrounding of this gesture recalls the importance of gestures in Akhmatova's early poetry, their crucial role in conveying emotion.[8] Movements of the mouth and lips are particularly prominent in the early lyrics. Smiles, for instance, serve to express a range of emotions—from happiness and pleasure, to mere civility, to contempt, to intense pain and anguish. As Boris Eikhenbaum observed, movements of the lips are not merely described, they are accentuated in the sound orchestration of the poetry.[9] This reflects the special valuation of the lips in the early period: besides conveying emotion, they figure as bearers of eros (e.g., "I ulybaesh'sia, o ne odnu pchelu/Rumianaia ulybka soblaznila" [*S*, 1: 207]/"And you smile, oh, this rosy smile/Has tempted more than one bee"; note also the recurrent motif of the *potselui* [kiss]); they are integral to speech and instrumental to the creative process (as expressed, for instance, in "V to vremia ia gostila na zemle"/"At that time I was a guest on earth," the first of the *Epic Motifs*).[10] The early lyrics paint lips in shades of red and pink, connoting vitality and sensuality (cf. "Rumianaia ulybka" [*S*, 1: 207]/"[This] rosy smile"; "Eti vishnevye videt' usta" [*S*, 1: 178]/"To see those cherry lips"; "Moi rot trevozhno zaalel" [*S*, 1: 81]/"My mouth turned crimson in agitation"), or else in pale hues, to express tension or anxiety. In "Instead of a Foreword," lips are first mentioned in the phrase "zhenshchina s golubymi gubami"/"woman with blue lips," which measures the change from the world of the early poetry to the lifeless world of *Requiem*: the unprecedented epithet *golubye* (blue) suggests numbness from a lack of air or from the cold, precluding sensation and hindering movement. Devoid of eros, these lips are impaired in their ability to convey emotion, and speech itself is threatened.

The last sentence of "Instead of a Foreword" portrays a movement made by these selfsame lips: "Togda chto-to vrode ulybki skol'znulo po tomu, chto nekogda bylo ee litsom."/"Then something like a smile slipped across what had once been her face." Estrangement operates on several levels here to undermine the semiotic effectiveness of this gesture. The indefinite locution "chto-to vrode ulybki"/"something like a smile" leaves in question the actual identity of the gesture by telling what it resembles but not naming it directly. The locus of this quasi-smile is described in similarly indefinite terms; it is named by what it was formerly ("nekogda") but is no longer—the woman's face. There is a play here on the idiom "net na nei litsa," a figurative expression used to describe momentary yet drastic changes in an individual's visage caused by an intense emotional or physical shock. Literally the phrase means "there is no face on her," and it is precisely this grotesque notion which is conveyed in "Instead of a Foreword" through the use of the past tense: the state of "facelessness" dominates the present and shows no signs of passing.[11]

The notion of facelessness has ominous implications, for the face has long been valued as the incarnation of spirituality, as in Cicero's aphorism "imago animi vultus est." Russian Orthodoxy teaches that the face embodies the highest spiritual qualities and values, imaging the divine in human beings;[12] accordingly, facelessness would betoken the loss of the spirit or soul and would represent yet another sign of lifelessness. By metonymy, the word *litso* also means "individual" or "person" (compare the latter's grammatical usage); from this perspective, loss of the *litso* would symbolize a loss of individuality, of personal identity. All those standing in line are indeed shown to be depersonalized, from the blue-lipped woman to the narrator herself, for the verb *opoznat'* in the text's second sentence "identifies" the narrator's former personal identity, which no longer applies in the given context.[13] All this bespeaks the absolute devastation of the lyric realm, the domain of the *lichnoe*— the personal and the individual. And yet there is faint hope in the fleeting glimpse of something resembling a smile on that "no-longer-face," a hint, however disfigured, of a solace that is possible if their shared suffering is not ceded to oblivion—faceless and nameless horror—but described and thus remembered as a testimonial to endurance and love.

What elicits the quasi-smile is a dialogue[14] that tells the story of the genesis of *Requiem*. By narrating the origins of *Requiem*, "Instead of a Foreword" sets forth the very nature and purpose of the *poema*.[15] The faculty of speech is imperiled in this setting, and the dialogue reflects this in two ways: for fear of reprisal, it is conducted in whispers ("tam vse govorili shepotom"), and it is maximally abbreviated, consisting of just six words. Brief as it is and softly as it is uttered, the dialogue does nevertheless occur, marking a break with the prevailing state of lifelessness. Symbolically, the dialogue represents the relationship between the author and her people, for its participants are the poet and a random, anonymous woman of the people. One crucial fact about the nameless woman's relation to the poet is given: "[ona], konechno, nikogda ne slykhala moego imeni"/"[she], of course, had never heard my name." [16] This statement reflects the poet's peripheral place in society during the 1930's: her work had been barred from publication since the mid-1920's, her readership for the most part no longer existed, and her life as a poet was generally believed to be over, another level of meaning implied in the verb *opoznat'*.

An ironic reversal of the Stalinist *sotsial'nyi zakaz* (social command), the woman's query—"A eto vy mozhete opisat'?"/"But can you describe this?"—challenges the poet to render the nightmarish reality of the Ezhov terror. The challenge is a daunting one. Those standing in line resemble the dead, and the task of describing the scene recalls Dante's task in the *Inferno*, with one crucial difference: Dante visited the underworld as a living man, but in "Instead of a Foreword," the poet is an inhabitant of the deathly realm. Nevertheless, the poet emphatically proclaims her ability to carry out the task: "Mogu."/"I can." This bold assertion of her verbal powers contrasts forcefully with the omnipresent enervation and lifelessness, foreshadowing the poet's ultimate triumph over death through the writing of *Requiem*.

Dante's importance as a model for Akhmatova in *Requiem* finds confirmation in the lyric entitled "Muza" ("The Muse"), dated 1924; its final lines record an exchange between the poet and her muse: "Ei govoriu: 'Ty l' Dantu diktovala/Stranitsy Ada?' Otvechaet: 'Ia'" (*S*, 1: 230)./"I say to her, 'Was it you who dictated to Dante/The pages of the Inferno?' She answers, 'It was I.'" The resemblance of this exchange to that recorded in "Instead of a Foreword" is striking: both consist of a brief question and a one-word affirmative response. Akhmatova is underscoring that her muse is identical with Dante's, establishing a parallel between Dante's *Inferno* and what she is fated to describe.[17]

Requiem's indebtedness to the *Inferno* merits separate treatment, but two striking connections between them are germane to the present discussion. First, as Dante reveals in Canto 29, his mission is to preserve the memory of the dead "nel primo mundo," among the living.[18] As revealed in the "Epilogue," Akhmatova's aim in *Requiem* is similar—to preserve for posterity the memory of those who suffered and perished in the inferno of the Ezhov terror. Second, the condition of the women as portrayed in "Instead of a Foreword" and elsewhere in *Requiem* recalls Dante's experience in the frozen ninth circle of hell. Their *otsepenenie* (torpor), for example, echoes the evocation of Dante's numbness in Canto 33: "sì come d'un callo,/per la freddura ciascun sentimento/cessato avesse del mio viso stallo." [19] In Canto 34, Dante describes his terror upon seeing Satan: "Io non mori' e non rimasi vivo;/pensa oggimai per te, s'hai fior d'ingegno,/qual io divenni, d'uno e d'altro privo." [20] Dante's fear deprives him of life yet does not kill him, a state paralleled by the women's lifelessness in "Instead of a Foreword." The "Dedication" goes on to describe the women as "mertvykh bezdykhannei" (*S*, 1: 362)/"more breathless than the dead," a phrase that separates the women from both the living and the dead, implying that their condition is worse than that of the dead.[21] The "Dedication" also qualifies the poet's years in Leningrad's prison lines as *osatanelye*, from the root *satana* (Satan), implying that the city was under Satan's dominion during that period; the epithet could be translated as "hellish," for it bears connotations of madness, evil, and frenzy. These links with Dante's *Inferno* point back to the title of *Requiem*, illuminating Akhmatova's intention in writing it: to bring *requiem aeternam* to the victims of the Ezhov terror.

Akhmatova's Song of the Motherland

The poet's declaration of her ability "to describe this" immediately raises questions as to the form such a description could take. What poetry could adequately express the depersonalized, lifeless state of those evoked in "Instead of a Foreword"? With what voice could Akhmatova, a lyric poet par excellence, convey the devastation of the lyric domain? These questions are addressed in the "Dedication," given below in full:

Перед этим горем гнутся горы,
Не течет великая река,
Но крепки тюремные затворы,
А за ними «каторжные норы»
И смертельная тоска.
Для кого-то веет ветер свежий,
Для кого-то нежится закат—
Мы не знаем, мы повсюду те же,
Слышим лишь ключей постылый скрежет
Да шаги тяжелые солдат.
Подымались как к обедне ранней,
По столице одичалой шли,
Там встречались, мертвых бездыханней,
Солнце ниже и Нева туманней,
А надежда все поет вдали.
Приговор... И сразу слезы хлынут,
Ото всех уже отделена,
Словно с болью жизнь из сердца вынут,
Словно грубо навзничь опрокинут,
Но идет... Шатается... Одна...
Где теперь невольные подруги
Двух моих осатанелых лет?
Что им чудится в сибирской вьюге,
Что мерещится им в лунном круге?
Им я шлю прощальный свой привет.

(S, 1: 362)

Before this woe mountains bend down,
The great river does not flow,
But strong are the prison bolts,
And beyond them are the "convicts' holes"
And mortal anguish.
For someone there blows a fresh wind,
For someone a sunset luxuriates,

We do not know, we are the same everywhere,
We hear just the hateful gnashing of keys
And the soldiers' heavy tread.
We would rise as if for early mass,
Walk through the capital turned savage,
Meet there, more breathless than the dead,
The sun is lower and the Neva more misty,
But hope still sings in the distance.
The sentence . . . And immediately the tears pour,
She's already separated from everyone,
As if the life had been painfully torn from her heart,
As if she had been coarsely thrown on her back,
But she walks . . . Staggers . . . Alone . . .
Where now are the involuntary friends
Of my two hellish years?
What appears to them in the Siberian blizzard,
What seems visible to them in the lunar circle?
To them I send my farewell greetings.

The "Dedication" begins impersonally, with a powerful double image of the misfortune that has struck—"eto gore"/"this woe"— as reflected in the natural world: the mountains' bending down (line 1) vividly images catastrophe (in the sense of an unexpected, violent change in the earth's surface), while the great river's ceasing to flow (line 2) suggests that life itself has been brought to a standstill, harking back to the theme of *otsepenenie* (torpor) in "Instead of a Foreword." [22] This natural imagery recalls the rendering of disaster in the Russian epic tradition, specifically in *Slovo o polku Igoreve* (*The Lay of Igor's Campaign*) and the *Zadonshchina*, which sing of national misfortune through the anthropomorphized image of trees bowing down to the earth in sorrow. Akhmatova's choice of mountains, which is motivated by the phonological similarity between *góre* (woe) and *góry* (mountains), accentuates the immensity of the misfortune. [23]

The catastrophe proper is revealed in the evocation of the prison realm (lines 3–5). The quotation " 'katorzhnye nory' " (line 4)/ " 'convicts' holes' " puts the scene into perspective: the source is Pushkin's 1827 lyric "Vo glubine sibirskikh rud"/"In the depths of

Siberian mines," an epistle to the Decembrists sentenced to hard labor in Siberia, exhorting them to endure in the first stanza and predicting relief in the final three quatrains:

Несчастью верная сестра,
Надежда в мрачном подземелье
Разбудит бодрость и веселье,
Придет желанная пора:

Любовь и дружество до вас
Дойдут сквозь мрачные затворы,
Как в ваши каторжные норы
Доходит мой свободный глас.

Оковы тяжкие падут,
Темницы рухнут—и свобода
Вас примет радостно у входа,
И братья меч вам отдадут.[24]

Misfortune's faithful sister,
Hope in the gloomy subterranean realm
Will awaken courage and good cheer,
The desired time will come:

Love and friendship
Will reach you through the dismal bolts,
As my free voice
Enters your convicts' holes.

The heavy fetters will fall,
The dungeons will collapse, and freedom
Will receive you joyfully at the entrance,
And your brothers will return to you your swords.

Far from simply reiterating Pushkin's words, Akhmatova foregrounds the fact of quotation by supplying his collocation with quotation marks. In addition, she preserves Pushkin's rhyme "zatvory"/"nory" ("bolts"/"holes"), accentuating the importance of "In the depths of Siberian mines" to the "Dedication."

Although both texts conjure up scenes of captivity, the striking differences between them contrast Stalin's rule with that of Nicholas I a century before. Pushkin's text is dominated by the antithesis between the inner realm of captivity—bounded by the "mrachnye zatvory"/"dismal bolts"—and the outer domain of freedom, and it traces freedom's incursion into the prison in the form of the poet's "svobodnyi glas"/"free voice." It concludes by envisaging freedom's complete triumph in the prison's destruction and the liberation of those incarcerated. The "Dedication" borrows Pushkin's "zatvory"/"bolts " to demarcate its prison realm, but while "In the depths" underscores the bolts' penetrability, Akhmatova emphasizes their strength ("No krepki tiuremnye zatvory"/"But strong are the prison bolts").[25] By naming what is situated behind those bolts with Pushkin's phrase "katorzhnye nory"/"convicts' holes" or "hard-labor holes," she alludes to the *katorga* (hard labor) in prison camps awaiting those within the Leningrad prison. Whereas the prison's gloom in "In the depths" is alleviated by the presence of hope, which inspires courage and good cheer, the prison realm in the "Dedication" is dominated by "smertel'naia toska" (line 5)/ "mortal anguish," suggesting that what the prisoners face is death, not liberation, as Pushkin predicts for his addressees.[26]

The grim import of the fifth line—"I smertel'naia toska"/"And mortal anguish"—is accentuated in its truncation: the line contains four, not five, feet, violating the metrical scheme of the poem.[27] This violation, the only one of its kind in the "Dedication," is motivated in another way as well, for Akhmatova is alluding to Pushkin's 1826 "Zimniaia doroga" ("Winter Road"):

Что-то слышится родное
В долгих песнях ямщика:
То разгулье удалое,
То сердечная тоска.[28]

Something native can be heard
In the coachman's long-drawn songs:
At times bold merrymaking,
At times anguish of the heart.

The echoing of the last line in the "Dedication"'s "I smertel'naia toska"/"And mortal anguish" once again contrasts Pushkin's age with Akhmatova's. Pushkin's "dull" winter road has been transformed a century later into the road to prison, the road to Siberia. Under Stalin, not only is Russian life devoid of "razgul'e"/"merrymaking" and full of misery, it is lived in extremis, as underscored in the replacement of the epithet "serdechnaia"/"heart's" by "smertel'naia"/"mortal", a change eloquently testifying to the devastation of the lyric domain.[29]

Another key difference between the "Dedication" and "In the depths" involves the portrayal of the world outside the prison: while "In the depths" represents it as the realm of freedom, in the "Dedication" life outside the prison mirrors that within. In the first stanza, the deep sorrow of the outer world (lines 1–2) reflects the "smertel'naia toska"/"mortal anguish" within the prison. In the second stanza, the adverb "povsiudu" (line 8) in the phrase "my povsiudu te zhe"/"we are everywhere the same" blurs the distinction between those outside and inside. That the women share the prisoners' captive state is also suggested in what they hear: "Slyshim lish' kliuchei postylyi skrezhet,/Da shagi tiazhelye soldat."/ "We hear just the hateful gnashing of keys,/And the soldiers' heavy tread." The mirroring of the prison in the outside world is likewise supported by the image of Leningrad evoked in the "Dedication." The third stanza's "Po stolitse odichaloi shli" (line 12)/"[We would] walk through the capital turned savage," as Sharon Leiter has observed, harks back to the beginning of Akhmatova's 1923 lyric "Sograzhdanam" ("To My Fellow Citizens"), which like much of the "Dedication" is spoken in the first-person plural:

И мы забыли навсегда,
Заключены в столице дикой,
Озера, степи, города
И зори родины далекой.
          (*S*, 1: 213)[30]

And we have forgotten forever,
Imprisoned in the savage capital,
The lakes, the steppes, the cities,
And the dawns of our distant motherland.

The city is pictured here as a place of confinement; later in the same text it is pointedly associated with the absence of freedom. In *Requiem*, the prisonlike nature of the former capital is explicitly expressed in the grotesque imaging of the city in the "Introduction":

И ненужным привеском болтался
Возле тюрем своих Ленинград.
И когда, обезумев от муки,
Шли уже осужденных полки
(S, 1: 362–63)

And, like a superfluous makeweight,
Leningrad dangled near its prisons.
And when, having lost their senses from torment,
There walked regiments of the already convicted.

Here, in a brilliant image of the prison lines, the city proper has been reduced to a useless appendage to its prisons; dominated by those prisons and the masses of convicts, the scene reeks of butchery, thanks to the use of the word "privesok"/"makeweight." [31]

One other difference between Pushkin's epistle and Akhmatova's "Dedication" concerns the status of the poet. "In the depths" emphasizes the poet's freedom when it pictures his "free voice" reaching the prisoners and inspiring them with courage. In the "Dedication," by contrast, the poet is just one of the many languishing in captivity, a point made directly in the last stanza, when the women who stood in line together are retrospectively called "nevol'nye podrugi"/"involuntary friends," companions through circumstances beyond their control, those circumstances themselves—*nevolia* (captivity)—named in the epithet "nevol'nye." The first-person plural *my*, which speaks in the second stanza, belongs to these women, and the poet is just one of their number. [32]

Pushkin is not the only Russian poet alluded to. Toward the beginning of the "Dedication" there is an enigmatic reference to some person or persons evidently untouched by suffering: "Dlia kogo-to veet veter svezhii,/Dlia kogo-to nezhitsia zakat" (lines 6–7)/"For someone a fresh wind blows,/For someone a sunset luxuriates." Set apart by their markedly unpoetic anaphora, flat diction, and banal imagery,[33] these lines conjure up a state of well-being that clashes with the prevailing misery and grief.[34] The solution to the riddle of these lines lies in a most unlikely source. "Dlia kogo-to veet veter svezhii"/"For someone a fresh wind blows" pointedly refers to the following: "Nad stranoi vesennii veter veet,/S kazhdym dnem vse radostnee zhit'"/"Over the country a spring wind blows,/"With every day living grows more joyful"—lines penned by Vasilii Lebedev-Kumach. The text in question is his "Pesnia o rodine" "Song of the Motherland," 1935),[35] a paean to Soviet life under Stalin. The song epitomizes the aggressively nationalistic, radiantly optimistic spirit of Stalinism in the late 1930's, when it achieved the status of a "sort of unofficial national anthem." [36] An exemplar of the propagandistic genre of the mass song, "Song of the Motherland" is mainly spoken in a first-person plural purporting to represent the voice of the Russian people. Written in the same meter—trochaic pentameter—as Lebedev-Kumach's song, the "Dedication" incorporates allusions to that Stalinist hymn in order to undermine its claim to speak for the people as a whole, most pointedly by replacing Lebedev-Kumach's *my* (we) with the indefinite pronoun *kto-to* (someone) in lines 6–7. When the first-person plural sounds forth immediately afterward in the "Dedication" for the first time ("My ne znaem, my povsiudu te zhe"/"We do not know, we are the same everywhere"), it represents the authentic voice of the Russian people, singing the truth about the motherland under Stalin's rule.[37]

The dirgelike "Dedication" gives the lie to Lebedev-Kumach's song, contradicting point by point the picture of Russian life drawn in it. Lebedev-Kumach rhapsodizes about the freedom enjoyed by all, as in these lines from the song's refrain: "Ia drugoi takoi strany ne znaiu,/Gde tak vol'no dyshit chelovek." [38]/"I don't know of any other country,/Where man breathes so freely." Akhmatova, by contrast, portrays the Russian people in a state of captivity; for the women of the "Dedication," the question of breathing freely does not even arise, for they are "mertvykh bezdykhannei"/"more breathless than the dead." "Song of the Motherland" extols the plenitude of Russian life in the following lines: "Vsiudu zhizn' i vol'no i shiroko,/Tochno Volga polnaia, techet." [39]/"Everywhere life flows both freely and broadly, like the full Volga." The "Dedication" pointedly recalls and contradicts Lebedev-Kumach's image in the line "Ne techet velikaia reka" (line 2)/"The great river does not flow." Two other lines from "Song of the Motherland" are pertinent to the representation of the women in the "Dedication": "Kak nevestu, rodinu my liubim,/Berezhem, kak laskovuiu mat'." [40]/"We love our motherland like a bride,/We cherish it like an affectionate mother." This hackneyed comparison of the motherland to bride and mother points toward the symbolic dimension of the women's depiction in the "Dedication": in their captivity and suffering, they stand for the nation as a whole, and their plight represents a travesty of the lofty pledge of love and protection sounded in "Song of the Motherland." [41]

Nowhere is this more evident than in the critical fourth stanza, the climax of the "Dedication." Throughout the first three stanzas, in keeping with the mass song model, the women are portrayed en masse, emphasizing their lack of individuality—a theme expressed explicitly in the phrase "my povsiudu te zhe." [42] In the fourth stanza, however, the focus unexpectedly shifts from the mass of women to just one of their number:

Приговор... И сразу слезы хлынут,
Ото всех уже отделена,
Словно с болью жизнь из сердца вынут,
Словно грубо навзничь опрокинут,
Но идет... Шатается... Одна...

The sentence . . . And immediately the tears pour,
She's already separated from everyone,
As if the life had been painfully torn from her heart,
As if she had been coarsely thrown on her back,
But she walks . . . Staggers . . . Alone . . .

Individuality is restored here to one woman through a brutal *prigovor* (sentence) isolating her from the rest. The reference is to the sentencing of a loved one within the prison, yet that sentence is portrayed solely as mirrored in its violent effect on the woman herself,[43] an effect that is likened both to a painful deathblow (line 18) and to her being thrown on her back (line 19), an oblique yet unmistakable reference to rape. On the symbolic level of Lebedev-Kumach's "bride" and "affectionate mother," Akhmatova is imaging here the murder and rape of the motherland. The barbarous inhumanity of this figurative murder and rape stands out in relief when it is recalled that the victim is, metaphorically speaking, dead already. Nevertheless, the woman does not win death's repose but must continue her existence, separated from the other women, alone in her suffering.

The "Dedication" hinges on this shift in focus from the group to the individual, for it traces an arc from a national catastrophe of epic proportions, as sketched in the first stanza, to the personal catastrophe of one woman, as evoked in the fourth stanza. This arc is inscribed in the text through a series of parallels between the two stanzas. Phonetically, the beginning of the first line—"*Pered* etim *gore*m"—is echoed in the first word of the fourth stanza, "*Prigovor.*" The dominant theme of the first stanza—the *gore* (woe) that has struck—is evidenced in the woman's reaction to the sentence, namely, in the flood of tears she sheds; in addition, the likening of the sentence's effect on the woman to a deathblow pointedly recalls the idiom "ubita gorem"/"killed by grief." Finally, the bending down of the mountains (line 1) is likewise mirrored in the image of the woman's being cast down (line 19). Through this series of correspondences, the national catastrophe is embodied in the fate of a single woman.[44] The movement traced in the "Dedication" from captivity to a sentencing cast as a figurative execution foreshadows the progression from arrest to execution in *Requiem*'s central sequence of ten poems.[45]

The mass song genre is abandoned in the fifth and final stanza, which gives rise to a new, truly lyric voice that speaks in the first-person singular of the present tense:

Где теперь невольные подруги
Двух моих осатанелых лет?
Что им чудится в сибирской вьюге,

Что мерещится им в лунном круге?
Им я шлю прощальный свой привет.

Where now are the involuntary friends
Of my two hellish years?
What appears to them in the Siberian blizzard,
What seems visible to them in the lunar circle?
To them I send my farewell greetings.

The theme of the suppression of the poet's voice, introduced through the multiple allusions to Pushkin's "In the depths," is reversed in these lines, for what sounds forth is the voice of the poet, speaking in a present tense that for the first time in the "Dedication" refers not to the time of narrated events but to the time of writing (emphasized in line 21's "teper'"/"now"). Having recollected the Ezhov terror in a voice speaking for all her people, the poet now speaks for herself, turning her attention to the present circumstances of the women who stood in the prison lines with her.

As anticipated in the fourth stanza's portrayal of one woman's isolation from the group, the poet has been separated from the other women. She speaks of them through a network of allusions to a different lyric by Pushkin, one that bares the profoundly lyric tenor of the concluding lines of the "Dedication." The text in question is the 1826 "Niane" ("To Nanny"), which was written shortly after the end of Pushkin's exile in Mikhailovskoe:

Подруга дней моих суровых,
Голубка дряхлая моя!
Одна в глуши лесов сосновых
Давно, давно ты ждешь меня.
Ты под окном своей светлицы
Горюешь, будто на часах,
И медлят поминутно спицы
В твоих наморщенных руках.
Глядишь в забытые вороты
На черный отдаленный путь:
Тоска, предчувствия, заботы
Теснят твою всечасно грудь.
То чудится тебе...[46]

Friend of my harsh days,
My old decrepit dear!
Alone, in the depths of pine forests,
You have long, long been waiting for me.
Beneath the window of your chamber
You grieve, as if standing watch,
And the knitting needles move ever more slowly
In your wrinkled hands.
You look through the forgotten gate
At the black, distant road:
Anguish, forebodings, worries
Crowd your breast with every hour.
At times there appears to you . . .

These lines invoke Arina Rodionovna, the poet's faithful companion in exile, about whom he wrote from Mikhailovskoe in 1824: "In the evening I listen to the tales of my nanny, the original of Tat'iana's nanny; . . . she is my only friend—and only with her am I not bored." [47] Akhmatova is echoing Pushkin's address to Arina Rodionovna—"Podruga dnei moikh surovykh"/"Friend of my harsh days"—when she names the women who stood with her outside the prison "podrugi/Dvukh moikh osatanelykh let"/"friends/ Of my two hellish years." Two years was the term of Pushkin's Mikhailovskoe exile, whereas Akhmatova actually spent just seventeen months in the prison lines, as the first sentence of "Instead of a Foreword" and the beginning of the fifth numbered text of *Requiem* ("Semnadtsat' mesiatsev krichu,/Zovu tebia domoi" [S, 1: 364]./"I have been shouting for seventeen months,/Calling you home") indicate. [48]

Akhmatova is establishing a parallel between Pushkin's exile and her own lack of freedom during the Ezhov terror, while highlighting the radical differences between their experiences through the two telling epithets in lines 21–22. First, her characterization of those years as *osatanelye* (hellish) contrasts with Pushkin's assessment of his days of exile as *surovye* (harsh, austere), pointing up the extreme cruelty of the Ezhov terror. Second, whereas Pushkin spent his exile in the company of his doting nurse, Akhmatova's companions were bound to her not by love but by force of circum-

stance, as the oxymoron "nevol'nye podrugi" (line 21)/"involuntary friends" suggests.[49] The stance of the poet, however, is identical in "To Nanny" and the "Dedication": just as Pushkin looks
back on the difficult period of his exile and evokes his faithful
nanny alone at Mikhailovskoe, so Akhmatova looks back on the
Ezhov terror and recalls those who stood in the prison lines with
her. Pushkin envisions Arina Rodionovna awaiting his return,
grieving for him, and fearing for his welfare, while Akhmatova is
uncertain of the women's fate and builds this uncertainty into the
text by posing three questions about them. The first question
echoes Pushkin's address to Arina Rodionovna; the second and
third are inspired by the line on which his text breaks off—"To
chuditsia tebe . . ."/"At times there appears to you . . ."; both artic-
ulate the question implicit in the truncation of "To Nanny" by ask-
ing what "appears" (the synonymous verbs *chudit'sia* and *mere-
shchit'sia* are used) to the women. The query "Chto im chuditsia v
sibirskoi v'iuge"/"What appears to them in the Siberian blizzard"
indicates that at least some of them are in Siberia, whether in prison
camp or in exile.[50]

The repetition of the pronoun *im* (to them) in each of the last
three lines of the "Dedication" sounds the theme of dedication,
harking back to the title of the text. Literary dedications are typically addressed to acquaintances or close personal friends of the
author as a sign of respect or affection. Pushkin, for example, dedicated *The Prisoner of the Caucasus* to his good friend N. N. Raev-
sky, *Poltava* to an unnamed but beloved woman, and *Eugene Onegin* to his friend and publisher P. A. Pletnev. The "Dedication" of
Requiem, by contrast, is addressed to a large group of nameless
women, yet it similarly expresses the author's feelings toward them,
suggesting that they provided the impetus for the writing of the
poema.[51] The story of the work's genesis presented in "Instead of a
Foreword" confirms this, as does the "To Nanny" subtext in the
"Dedication."[52] "To Nanny" gives at least a partial answer to the
questions posed by Akhmatova about the fate of her addressees.
Pushkin writes to Arina Rodionovna, "Davno, davno, ty zhdesh'
menia"/"You have long, long been waiting for me." On one level,

this indicates that the women from the prison lines are alone, still separated from their loved ones. On another level, however, it implies that they are waiting for the poet, for Akhmatova, to describe their shared experience.[53] Still troubled ("Toska, predchuvstviia, zaboty/Tesniat tvoiu vsechasno grud'."/"Anguish, forebodings, worries/Crowd your breast with every hour."), they await the peace that *Requiem* will bring.

Through the allusions to Pushkin's lyric, Akhmatova likens her addressees to Arina Rodionovna, suggesting their importance as a source not only of comfort but of inspiration as well. Pushkin drew many memorable verse portraits of Arina Rodionovna, but what distinguishes "To Nanny" among them is its heightened lyricism; the poet's strong affection for his nanny is expressed in the text's tender forms of address, as well as in the sharp detail with which her image is evoked. By couching her questions about her addressees in terms of Pushkin's lyric, Akhmatova demonstrates her profound respect, concern, and solicitude for them, elevating them to the status of intimate friends. Concomitantly, she restores to them their human dignity, symbolically redressing the wrongs they suffered during the Ezhov terror.

The Shroud and the Monument

This restorative, consolatory impulse is the mainspring of *Requiem*. Prefigured in "Instead of a Foreword" and openly expressed in the concluding lines of the "Dedication," it resurfaces at the end of the work to dominate the two-part "Epilogue," where it is manifested in the poet's stance as intercessor for herself and her "captive friends": "I ia molius' ne o sebe odnoi,/A obo vsekh, kto tam stoial so mnoi"[54] (*S*, 1: 370)/"And I pray not for myself alone,/But for all who stood there with me." The restorative impulse is likewise embodied in the poet's commemoration of their shared ordeal, in her perpetuation of its memory, reversing the movement traced in the central lyrical sequence from remembrance—the first poem culminates in the pledge "Not to forget!" ("Ne zabyt'!" [*S*, 1: 363])— to amnesia, predicted in the ninth poem, "Uzhe bezumie krylom"/

"Already the wing of madness." [55] The resurgence of memory in the "Epilogue" is borne out in its very texture, for it is interwoven with allusions to the rest of *Requiem*, retrospective gestures harking back to earlier moments in the text.

The first part of the "Epilogue" recapitulates all that precedes it by conjuring up a collective portrait of the poet and her addressees, a portrait focusing entirely on their faces:

> Узнала я, как опадают лица,
> Как из-под век выглядывает страх,
> Как клинописи жесткие страницы
> Страдание выводит на щеках.
>
> (*S*, 1: 368)

> I found out how faces sink in,
> How fear peers out from under eyelids,
> How suffering painstakingly draws on cheeks
> The hard pages of cuneiform.

A technique reminiscent of time-lapse photography is used to sketch the transformation of the women's faces through suffering, effectively glossing the concluding words of "Instead of a Fore-word"—"across what had once been her face." The first line's "opadaiut litsa"/"faces sink in" harks back to the beginning of the "Dedication"—"Pered etim gorem gnutsia gory" (*S*, 1: 362)/"Before this woe mountains bend down"—measuring the impact of that same *gore* (woe) on the fragile human visage. [56] The "strakh"/ "fear" peering out from under the women's eyelids constitutes a transparent reference to the historical context; [57] at the same time, it recalls the persona's description of her son's eyes in the ninth poem of the sequence: "syna strashnye glaza—/Okameneloe stra-danie" (*S*, 1: 367)/"my son's terrible eyes—/The petrified suffer-ing." The imagery of petrification, which harks back to the state of lifelessness evoked in "Instead of a Foreword" and the "Dedica-tion," pervades the last poems of the central sequence, describing the experience both of those incarcerated (as in the ninth poem) and of those who love them, as expressed in the persona's utterance in the seventh poem, "Nado, chtob dusha okamenela" (*S*, 1: 365)/

"My soul must turn to stone," as well as in the tenth poem's "Uch-enik liubimyi kamenel" (*S*, 1: 368)/"The favorite disciple was becoming petrified"). This imagery is recapitulated in the "Epilogue" in the phrase "klinopisi zhestkie stranitsy"/"hard pages of cuneiform," likening the women's cheeks to stone or clay tablets covered with cuneiform writing; the wedge-shaped, serried indentations of cuneiform characters are a powerful metaphor for deep wrinkles, which in turn figure as a textual record of the women's suffering.

The second part of the "Epilogue" explicitly advances memory and remembrance in response to the devastation wrought by the Ezhov terror:

Опять поминальный приблизился час.
Я вижу, я слышу, я чувствую вас:

И ту, что едва до окна довели,
И ту, что родимой не топчет земли,

И ту, что, красивой тряхнув головой,
Сказала: «Сюда прихожу, как домой.»

Хотелось бы всех поименно назвать,
Но отняли список, и негде узнать.

(S, 1: 369)

Again the memorial hour has drawn near.
I see, I hear, I sense you:

Both the one whom they barely led up to the window,
And the one who does not tread on native soil,

And the one who, shaking her beautiful head,
Said, "Coming here is like coming home."

I would like to call them all by name,
But the list has been taken away, and there's
      nowhere to find out.

The phrase "pominal'nyi chas"/"memorial hour" refers to the Russian Orthodox "pominal'nye dni"/"memorial days," when prayers are offered for the welfare of the souls of the deceased—the third, ninth, and fortieth days after death and then every year on the anniversary of the death. The replacement of *den'* (day) with *chas* (hour) signals that the ritual is observed at least daily, a situation anticipated in a 1915 text written in response to losses suffered in World War I: "Tak chto sdelalsia kazhdyi den'/Pominal'nym dnem" (*SP*, 84)/"So that every day has become/A memorial day." In contrast to the collective portrait evoked in the first part of the "Epilogue," the poet conjures up brief yet individualized portraits of three of her addressees and then articulates her unrealizable wish to call all of the women by name, thereby commemorating them individually—the antithesis of their depersonalization during the Ezhov terror.

The restorative impulse underlying *Requiem* is emblematized in the image of the text of *Requiem* as a *pokrov* (shroud) for the poet's former companions: "Dlia nikh sotkala ia shirokii pokrov/Iz bednykh, u nikh zhe podslushannykh slov" (*S*, 1: 369)/"For them I have woven a broad shroud/Of poor words overheard from them." *Requiem*, Akhmatova's *pokrov*, is a shroud woven of words—a text, a verbal fabric created in the place of a void, bringing deliverance from silence and oblivion. Even more important, the *pokrov* (shroud) represents the burial shroud that both sanctifies and preserves in anticipation of a coming resurrection. The image of the shroud figures prominently in the first part of the diptych "Iul' 1914" ("July 1914," *S*, 1: 133–34), which predicts in apocalyptic terms the horrors to be suffered by Russia in World War I, horrors anticipating those of the Ezhov terror, as the following quotation suggests: "Skoro/Stanet tesno ot svezhikh mogil" (*S*, 1: 134)/ "Soon/Fresh graves will crowd the earth." The final stanza of the text foretells, in the words of an ominous "one-legged passerby," the saving intervention of the Virgin Mary:

«Только нашей земли не разделит
На потеху себе супостат:
Богородица белый расстелет
Над скорбями великими плат».

"Only our land the adversary
Will not divide for his own amusement:
The Virgin Mary will spread a white
Shawl over the great sorrows."

The stanza alludes to a legend about the Saracens' fierce attack on Constantinople in the tenth century. According to the legend, the Virgin Mary appeared to the Christian faithful during the attack and "spread her shroud [*pokrov*] over the Christians," who took heart and repelled the enemy.[58] The second part of "July 1914" realizes the apocalyptic predictions of the first part in a vivid, present-tense description of Russia at war; it likens the ordeal of the Russian land to the crucifixion of Christ, anticipating the symbolic import of the tenth poem of *Requiem*, "Raspiatie" ("The Crucifixion"). Like "July 1914," *Requiem* commemorates the "velikie skorbi"/"great sorrows" of the Russian land, but it is the poet who plays the role of intercessor for Russia by fashioning a metaphorical burial shroud for it, a shroud that will preserve and sanctify, ensuring Russia's future resurrection.

The assertion that *Requiem* was woven from the words of the ordinary women of the prison lines is confirmed in the quotation of one of the women's utterances a few lines earlier: "'Siuda prikhozhu kak domoi'"/"'Coming here is like coming home.'" Through this claim, Akhmatova emphasizes once again that *Requiem* is a mass *poema* representing the true voice of the Russian people. The poverty of the women's words ("bednye slova"/"poor words") contrasts sharply with the "grandeur and glory" from which official mass literary works are made, as exemplified in the empty clichés of Lebedev-Kumach's "Song of the Motherland":

Этих слов величие и славу
Никакие годы не сотрут:
—Человек всегда имеет право
На ученье, отдых и на труд![59]

The grandeur and glory of these words
No years will erase:
"Man always has the right
To study, rest, and labor!"

Just two lines after the mention of the women's "poor words" in the "Epilogue," the mass *poema* theme finds direct expression in the text: "I esli zazhmut moi izmuchennyi rot,/Kotorym krichit stomil'onnyi narod" (*S*, 1: 369)/"And if they shut my tortured mouth,/Through which a nation of a hundred million shouts."

Akhmatova's claim that she speaks for the entire Russian nation is couched in an allusion to a different poet of the masses, Vladimir Mayakovsky, and specifically to his first mass *poema 150,000,000* (1919–20). The title's millions—Russia's population in 1919[60]—represent not only the collective hero of the work but also its collective author, according to Mayakovsky's initial line: "150 000 000 mastera etoi poemy imia."/"150,000,000 is the name of the master of this *poema*." [61] The "Epilogue" specifically refers to Mayakovsky's fourth line, which constitutes a variation on the theme of collective authorship: "150 000 000 govoriat gubami moimi." [62]/"150,000,000 speak through my lips." [63]

For all the obvious differences between them, *Requiem* and *150,000,000* are linked by surprising similarities. First, their points of departure are identical, for both sing, albeit in radically different tonalities, the ruin of the Russian nation. Compare Akhmatova's characterization of Russia's suffering during the Ezhov terror—"I bezvinnaia korchilas' Rus'/Pod krovavymi sapogami/I pod shinami chernykh marus'" (*S*, 1: 363)./"And innocent Russia writhed/ Under bloody boots/And under the tires of Black Marias"—with Mayakovsky's description of the toll taken by the revolution and civil war—"Propala Rosseichka!/Zagubili bednuiu!" [64]/"Dear little Russia is done for!/They've ruined the poor thing!" Mayakovsky is in fact only mocking someone else's complaint, for he calls immediately for the creation of a "new Russia," a "universal" one ("Novuiu naidem Rossiiu./Vsekhsvetnuiu!"),[65] which in turn gives rise to the plot of *150,000,000*—an allegorical treatment of worldwide class struggle, culminating in the inevitable victory of the working class.

The concluding chapter of *150,000,000* serves as an epilogue to the *poema*, and it contains, unexpectedly, a series of salient parallels with Akhmatova's *Requiem*. Set in a communist utopia of the distant future, it envisages a "ezhegodnee torzhestvo"/"annual celebration" in honor of, "perhaps, the hundredth anniversary of the October revolution." [66] The celebration is described as a "mira torzhestvennyi rekviem" [67]/"festive requiem of the world" and cast as a monumental parade memorializing those who suffered and died in the struggle to create the utopia. Mayakovsky focuses on the suffering of his contemporaries during the "famine years" of 1919 and 1920, the very years he was writing *150,000,000*. Among others, he commemorates "za nas zamuchennye ... milliony ... Ivanov" [68]/"the millions of ... Ivans ... tortured for us," as well as

женщины,
            рожденные под горностаевые
мантии,
            тело в лохмотья рядя,
падавшие замертво,
                        за хлебом простаивая
в неисчислимых очередях.[69]

women,
        born fit for ermine
mantles,
        dressing your bodies in rags,
collapsing in dead faints,
                    standing for bread
in innumerable lines.

Akhmatova's *Requiem* commemorates events set some two decades after the revolution Mayakovsky celebrates in *150,000,000*, yet little has changed. "Ivans" are literally being martyred ("a skol'ko tam/Nepovinnykh zhiznei konchaetsia" (*S*, 1: 364)/"but how many/Innocent lives are ending there"), poor women (compare the phrase from the "Epilogue" "bednye slova"/"poor words") are standing in "innumerable lines"—not bread lines, to be sure, but prison lines. Among the martyrs of the revolution celebrated by Mayakovsky are poets "rasstreliannye na barrikadakh dukha,/ chtob dni segodniashnie byli propety" [70]/"executed on the barricades of the spirit/in order to celebrate today's days." Viewed from the perspective of the late 1930's, these figurative executions ironically anticipate the persecution and destruction of poets by the Soviet state after the revolution, as expressed in Akhmatova's "A esli zazhmut moi izmuchennyi rot"/"And if they shut my tortured mouth."

Almost as soon as it begins, Mayakovsky's oxymoronic "requiem parade" is abruptly terminated, giving way in the final lines of the text to general merriment:

Парад мировой расходился ровно,—
ведь горе давнишнее душу не бесит.
Годами
        печаль
               в покой воркестрована
и песней брошена ввысь поднебесить.
Еще гудят голосов отголоски
про смерти чьи-то,
                    про память вечную.
А люди
       уже
            в многоуличном лоске
катили минуту, весельем расцвеченную.
Ну и катись средь песенного лада,
цвети, земля, в молотьбе и в сеятьбе.[71]

The world's parade dispersed smoothly,—
after all, grief long past doesn't enrage the soul.
By the years
        sorrow
              has been orchestrated into peace
and cast up as a song to be aloft in the heavens.
The echoes of voices still hum
about the deaths of some people,
                  about eternal memory.
While people
       already
            in a many-streeted luster
have rolled the minute, colored with gaiety.
So roll on amidst the song's harmony,
bloom, earth, in threshing and in sowing.

This celebration justifies the loss of those commemorated in the "requiem parade" as a necessary sacrifice, a means to a glorious end. For Mayakovsky, the suffering of his day is meaningful only in relation to—and from the perspective of—the utopia of the future. Projected a century into the future, his "requiem parade" for his times minimizes the enormity of the loss suffered, recalling it as a remote fait accompli: "gore davnishnee dushu ne besit"/"grief long past doesn't enrage the soul." Those whose sacrifice is recalled are memorialized only abstractly, in huge masses, in "legions," in "millions." [72] Their depersonalization is epitomized in the fact that the sole personal name mentioned in the requiem is Ivan, the most impersonal of Russian names, and it appears only in the plural, when the sacrifices of "millions of . . . Ivans" are extolled. In this travesty of a genuine requiem, Mayakovsky simulates remembrance while truly remembering no one and does not even feign to mourn, claiming cavalierly in the closing lines that sorrow and grief have been effaced by time.

Akhmatova does not share Mayakovsky's faith in a future earthly paradise; for her, nothing can justify the suffering, and only constant remembrance can redeem it. *Requiem* as a whole was written to ensure that the sorrow and grief of the Russian people during the Ezhov terror would not be effaced by time. In contrast to Mayakovsky's memorialization of the revolution's "legions" and "millions" of victims, Akhmatova conjures up three of her addressees individually, expresses her desire to call them all by name, and incorporates their words into her text, expressing her respect for their dignity as individuals, something incomprehensible to Mayakovsky.

In the concluding lines of *150,000,000*, the words "vechnaia pamiat' "/"eternal memory"—the refrain of the Russian Orthodox funeral service—echo momentarily, only to be overwhelmed by the sounds of the mass festivities. The consolation offered by Akhmatova in *Requiem*, on the contrary, lies wholly in this notion of "eternal memory," as expressed programmatically in the poet's declaration of her unconditional faithfulness to the memory of her addressees: "O nikh vspominaiu vsegda i vezde,/O nikh ne zabudu i v novoi bede" (*S*, 1: 369)/"Always and everywhere I recollect them,/Even in new misfortune I will not forget them." The possibility of the poet's silencing by the authorities is portrayed as a threat to "eternal memory," and this prompts the turn, precisely in the middle of the second part of the "Epilogue," to the classical topos of the poet's monument, a topos initiated in Horace's ode "Exegi monumentum aere perennius," and imitated in Russia first by Derzhavin ("Ia pamiatnik sebe vozdvig chudesnyi, vechnyi"/"I have erected to myself a monument wonderful, eternal") and then definitively by Pushkin in 1836 ("Ia pamiatnik sebe vozdvig neru-kotvornyi"/"I have erected to myself a monument not made by human hands"): "A esli kogda-nibud' v etoi strane,/Vozdvignut' zadumaiut pamiatnik mne" (*S*, 1: 369)/"And if ever in this coun-try/They think of erecting a monument to me." The necessary com-ponents of the topos—*vozdvignut'* (to erect) and *pamiatnik* (mon-ument)—are present, but Akhmatova turns the topos on its head by speaking not metaphorically of her poetry as a figurative mon-ument, but literally of a future monument to be erected by her na-tive land in her memory. Instead of being "aere perennius"/"more durable than bronze," like the monument Horace sings of, or "ne-rukotvornyi"/"not made by human hands," like Pushkin's, Akh-matova's future monument will be made of bronze: "A pust' s ne-podvizhnykh i bronzovykh vek . . ." (*S*, 1: 370)/"And let from its immobile and bronze eyelids. . . ."

Akhmatova then stipulates that the monument is to be placed "zdes', gde stoiala ia trista chasov/I gde dlia menia ne otkryli za-sov" (*S*, 1: 370)/"here, where I stood three hundred hours,/And where they did not open the bolt for me." The word *zdes'* (here) reveals the poet's locus in the second part of the "Epilogue" to be outside the Leningrad prison where her son was incarcerated. This is a situational refrain in *Requiem*: it figures in both "Instead of a Foreword" and the "Dedication," as well as in the fourth poem of the central sequence: "Kak trekhsotaia . . . /Pod Krestami budesh' stoiat'" (*S*, 1: 364)/"As the three-hundredth . . . /Under the Crosses you will stand." The appearance of the word *Kresty* (the Crosses), the name of the prison where Lev Gumilev was held, pre-figures the tenth poem's treatment of the crucifixion of Jesus, with its minus portrait of the Virgin Mary at the foot of the crosses. The motif recurs in the concluding lines of the first part of the "Epilogue":

> И я молюсь не о себе одной,
> А обо всех, кто там стоял со мною,
> И в лютый холод, и в июльский зной,
> Под красною ослепшею стеною.
> (S, 1: 369)

But I pray not for myself alone,
But for all who stood there with me,
Both in the fierce cold and in July's heat,
Under the red wall that had gone blind.

By its very location, the monument will memorialize the seventeen months Akhmatova spent in the prison lines and will mourn and commemorate all of the victims of the Ezhovshchina. The "Epilogue" was written just three years after the Pushkin jubilee in 1937, a graphic reminder of how the state could exploit for its own ends the celebration (*torzhestvo*) of the memory of a great poet, misrepresenting the poet's legacy to suit its own version of history. The condition dictated in the "Epilogue" is intended to prevent such a distortion: situated outside the Kresty Prison, the statue will embody a silent protest against tyranny by preserving the memory of the Ezhov terror and its victims.

Chapter 3

"Prehistory": A Russian Creation Myth

"You know, I think," said Natasha in a
whisper . . . , "that when you remember,
remember, remember everything, then you
remember back far enough to remember
what there was before I was in the world."
—Lev Tolstoy, *War and Peace*

In my beginning is my end.
—T. S. Eliot, "East Coker"

Мне ведомы начала и концы.
To me are known beginnings and ends.
—Anna Akhmatova, the fifth Northern
Elegy

"Predystoriia" ("Prehistory"), a 58-line text written in blank
verse, exemplifies a distinctive trait of Akhmatova's poetry—the privileging of the category of beginnings, of origins. The
poet first demonstrated her predilection for origins, for "first
times," in "V to vremia ia gostila na zemle" ("At that time I was a
guest on earth," 1913), the first of the three blank-verse *Epicheskie
motivy* (*Epic Motifs*). Like Akhmatova's first narrative poem, *U
samogo moria* (*Right by the Sea*, 1914), "At that time" is based on
the years the poet spent by the Black Sea in her youth, a period
both texts evoke in relatively idyllic terms. "At that time" mythol-
ogizes the origins of Akhmatova's poetic talents: the young heroine's reception of the poetic gift from a muse figure is cast as a
blissful fall from a state of innocence, the loss of a paradisiacal
wholeness and plenitude. At the same time, this myth of origins
comments on Akhmatova's own poetry. Of particular metapoetic

import is the identification of the poetic gift with memory, for memory is a theme of paramount significance in her work, especially in the later period. The comparison of the muse's speech to the sound of bagpipes that "Vdali poet o vechere razluk" (*SP*, 324)/ "In the distance sings of the evening of partings" can also be interpreted metapoetically, for the themes of separation and loss figure prominently in Akhmatova's work.[1]

In March 1940 Akhmatova returned to the question of her origins in the *malen'kaia poema* (little narrative poem) *Putem vseia zemli* (*The Way of All the Earth*), which portrays a series of attempted returns to the past, including a visit to the shore of the Black Sea. The persona finds the once idyllic landscape disfigured by death[2] and encounters a mocking, incredulous muse, the antithesis of the nurturing muse figure in "At that time." The failed return to the Black Sea idyll in *The Way of All the Earth* is emblematic of a rupture with the past, a rupture also articulated in *Requiem*'s "Epilogue," which was likewise composed in March 1940. In it the poet recalls the "sea, where [she] was born," only to state categorically: "Posledniaia s morem razorvana sviaz'" (*S*, 1: 370)/"The last tie with the sea has been broken." The failure enacted in *The Way of All the Earth* bespeaks the inadequacy of "At that time" as a personal myth of origins for Akhmatova in 1940. From the perspective of 1913, when "At that time" was written, the world Akhmatova inhabited in 1940 was virtually unrecognizable. Her poetry had changed radically, too, as had her sense of herself as a poet, and 1940 was a time of unparalleled creativity and bold experimentation.

"Prehistory" constitutes Akhmatova's new myth of her origins, one expressive of her identity as a poet in 1940. It was written mainly in September 1940, in Leningrad, and was completed in 1943 in Tashkent. In it, Akhmatova does what Natasha Rostova imagines in the first epigraph to this chapter: she remembers back past her childhood on the Black Sea in the 1890's, back beyond her birth in 1889, to conjure up a picture of the world into which she was soon to be born—Russia in the 1870's. J. P. Vernant's description of the nature and purpose of ancient creation myths illuminates Akhmatova's design in "Prehistory," her furthest poetic foray into the past:

The Muses sing, beginning with the beginning—*éx arkhēs* ([Hesiod's] Theogony, 45, 115)—, the first appearance of the world, the genesis of the gods, the birth of humanity. The past is thus revealed as much more than the antecedent of the present; it is its source. In going back to it, recollection does not seek to situate events in a temporal frame, but to reach the depth of being, to discover the original, the primordial reality from which the cosmos issued and which makes it possible to understand becoming as a whole.[3]

Akhmatova ventures into the past in imagination so as to understand her present, for as Vernant's last phrase—"to understand becoming as a whole"—suggests, to indicate the origins of a phenomenon is to explain it.[4] "Prehistory" makes sense of the vast changes in Akhmatova's life and work, expressing her new identity as a poet and metapoetically defining the new fundamentals of her art.

Предыстория

Я теперь живу не там...
Пушкин

Россия Достоевского. Луна
Почти на четверть скрыта колокольней.
Торгуют кабаки, летят пролетки,
Пятиэтажные растут громады
В Гороховой, у Знаменья, под Смольным.   5
Везде танцклассы, вывески менял,
А рядом: «Henriette», «Basile», «André»
И пышные гроба: «Шумилов-старший».
Но, впрочем, город мало изменился.
Не я одна, но и другие тоже   10
Заметили, что он подчас умеет
Казаться литографией старинной,
Не первоклассной, но вполне пристойной,
Семидесятых, кажется, годов.
   Особенно зимой, перед рассветом   15
   Иль в сумерки—тогда за воротами
Темнеет жесткий и прямой Литейный,

Еще не опозоренный модерном,
И визави меня живут—Некрасов
И Салтыков... Обоим по доске   20
Мемориальной. О, как было б страшно
Им видеть эти доски! Прохожу.
А в Старой Руссе пышные канавы,
И в садиках подгнившие беседки,
И стекла окон так черны, как прорубь,   25
И мнится, там такое приключилось,
Что лучше не заглядывать, уйдем.
Не с каждым местом сговориться можно,
Чтобы оно свою открыло тайну
(А в Оптиной мне больше не бывать...)   30

Шуршанье юбок, клетчатые пледы,
Ореховые рамы у зеркал,
Каренинской красою изумленных,
И в коридорах узких те обои,
Которыми мы любовались в детстве,   35
Под желтой керосиновою лампой,
И тот же плюш на креслах...
    Всё разночинно, наспех, как-нибудь...
    Отцы и деды непонятны. Земли
    Заложены. И в Бадене—рулетка.   40

И женщина с прозрачными глазами
(Такой глубокой синевы, что море
Нельзя не вспомнить, поглядевши в них),
С редчайшим именем и белой ручкой,
И добротой, которую в наследство   45
Я от нее как будто получила,—
Ненужный дар моей жестокой жизни...

Страну знобит, а омский каторжанин
Всё понял и на всем поставил крест.
Вот он сейчас перемешает всё   50
И сам над первозданным беспорядком,
Как некий дух, взнесется. Полночь бьет.
Перо скрипит, и многие страницы
Семеновским припахивают плацем.

Так вот когда мы вздумали родиться   55
И безошибочно отмерив время,
Чтоб ничего не пропустить из зрелищ
Невиданных, простились с небытьем.

Prehistory

I live elsewhere now . . .
—Pushkin

Dostoevsky's Russia. The moon
Is almost a quarter hidden by a bell tower.
Taverns are trading, horsecabs fly by,
Five-storied masses rise up
On Gorokhovaia, by Znamen'e, near Smol'nyi.   5
Everywhere there are dance classes, money
           changers' signs,
And next door: "Henriette," "Basile," "André,"
And luxurious coffins—"Shumilov, Senior."
But, incidentally, the city has changed little.
Not I alone, but others as well,   10
Have noticed that it sometimes is able
To appear to be an antique lithograph,
Not a first-class one, but quite acceptable,
Of the seventies, it seems.
     Especially in winter, before dawn,   15
     Or at dusk—then beyond the gates
     Is darkly visible the rigid and straight Liteinyi,
     Not yet disgraced by the modern style,
     And opposite me live—Nekrasov
     And Saltykov . . . For each of them   20
     A memorial plaque. Oh, how terrible it would be
     For them to see these plaques! I pass by.
And in Staraia Russa there are luxuriant ditches,
And in little gardens half-rotted summerhouses,
And the windows' glass panes are as black as an ice hole,   25
And it seems that some such thing happened there
That it's better not to glance in, let's leave.
Not with every place is it possible to make a deal

For it to reveal its mystery
(And I can visit Optina no more . . .).   30

The rustling of skirts, checkered plaids,
Walnut frames of mirrors
Amazed by Kareninesque beauty,
And in narrow corridors the same wallpaper
That we admired in childhood,   35
Under the yellow kerosene lamp,
And the same plush on the armchairs . . .
   Everything is jumbled, slapdash, any old way . . .
   Fathers and grandfathers are incomprehensible. The lands
   Have been mortgaged. And in Baden there's roulette.   40

And a woman with transparent eyes
(Of such deep dark blue, that on looking into them
It's impossible not to recall the sea),
With a most rare name and small white hands,
And a kindness that I evidently   45
Received from her in inheritance—
An unnecessary gift of my cruel life . . .

The country is feverish, and the Omsk convict
Understood everything and gave it all up for lost.
In a moment he will mix up everything,   50
And over the primordial disorder he himself,
Like some spirit, will soar. Midnight strikes.
The pen scratches, and many pages
Smell faintly of Semenovskii Square.

That's when we took it into our heads to be born   55
And, having measured off the time unerringly,
So as to miss nothing of the spectacles
Unprecedented, we bid farewell to nonbeing.

Akhmatova's Genesis

The seminal role of Dostoevsky in "Prehistory" is proclaimed in
the first two words of the text: "Rossiia Dostoevskogo"/"Dostoevsky's Russia." This phrase can be interpreted as referring both to

the Russia of Dostoevsky's lifetime and to Russia as depicted by him in his art; whereas the former reading takes Dostoevsky as a historical figure, the latter stresses his work as a creative artist. The conjunction of these two emphases—biographical and literary—defines the portrait of Russia which emerges in "Prehistory": it is shown through the prism of Dostoevsky's life and works.[5] The focus on his life and art is evidenced in the places evoked or simply mentioned in the text: St. Petersburg's various landmarks, Staraia Russa, the Optina Hermitage, Baden-Baden, and Omsk, all figured prominently in Dostoevsky's life and are directly or indirectly portrayed in his art.

Dostoevsky's name occurs just once in the text, and its appearance in the genitive case introduces on a purely grammatical level the central theme of "Prehistory"—genesis, the genesis of the world into which Akhmatova and her generation were born. The theme of genesis finds direct expression toward the end of "Prehistory" (lines 48–54):

> Страну знобит, а омский каторжанин
> Все понял и на всем поставил крест.
> Вот он сейчас перемешает все
> И сам над первозданным беспорядком,
> Как некий дух, взнесется. Полночь бьет.
> Перо скрипит, и многие страницы
> Семеновским припахивают плацем.

> The country is feverish, and the Omsk convict
> Understood everything and gave it all up for lost.
> In a moment he will mix up everything,
> And over the primordial disorder he himself,
> Like some spirit, will soar. Midnight strikes.
> The pen scratches, and many pages
> Smell faintly of Semenovskii Square.

Dostoevsky, called the Omsk convict in reference to his years of penal servitude in Siberia, is portrayed in the process of literary creation. The key to this segment of "Prehistory," as Kees Verheul has noted, lies in an allusion to the Old Testament account of the creation, specifically to the second verse of Genesis:[6]

Земля была безвидна и пуста, и тьма над бездною; и Дух Божий носился над водою.

The earth was without form, and void; and darkness was upon the face of the deep. And the Spirit of God moved upon the face of the waters.

The collocation "Kak nekii dukh, vznesetsia"(line 52)/"Like some spirit, will soar" likens Dostoevsky to the Old Testament divinity on the first day of creation. In "Prehistory," the act of writing is equated with the cosmogony; cast as demiurge, Dostoevsky reenacts the creation of the world in his art.[7]

The allusion to the biblical creation story points up the mythopoetic thrust of Akhmatova's text. "Prehistory" constitutes a "vertiginously brief" yet full-fledged creation myth, for its description of Dostoevsky at work manifests the essential features of cosmogonical myths. Mircea Eliade has identified three such components, the first of which is the "restoration of primordial chaos" through the "abolition of contours, fusion of all forms, [and] return to the formless."[8] "Prehistory" shows Dostoevsky restoring the "pervozdannyi besporiadok"/"primordial chaos" by mixing together all forms: "Vot on seichas peremeshaet vse"/"In a moment he will mix up everything."[9] A second feature of cosmogonical myths and rituals, and a concomitant of the restoration of primordial chaos, is the "abolition of past time," that is, the suspension of linear time, producing a coexistence of past and present.[10] In "Prehistory," this is patently manifested in the sudden shift to the present tense in the words "Polnoch' b'et"(line 52)/"Midnight strikes"; this phrase effectively suspends the passage of time, for no completion of the striking is indicated. Akhmatova's choice of hour is likewise integral to the creative process, for midnight marks the boundary between the old day and the new and is a time when "limits, contours, and distances are indiscernible."[11] The third and final component of cosmogonic myths and rituals is the conquering of chaos and the emergence of cosmos.[12] In "Prehistory," this is implicit in Dostoevsky's rising up over the chaos and explicit in the depiction of him writing. In the last four lines of the text, the focus shifts from creation to genesis in the etymological sense of the word (it derives from the Greek *gignesthai* [to be born]):

Так вот когда мы вздумали родиться
И, безошибочно отмерив время,
Чтоб ничего не пропустить из зрелищ
Невиданных, простились с небытьем.

That's when we took it into our heads to be born
And, having measured off the time unerringly,
So as to miss nothing of the spectacles
Unprecedented, we bid farewell to nonbeing.

Proclaiming the birth of the poet's generation, the phrase "prostilis' s nebyt'em"/"bid farewell to nonbeing" names in a negative circumlocution the issue at hand—genesis (*bytie*), the emergence of life from primordial chaos.

Akhmatova's account of her generation's birth in "Prehistory" is indebted to an earlier literary treatment of the same event—Boris Pasternak's "Ottsy" ("Fathers"), one of the "epic fragments" making up *Deviat'sot piatyi god* (*Nineteen Hundred Five*, 1925–26), his "chronicle of the year 1905 in verse form."[13] Set, like "Prehistory," in the 1870's, "Fathers" proclaims as its subject the "povest' nashikh ottsov"[14]/"tale of our fathers," and it records the birth of the author's generation. "Prehistory" was definitely created with a backward glance at "Fathers."[15] Not only does Akhmatova treat the same themes as Pasternak—Russia of the 1870's, the birth of their generation—she echoes specific imagery from Pasternak: compare, for instance, Pasternak's "Za Nevoiu proletka gremit"[16]/ "Beyond the Neva a horsecab roars" with Akhmatova's "Torguiut kabaki, letiat proletki" (line 3)/"Taverns are trading, horsecabs fly by." "Prehistory" in fact polemicizes with Pasternak's portrayal of the 1870's. "Fathers" incorporates a plethora of references to typical phenomena of that decade, chosen for their relevance to the revolution of 1905. In "Prehistory," the historical facts mentioned and geographical names invoked were selected for their pertinence to literary history and, more specifically, to the life and art of Dostoevsky. In "Fathers," Dostoevsky's name is mentioned only in passing, in the course of a description of the revolutionary underground:

Двадцатипятилетье—в подпольи.
....
Тут бывал Достоевский.
Затворницы ж эти,
Не чаяв,
Что у них,
Что ни обыск,
То вывоз реликвий в музей,
Шли на казнь.[17]

Twenty-five-year-olds are in the underground.
....
Dostoevsky used to come here.
These hermits,
Not knowing
That with them
Every search
Was a removal of relics to the museum,
Went to their execution.

Pasternak's underground is inhabited by Sof'ia Perovskaia and the People's Will Party, as well as by the terrorist S. G. Nechaev, on whose activities Dostoevsky modeled his portrayal of the revolutionaries in *Besy* (*The Devils*, 1871–72). For Pasternak, Dostoevsky's significance lies in his close connection with the radical youth of his day, whose activities paved the way for the revolution of 1905. Akhmatova's evaluation of Dostoevsky's significance is radically different: his presence dominates "Prehistory," and he is portrayed as the father of the world into which the poet's generation is born.[18]

The other pivotal difference between "Prehistory" and "Fathers" involves the rendering of the birth of the poets' generation. Pasternak evokes that birth as follows:

Мы родимся на свет.
Как-нибудь
Предвечернее солнце
Подзовет нас к окну.
Мы одухотворим наугад

Непривычный закат,
И при зрелище труб
Потрясемся,
Как потрясся,
Кто б мог
Оглянуться лет на сто назад.[19]

We will be born into the world.
One day
The early evening sun
Will call us to the window.
We will animate at random
The unusual sunset,
And at the spectacle of the chimneys
We will be shaken,
As would be shaken
One who could
Look back a hundred years.

Here, as in the closing lines of "Prehistory," the motifs of birth and vision are intertwined: the moment of birth is linked with subsequent events—named by the word *zrelishche* (spectacle)—to be witnessed by the poets' generation. In both cases, those events have apocalyptic overtones: in Pasternak's *zrelishche trub* (spectacle of the chimneys), the second word could also be read as "trumpets," as in the trumpets that sound in the book of Revelation; Akhmatova's *zrelishcha nevidannye* (spectacles unprecedented) is stylistically more elevated, suggesting a series of great and terrible historical events.[20]

The conjunction of the motifs of vision and spectacle in both texts derives from one source—Fedor Tiutchev's famous poem "Tsitseron" ("Cicero," 1830), in which the Roman orator is called the "zritel'"/"spectator" of the "zrelishcha"/"spectacles" prepared by the gods. Cicero's greatness is shown to depend on the tragic historical events he witnessed, culminating in the fall of the Roman republic, or, in Tiutchev's words, "Zakat zvezdy ee krovavyi"/"the bloody setting of the star [of Roman glory]."[21] Pasternak translates Tiutchev's solemn rhetoric into a concrete, urban scene, while preserving the catastrophic connotations of the imagery: the metaphorical setting (*zakat*) of the star of Roman glory is transformed into a literal sunset (*zakat*) framed by a window; Tiutchev's "vysokie zrelishcha"/"lofty spectacles" are recast as the "zrelishche trub"/"spectacle of the chimneys," where height is meant literally, in the sense of a rooftop view of the city. Akhmatova's employment of the word "zrelishcha"/"spectacles" is much more in keeping with Tiutchev's use of the word. She intensifies the motif of vision through the epithet "nevidannye"/"unprecedented" (literally, never seen before), situating her generation's arrival in this world precisely on the eve of a series of history's "fateful moments." [22] "Fathers" treats the same birth as just one event among others, announcing it without ado ("My rodimsia na svet"/"We will be born into the world") and then immediately envisioning the witnessing of the future sunset. "Prehistory," by contrast, strongly foregrounds the birth, for the entire text culminates in the lines devoted to it. The destiny of Akhmatova's generation, determined by the moment of its birth, is akin to that of Tiutchev's Cicero—to see the fall of the Russian empire and its aftermath. Yet though for Tiutchev Cicero's fate is enviable ("Schastliv, kto posetil sei mir/V ego minuty rokovye!"/"Happy is he who visited this world/In its fateful moments!") in that it immortalized him, for Akhmatova the destiny of her generation is unenviable, as expressed in the ironic *vzdumali* ("took it into our heads," line 55); the moment of her generation's birth ensured not its immortality but its destruction, as expressed in the 1944 lyric "De profundis . . . Moe pokolenie" (*SP*, 295)/"De profundis . . . My generation." [23]

The title that Akhmatova chose for "Prehistory" does much to explain the significance of its truncation immediately after the description of the birth. In Russian, *predystoriia* (prehistory) signifies an account of events or conditions predating written or recorded history. This bespeaks Akhmatova's concern with antecedents, with the origins of her generation and the world into which it was born. It also reflects the text's fundamentally ahistorical, mythical bias. In narrative theory, *predystoriia* denotes what is known as *Vorgeschichte*—those events occurring before the start of the dramatic action, which are referred to in the course of the narrative. In her essay "'Kamennyi gost'' Pushkina" ("Pushkin's *Stone Guest*"), Akhmatova discusses Pushkin's use of *Vorgeschichte*, and her remarks shed considerable light on "Prehistory." Noting the important role of *Vorgeschichte* in *The Stone Guest*, she draws a parallel with Dostoevsky's use of the same device:

This little tragedy presupposes a very big *Vorgeschichte* [*predystoriia*], which . . . is accommodated in a few lines interspersed here and there in the text. In Russian literature this device was magnificently and uniquely developed by Dostoevsky in his novels-tragedies: in essence the reader-viewer is invited to be present only at the denouement. So it is in *The Devils, The Idiot*, and even *The Brothers Karamazov*. Everything has already occurred somewhere beyond the bounds of the given work—love, hatred, betrayal, friendship. The same is true of Pushkin's *Stone Guest*.[24]

In both authors Akhmatova identifies the employment of the device specifically with the tragic: *The Stone Guest* is one of Pushkin's "little tragedies,"[25] while Dostoevsky's novels she terms "novels-tragedies," following Viacheslav Ivanov.[26] In both Pushkin and Dostoevsky, the dramatic action commences on the verge of the tragic denouement: the sequence of events leading up to that moment is not dramatized but is simply "touched on"[27] to a greater or lesser degree. According to Akhmatova, Pushkin and Dostoevsky radically curtail the dramatic action by incorporating so much of it into the *Vorgeschichte* that "everything begins . . . when everything has [already] ended."[28] The paradoxical nature of this utterance stems from a conflation of elements relating to form and plot: "everything begins" refers to the commencement of the work proper, while "everything has ended" refers to the tragic denouement, usually positioned at the end of the literary work. The paradox of "Prehistory" is just the reverse: to paraphrase Akhmatova, everything ends when everything has just begun. Here, however, the relations between the elements of form and plot are likewise reversed: the text formally concludes with birth, an event traditionally associated with the beginnings of plots and narratives that is, ostensibly, the antithesis of the traditional tragic denouement—death. The birth in "Prehistory," however, is informed with tragic significance, for Akhmatova telescopes into the single moment of birth the story of her generation, destined to live through a series of cataclysmic historical events.

Dostoevskian Facts and Fictions

In "Prehistory," the *Vorgeschichte* is expanded into a self-sufficient work of art, while the story, the *Geschichte*, of the fate of Akhmatova's generation, is compressed into the moment of its birth. "Prehistory" prefigures the fate of Akhmatova's generation through an intricate network of references, some explicit and others ingeniously indirect, to the life and art of Dostoevsky. So comprehensive is this network of references that it constitutes a compressed literary biography of the novelist.

These references begin in the second sentence of the text—"Luna/Pochti na chetvert' skryta kolokol'nei"/"The moon/Is almost a quarter hidden by a bell tower"—which renders the view from the window of Dostoevsky's study in his apartment on Kuznechnyi Lane, a view of the Church of Vladimir.[29] Dostoevsky lived and worked in the apartment from 1878 until his death in 1881, so that "Prehistory" begins with Dostoevsky's view of Petersburg at the very end of his life; Akhmatova's point of departure in the text is, as Verheul has written, "the working table of Dostoevsky," or quite literally Dostoevsky's view of the world.[30] The first eight lines of "Prehistory" evoke a dynamic portrait of the city inextricably linked with Dostoevsky. St. Petersburg is not named in the text, but it is easily identifiable from the toponyms enumerated. Although Dostoevsky continually changed addresses, during most of his Petersburg years he resided in the area around Gorokhovaia, and the street figures time and again in his fiction.[31] The action of *Crime and Punishment* (1866) revolves around Gorokhovaia, Rogozhin's house in *The Idiot* (1868) is located on Gorokhovaia, and in *The Devils* (1872) Stavrogin confesses to having committed a crime in a house situated there.[32] The reference to coffins in Dostoevsky's Petersburg ("I pyshnye groba: 'Shumilov-starshii'." / "And luxurious coffins: 'Shumilov, Senior'.") recalls the writer's morbid penchant for coffins and coffinmakers' shops.[33] Literal and metaphorical coffins abound in Dostoevsky's fiction: his tortured protagonists often live in quarters reminiscent of coffins or tombs (Raskol'nikov, Arkadii Dolgorukii).[34]

Toward the middle of the text, the setting shifts to Staraia Russa (lines 23–29), a town closely linked with Dostoevsky in the 1870's. Starting in 1872, the writer and his family passed the summers there in a "spacious manor house" they rented on the edge of town; Dostoevsky spent a whole year (1874–75) there writing *The Adolescent*.[35] Dostoevsky purchased a residence in Staraia Russa in 1876 and spent the summers of 1878 and 1879 there at work on *The Brothers Karamazov*. That novel reproduces the topography of Staraia Russa in its rendering of the provincial town in which Fedor Karamazov lives; Karamazov's house is modeled on Dostoevsky's.[36] The parenthetical reference in line 30 to the Optina Hermitage recalls Dostoevsky's visit to the famous monastery in 1878 after the death of his young son. He was granted a private interview with Amvrosii, an elder in the monastery who subsequently served as one of the prototypes for Father Zosima in *The Brothers Karamazov*.[37] Toward the beginning of the novel, the Optina Hermitage is mentioned by name as a monastery in which the institution of the *starets* flourished in Russia.[38] As is well known, Dostoevsky based the description of the monastery on his impressions of Optina. According to the writer's wife, Zosima's famous speech to the peasant woman grieving over the death of her child (part I, book 2, chapter 3) replicates Amvrosii's words of comfort to Dostoevsky during his visit.[39]

Dostoevsky's repeated pronouncements on the forces of chaos and disintegration at work in Russian society are recalled in lines 38–40: "Vse raznochinno, naspekh, kak-nibud' . . . /Ottsy i dedy neponiatny. Zemli/Zalozheny. A v Badene—ruletka." / "Everything is jumbled, slapdash, in any old way . . . /Fathers and grandfathers are incomprehensible. The lands/Have been mortgaged. And in

Baden there's roulette." [40] The word "raznochinno," rendered above as "jumbled," lacks an adequate counterpart in English. A neologism, it derives from the noun *raznochinets*, which denotes a member of the intelligentsia of non-noble origins—for instance, the educated children of priests or merchants who entered the civil service or the professions. Like most of his protagonists, Dostoevsky himself was a *raznochinets*. As a modifier, "raznochinno" would signify "in the manner of a *raznochinets*," but the novelty of its form foregrounds the meanings of its component parts—*razno-* (various) and *chin* (rank)—suggesting the yoking of disparate, conflicting phenomena—a fundamental trait of Dostoevsky's poetics. Accordingly, the line could be read as a comment on his propensity for juxtaposing in his art disparate and contradictory facts from all realms of life, for blending the realistic and the fantastic, the grotesque and the tragic.

"Ottsy i dedy neponiatny" (line 39)/"Fathers and grandfathers are incomprehensible" echoes the title of Turgenev's *Ottsy i deti* (*Fathers and Children*, 1862), a novel admired by Dostoevsky. [41] Throughout the 1870's, Dostoevsky was obsessed with the problem of relations between the generations: the theme plays an important role in *The Devils* and dominates *The Adolescent* and *The Brothers Karamazov*. [42] According to the January 1876 installment of the *Diary*, his last novel was to portray "fathers and children . . . from all strata of society," "trac[ing] the children from their very earliest childhood." [43] Like the reference to Turgenev's novel, the terse sentences—"Zemli/Zalozheny. A v Badene—ruletka"/"The lands/ Have been mortgaged. And in Baden there's roulette"—point back to the 1860's: they recall the thematics and plot of *The Gambler* (1866), a novella based on Dostoevsky's ruinous obsession with gambling in the 1860's. [44]

The phrase "omskii katorzhanin" (line 48)/"Omsk convict" points back yet another decade to the 1850's, for it refers to Dostoevsky's penal servitude at Omsk from January 1850 to January 1854. His prison experiences received artistic treatment in *Notes from the House of the Dead* (1861–62). The furthest point of incursion into the past comes with the mention of Semenovskii

Square (line 54), the site of the mock execution of the members of the Petrashevsky circle on December 22, 1849.[45] Dostoevsky described his feelings and thoughts during the event in a letter to his brother Mikhail on that same night[46] and subsequently rendered it twice in his artistic prose—first in *The Idiot*, where Prince Myshkin tells of the last minutes of a man condemned to death, and later in a first-person reminiscence included in the *Diary* (January 1873).[47] Simultaneously, Semenovskii Square leads full circle back to the end of the 1870's, for its name is incorporated into the representation of Dostoevsky writing, signaling the return to Kuznechnyi Lane and the study of the master.

A particularly striking feature of this elliptical literary biography is its reverse chronology: it traces the writer's life back from his very last years to the events of December 22, 1849. This ordering underscores the pivotal role of the mock execution and penal servitude in Dostoevsky's life, a role he explicitly acknowledged on several occasions: the mock execution he experienced as a figurative death, while the years in prison saw the gradual "regeneration of [his] convictions,"[48] leading to his conversion to Russian Orthodoxy and his new understanding of the Russian people, to the worldview that informs his post-Siberian writings.[49] Hence the novelist's superior understanding of his age: "omskii katorzhanin/ Vse ponial i na vsem postavil krest"/"the Omsk convict/Understood everything and gave it all up for lost" (lines 48–49). The phrase "na vsem postavil krest" is deeply ambiguous: idiomatically, it means to abandon all hope or faith in everything, but literally it means to place a cross on everything, as in blessing or burying it, and thus alludes to Dostoevsky's religious faith. As a Christian symbol, the cross is emblematic of Jesus' sufferings; accordingly, Dostoevsky's action here could be read as a prediction of inevitable suffering for Russia and of redemption through that suffering.[50]

This compressed literary biography is definitive in yet another key respect: Dostoevsky's life prefigures the lives of writers of Akhmatova's generation. In the twentieth century, the mock execution on Semenovskii Square gave way to the real executions of poets and writers. The words "Omsk convict" are prophetic of the fate of the many writers sent to Siberia after the revolution, who died literal, not figurative, deaths. Furthermore, just as Dostoevsky's art was decisively influenced by the mock execution and the years of imprisonment, so the pages of poets and writers of Akhmatova's generation "smell faintly"—and not so faintly—of executions.

In "Prehistory," Dostoevsky's art, too, is portrayed as prefiguring what was to come. It is well known that Dostoevsky prided himself on the prophetic, revelatory powers of his art. By his special brand of realism—"realism, only deeper"—he strove to depict reality so as to anticipate, in his words, "the future results of present events."[51] "Prehistory" portrays Dostoevsky at the very end of his life, when he was writing *The Brothers Karamazov*. Although there is no explicit reference to that novel in "Prehistory," the Staraia Russa segment contains a cluster of striking allusions to it:

А в Старой Руссе пышные канавы,
И в садиках подгнившие беседки,
И стекла окон так черны, как прорубь,   25
И мнится, там такое приключилось,
Что лучше не заглядывать, уйдем.
Не с каждым местом сговориться можно,
Чтобы оно свою открыло тайну
(А в Оптиной мне больше не бывать...).   30

And in Staraia Russa there are luxuriant ditches,
And in little gardens half-rotted summerhouses,
And the windows' glass panes are as black as an ice hole,   25
And it seems that some such thing happened there
That it's better not to glance in, let's leave.
Not with every place is it possible to make a deal
For it to reveal its mystery
(And I can visit Optina no more . . .).   30

Staraia Russa is evoked in just three lines, each of which features a separate motif: the ditches, the summerhouses, and the windows of a house.[52] The text cautions against looking into the windows, immediately offering an enigmatic rationale: "Ne s kazhdym mestom sgovorit'sia mozhno,/Chtoby ono svoiu otkrylo tainu"/"Not with every place is it possible to make a deal/For it to reveal its mystery."[53] These gnomic lines assert the impossibility of penetrating every interior, of solving every riddle. They are ostensibly calculated to disengage the reader's attention from the mysterious interior by declaring it impenetrable; they have, however, the opposite effect. By presenting the reader with a darkened interior, alluding to an event that occurred there, and then refraining from divulging its nature and calling it a mystery, Akhmatova is creating a mystery and marking it as such. The two lines just quoted have a metapoetic significance: the word *mesto* is used ambiguously, with reference both to the interior hidden by the darkened windowpanes and to this very segment of the text. In the terminology of Charles S. Peirce, the passage as a whole constitutes an icon, or iconographic sign, of a *temnoe mesto*; literally, *temnoe mesto* means "dark place," but idiomatically it denotes a textual obscurity, some part of a text that resists comprehension.

The solution to the riddle of this passage lies in *The Brothers Karamazov*. The three Staraia Russa motifs are central to the novel's action. The ditches not only conjure up the topography of the town where Fedor Karamazov lives,[54] they metonymically recall a crucial episode in the plot—Alesha Karamazov's first encounter with the schoolboys (part II, book 4, chapter 3).[55] The second motif—"podgnivshie besedki"/"half-rotted summerhouses"—alludes to the ramshackle, half-rotting summerhouse (*besedka*) where Dmitrii makes his confession to Alesha (part I, book 3, chapter 3), revealing his motives for murder and declaring his readiness to kill his father if necessary.[56] In the same summerhouse on the very next day, Alesha overhears Smerdiakov proclaim his hatred both for his fatherland and for the circumstances of his birth and flaunt his potential for rebellion.[57] Both summerhouse episodes have a direct bearing on the dramatic action of the novel, supplying different motives for the murder of Fedor Karamazov.

The source of the third motif—the dark windows—is the chapter metapoetically entitled "V temnote" ("In the Dark," part III, book 8, chapter 4), in which Dmitrii rushes to his father's house, tormented by the fear that Grushen'ka is there. From afar he sees the lighted windows of the house, and then he steals right up to one of them and knocks. The knock brings old Fedor to the window, which he opens, thrusting his head through it and almost climbing out of it.[58] Later, during the preliminary investigation of the crime, the detail of the window assumes great importance (part III, book 9, chapter 5). The prosecutor states that the murder was committed "v komnate, a *ne cherez okno*"[59]/"in the room, and *not through the window.*" The prosecutor's assertion that the murder took place in the room may be read as a definitive commentary on the dark windows of "Prehistory," obliterating all doubt as to what they conceal. On the night of the murder, the windows were brightly lit. In the return to the scene of the crime in "Prehistory," the windows have gone dark, obscuring the interior. Akhmatova's obfuscation here is far from arbitrary, for it is modeled on Dostoevsky's poetics. The actual commission of the crime is not dramatized in the novel; although the nature of the crime is revealed almost immediately, the question of exactly how and by whom it was committed forms the mainspring of the rest of the plot.

The event alluded to by Akhmatova—patricide—stands at the core of Dostoevsky's treatment of the conflict between the generations in *The Brothers Karamazov*. Situated precisely in the center of "Prehistory," the Staraia Russa passage constitutes Akhmatova's metonymic recapitulation of *The Brothers Karamazov*[60] and contains the key to the poet's understanding of the fate of her generation. Driven as the novel is by the violent conflict between the generations, by the rebellion of the sons against the father and the revolt against all forms of authority, *The Brothers Karamazov* with uncanny accuracy prefigures the Russian revolution and its aftermath. The enigmatic visit to Staraia Russa thus foreshadows the series of catastrophic events to be witnessed by Akhmatova's generation. This prefigurement is suggested in another way as well: the concealed murder of Fedor Karamazov is a *zrelishche ne vidannoe*—literally, an unseen spectacle—anticipating the *zrelishcha nevidannye* (spectacles never-seen-before) mentioned at the end of "Prehistory."

The Portrait of a Woman

In one of her prose notes, Akhmatova terms "Prehistory" a "non-lyric piece" (*SP,* 511). One lyrical theme, however, permeates the work as a whole—the theme of change and the poet's attempt to come to terms with it. The theme is introduced in a mediated form, through the epigraph "Ia teper' zhivu ne tam . . ."/"I live elsewhere now . . . ," which is taken from Pushkin's narrative poem "Domik v Kolomne" ("The Little House in Kolomna"). What immediately follows the epigraph is of paramount importance to "Prehistory":

> ...Я живу
> Теперь не там, но верною мечтою
> Люблю летать, заснувши наяву,
> В Коломну, к Покрову—и в воскресенье
> Там слушать русское богослуженье.[61]

> . . . I live
> Elsewhere now, but in a faithful dream
> I love to fly, drowsing while awake,
> To Kolomna, to Pokrov—and on Sunday
> To listen there to a Russian liturgy.

Here change is transcended through memory, through an imaginative flight into the past. Pushkin's narrator immediately embarks on such a flight, serving up a humorous recollection of his impious behavior during one such divine service. In the St. Petersburg evoked in "Prehistory," just as in the St. Petersburg of Pushkin's day, the city's many churches were open and operating. In the city of 1940, by contrast, religious persecution was the order of the day, and most of those very churches had been closed or destroyed by the Soviet authorities.

The Pushkinian epigraph resonates particularly strongly in one line of "Prehistory," the authorial aside in the middle of the text: "(A v Optinoi mne bol'she ne byvat' . . .)"/"(And I can visit Optina no more . . .)." Akhmatova is contrasting her fate with Dostoevsky's: he had traveled to Optina for spiritual guidance in the

1870's, but such a journey was an impossibility for Akhmatova in 1940. The Optina Hermitage, the object of innumerable pilgrimages by the Russian Orthodox faithful, had been virtually destroyed after the revolution: in 1923 its buildings were ransacked, its monks and elders persecuted and expelled. In *The Brothers Karamazov* the monastery is not idealized, but it is a holy place opposed to the sinful world of Fedor Karamazov and identified with the teachings of Zosima and the human striving toward the ideal. The destruction of Optina signifies a complete rebellion against divine authority and the sanctioning of any deed, any act, no matter how sinful, when expediency requires.[62]

The Pushkinian epigraph sets the stage for Akhmatova's much more serious foray into the past. That foray is not expressly presented as a recollection, and the narrative stance is generally distanced and often ironic. The opening portrait of Dostoevsky's Petersburg (lines 1–8) is a good example, for on the surface it is highly unlyrical. In fact, it is based on Akhmatova's earliest memories of Petersburg, as the following prose recollection of the city, recorded by Akhmatova in 1962, demonstrates:

The first (lowest) layer for me is Petersburg of the nineties, Dostoevsky's Petersburg. It was covered from head to toe in tasteless signboards—lingerie, corsets, hats; it was totally devoid of greenery, of grass, of flowers; it was all in a drum beat, so reminiscent always of an execution, it was in the good capital-city French, in the grandiose funeral processions, and in the royal cavalcades described by Mandelstam.[63]

The numerous parallels with the opening lines of "Prehistory" reveal that Akhmatova was drawing on her earliest memories of Petersburg, but the role of these memories is concealed, and personal recollection emerges as a theme only much later in the text.[64]

The categorical phrase "Dostoevsky's Russia" identifies the dynamic present-tense portrait of St. Petersburg as a thing of the past, declaring its difference from the city of the author's present, 1940, in keeping with the sense of the epigraph. In fact, every aspect of the city's description bespeaks change. Horse-drawn cabs have been replaced by motorized vehicles; Gorokhovaia Street has been renamed—after Dzerzhinsky, no less, the first head of the Soviet secret police; Smol'nyi has been transformed from a convent and women's school into a government headquarters; no trace of anything French survives; the once omnipresent dance studios and money changers' shops no longer exist; the funeral business, now nationalized, has become invisible; signboards with personalized names have been replaced by those bearing generic names and supplemented by banners and posters carrying political and ideological slogans. The key change, of course, is not mentioned in the text—the renaming of the city from St. Petersburg to Leningrad.[65]

Although the lyrical impulse is veiled in most of "Prehistory," it does surface to dominate two important passages. The first sketches a domestic interior, the second draws the portrait of a woman. Together, the two passages represent the feminine principle, the feminine source, in Akhmatova's myth of origins. The first segment (lines 31–37) immediately follows and sharply contrasts with the Staraia Russa segment. There the reader was excluded from the dark interior and denied a glance inside, which would have recollected the central event of *The Brothers Karamazov*—the murder of Fedor Karamazov. The next part of "Prehistory" (lines 31–37) conjures up in great detail a very different interior, one suffused by the light of a kerosene lamp:

Шуршанье юбок, клетчатые пледы,
Ореховые рамы у зеркал,
Каренинской красою изумленных,
И в коридорах узких те обои,
Которыми мы любовались в детстве,
Под желтой керосиновою лампой,
И тот же плюш на креслах...

The rustling of skirts, checkered plaids,
Walnut frames of mirrors
Amazed by Kareninesque beauty,
And in narrow corridors the same wallpaper
That we admired in childhood,
Under the yellow kerosene lamp,
And the same plush on the armchairs . . .

The theme of recollection sounds in the reference to childhood; the sensations and *realia* enumerated are recognizable from childhood memories, as accentuated in the phrases "te oboi"/"the same wallpaper" and "tot zhe pliush"/"the same plush."[66] In contradistinction to the masculine realm concealed in the Staraia Russa segment, this interior is identified as the feminine domain, both through the mention of the sound of skirts and the reference to Tolstoy's *Anna Karenina*, one of the monumental literary events of the 1870's.[67] The walnut-framed mirrors point to the tradition of the Russian realistic novel, which claimed to mirror society by drawing a typical picture of it. The evocation as a whole has a generalized flavor; for all the specificity of the individual details, they figure as typical traits of domestic interiors of the 1870's.

The illuminated interior is a realm of pleasure and beauty, but it is not entirely secure. The reference to Tolstoy's novel conceals a threat to the domestic realm, for *Anna Karenina* depicts the disintegration of the family, making it the counterpart of *The Brothers Karamazov* in the text.[68] The threat to the interior is realized in the sudden truncation of the last line of the passage on the third foot and the abrupt shift to the exterior world in the next three lines:

Все разночинно, наспех, как-нибудь...
Отцы и деды непонятны. Земли
Заложены. И в Бадене—рулетка.

Everything is jumbled, slapdash, any old way . . .
Fathers and grandfathers are incomprehensible. The lands
Have been mortgaged. And in Baden there's roulette.

Chaos and disorder are expressed here lexically, thematically, as well as rhythmico-syntactically, a striking contrast to the fluidity, orderliness, and harmoniousness of the preceding passage.

The feminine element returns in the next part of "Prehistory," and with it the vein of personal recollection reaches its apogee:

И женщина с прозрачными глазами
(Такой глубокой синевы, что море
Нельзя не вспомнить, поглядевши в них),

С редчайшим именем и белой ручкой,
И добротой, которую в наследство
Я от нее как будто получила,—
Ненужный дар моей жестокой жизни...

And a woman with transparent eyes
(Of such deep dark blue, that on looking into them
It's impossible not to recall the sea),
With a most rare name and small white hands,
And a kindness that I evidently
Received from her in inheritance—
An unnecessary gift of my cruel life . . .

Constructed as a single complex sentence, this passage evokes the portrait of a woman whose realm was described earlier, albeit in generalized terms, whose appearance was prefigured in the mirror reflection of feminine beauty. Everything about the portrait is individualized, attesting to the unique nature of its subject.

The transparency of the woman's eyes is the antithesis of the impenetrability attributed to the male forebears in the sentence "Ottsy i dedy neponiatny"/"Fathers and grandfathers are incomprehensible." The transparency also contrasts with the black windowpanes of the Staraia Russa segment, windowpanes concealing the realm of the father. A glance into those windows is both warned against and denied, yet here a glance into the eyes is given, triggering an involuntary recollection of the sea. This recollection in turn activates a complex network of intertextual reminiscences. The sea in Akhmatova's poetry is associated with first times, with origins, with birth. The poet was born on the coast of the Black Sea,[69] and the summers of her childhood and youth were spent on the Black Sea near Sevastopol, where she, as an autobiographical sketch puts it, "podruzhilas' s morem"(*S*, 1:43)/"made friends with the sea." [70] These early memories left their impression on her first narrative poem, *Right by the Sea* (1914), as well as on "At that time I was a guest on earth" (1913), both of which are set by the sea.[71] In her later poetry, Akhmatova as a rule recollects the sea only to express a sense of dislocation, of alienation from her origins, as, for instance, in *The Way of All the Earth* and in the second part of *Re-*

quiem's "Epilogue." In "Prehistory," memory overcomes alienation and disjunction: the fleeting recollection of the sea rejoins the poet with her origins and childhood.

This recalls the text's primary concern with genesis and simultaneously offers a clue to the woman's identity, which is presented as something of a riddle. The epithet attached to her name—*redchaishee* (most rare)—underscores her uniqueness, and the fact that her name is described but not uttered bespeaks a reverential attitude toward her. The motif of *nasledstvo* (inheritance) indicates that the woman is a blood relation of the poet. The recollection of the sea prompted by the glance into her eyes makes possible her precise identification, for as the "source of the generation of all life," the sea is symbolically associated with the mother, particularly "in the formless aspect of its waters." [72] The portrait is indeed that of the poet's mother, Inna Erazmovna Gorenko. [73] The maternal inheritance is specified to be the trait of *dobrota* (kindness, goodness), which in turn is defined in the line: "Nenuzhnyi dar moei zhestokoi zhizni"/"An unnecessary gift of my cruel life." The word *zhizn'* (life) occurs but once in "Prehistory," appropriately in connection with the mother, and the epithet attached to it expresses the poet's evaluation of her life from the perspective of 1940, at the age of 51. The antithesis between kindness and cruelty sketches the bitter trajectory of the poet's life, from a timeless childhood idyll into a dreadful sequence of "unprecedented spectacles."

Pasternak devotes a few lines of his "Fathers" to mothers, and the comparison with Akhmatova's portrait is instructive:

Это было вчера,
И, родись мы лет на тридцать раньше,
Подойди со двора,
В керосиновой мгле фонарей,
Средь мерцанья реторт
Мы нашли бы,
Что те лаборантши—
Наши матери
Или
Приятельницы матерей. [74]

That was yesterday,
And had we been born some thirty years earlier,
Were we to approach from the courtyard,
In the lanterns' kerosene haze,
Midst the flickering of retorts,
We would find
That those laboratory assistants were
Our mothers
Or
The friends of our mothers.

Instead of portraying his own mother, Rosa Kaufman—"an outstanding pianist," in Pasternak's words[75]—he conjures up a generalized portrait of "Our mothers/Or/The friends of our mothers." Pasternak's "lanterns' kerosene haze" recalls the "yellow kerosene lamp" lighting the domestic interior in "Prehistory," yet it illuminates not a home but a laboratory. Through this picture of women at work in the laboratory, Pasternak alludes to the emancipation of women that was so prominent a part of social change in Russia in the second half of the nineteenth century. Akhmatova entirely excludes from her mother's portrait such sociohistorical allusions. Like many young women of her day, Inna Erazmovna left home to go to college, and she even joined a circle of the People's Will Party for a time,[76] but these facts find no reflection in "Prehistory." The portrait proper is devoid of details tying it to a specific milieu, and it is bound to the age in which its subject lived only by the context in which it appears. The portrait of Inna Erazmovna marks a radical departure from the kaleidoscopic shifting of imagery and of temporal and spatial coordinates that characterizes "Prehistory" as a whole: it is singular, focused, and atemporal, utterly static, all of which traits bespeak the portrait's iconic nature. Like the icon, Akhmatova's image of her mother partakes of the timeless and the unchanging and is an object of veneration and yearning. This idealization is accentuated because the sole psychological trait attributed to Inna Erazmovna is kindness or goodness, which testifies to her spiritual excellence, recalling the primary trait of the Virgin Mary—compassion.

The portrait of Inna Erazmovna seems detached from the picture of Dostoevsky's Russia evoked in "Prehistory," but its form and appearance in the text are closely related to Dostoevsky's art. Robert Louis Jackson, who has written extensively on the role of the *obraz* (form, shape, image, icon) in Dostoevsky's art, has defined the icon's significance in Dostoevsky: "The icon, particularly the iconographic representation of the Madonna, appears in Dostoevsky's artistic universe as a religious-aesthetic symbol of great importance—a literal image of beauty toward which man turns in reverence and longing." [77] The icon of the *Theotokos* (Mother of God) figures prominently in Dostoevsky's work, but there is a related image that is also prominent in the later novels—an early visual memory of a character's natural mother, a memory cherished by the character. Two early memories of mothers in Dostoevsky's writings of the 1870's seem particularly germane to Akhmatova's portrait of hers in "Prehistory"—those of Arkadii Dolgorukii and Alesha Karamazov.

Separated from his mother at birth, Arkadii Dolgorukii saw her just three times during his early years. In part I of *The Adolescent*, Arkadii tells his mother what he remembered from her early visits:

"I don't remember or know anything, it's just that something of your face remained in my heart for the rest of my life, and furthermore there remained the knowledge that you were my mother. . . .

"Your face, or something of it, the expression, remained in my memory so distinctly that five years later in Moscow I recognized you immediately, although nobody told me that you were my mother." [78]

Arkadii reveres the memory of his mother's face as his sole link with her, his only tie with his origins.

In *The Brothers Karamazov*, Alesha Karamazov preserves and reveres an even keener early memory of his mother. The narrator's insistence on the singular significance of this memory in Alesha's life is of particular relevance to "Prehistory":

Although he was only in his fourth year at his mother's death, he remembered her afterward for his whole life, her face, her caresses, "precisely as if she were standing alive before me." Such memories may be preserved (and this is a well-known fact) even from an earlier age, even from the age of two, but just protruding all one's life like spots of light out of the darkness, like a corner torn out of a huge picture that has gone entirely dark except for that little corner itself. That is exactly how it was with him.[79]

The sacrosanct nature of the memory of the mother is emphasized in the narrator's metaphors, particularly in the contrast between light and darkness. The comparison of the memory to a "spot of light" suggests that it is a source of support, comfort, and deliverance. The memory proper, which is of an incident in Alesha's early childhood, bears this out: sobbing hysterically on her knees, Alesha's mother holds him up to an icon of the *Theotokos*, praying for the Mother of God to protect him.[80] Akhmatova's portrait of Inna Erazmovna—unparalleled in all her work and so enigmatic within "Prehistory"—appears to have been inspired by Dostoevsky's iconography; like Alesha's memory of his mother, it represents a source of support and comfort, of spiritual strength.[81]

The Poet's Genealogy

Akhmatova pays homage to her mother in the iconographic portrait of Inna Erazmovna, but "Prehistory" lacks a complementary portrait of Akhmatova's biological father, Andrei Antonovich Gorenko. Amanda Haight's description of a decisive point in the poet's relations with her father helps to explain the absence of such a portrait:

Hearing of her poems, when she was seventeen, he told her not to bring shame upon his name. "I don't need that name," she answered and chose a Tatar name—that of the last Tatar princess of the Golden Horde. A strange choice, as she said later, for a Russian poetess, but Akhmatova was the name of her Tatar great-grandmother and the Tatars in the south had always seemed mysterious and fascinating.[82]

From the very beginning of her career, Akhmatova's identity as a poet was bound up with the renunciation of her biological father and his legacy, as epitomized in her rejection of his family name for that of a female ancestor.[83] The place of the father in Akhmatova's account of her origins is filled by Dostoevsky: his portrait complements Inna Erazmovna's, which immediately precedes it in the text. Although both portraits are drawn in seven lines, they differ profoundly. Whereas the image of Inna Erazmovna is static, Dostoevsky is portrayed as the embodiment of action, with a proliferation of verbs describing him engaged in the act of creation. The portrait of the mother is atemporal, and that of Dostoevsky is firmly anchored in a specific sociohistorical context: the initial phrase "Stranu znobit" (line 48)/"The country is feverish" situates him in a Russia in ferment, Russia of the 1870's. His portrait is, moreover, framed by those facts of his biography—the mock execution and the years of penal servitude—that shaped his worldview.

The close parallels between Akhmatova's depiction of Dostoevsky and cosmogonic myths were discussed above, but the question of the function of such myths has not been addressed. According to Eliade, creation myths and rituals have a deeply therapeutic, life-affirming function: they renew and revitalize the world by effecting what he terms a "regeneration of time." [84] Akhmatova's creation myth has a fundamentally different thrust. Instead of reaffirming the structure of the world in which the poet found herself in 1940, "Prehistory" reveals the origins of a world "out of joint." Judith Shklar, in her essay "Subversive Genealogies," has identified a tradition of writers from Hesiod to Rousseau, Nietzsche, and Freud, who have questioned and condemned the established order by rendering a myth of origins. These writers turned to the creation myth "in order to convey, in elaborate forms, their felt discord with their surroundings. . . . Actuality is to be revealed, shown, and shown up by a review of its origins that does not delineate the causes, but the awful character of this aging world." [85] Shklar locates the force of these subversive genealogies in what distinguishes them from history: "Unlike history, 'genealogy' refers both to the past and the present simultaneously. . . . It is an account of the past as an integral part of the present." [86] "Prehistory" belongs to the tradition of subversive genealogies identified by Shklar, for it conjures up the past in order to pass judgment on the present. The line "Vse ponial i na vsem postavil krest" (line 49)/"Understood everything and gave it all up for lost" is particularly revealing in this regard. It represents Dostoevsky's assessment of his age, but it simultaneously expresses Akhmatova's own stance in "Prehistory": she, too, is judging her age and revealing it to be fraught with suffering, violence, and death.

"Prehistory" diverges from the tradition defined by Shklar in one important respect—the highly lyrical, autobiographical vein that runs through it, culminating in the portrait of Akhmatova's mother. In addition to examining the origins of the world around her, the poet is exploring her own personal origins as well. Her maternal inheritance is defined as the trait of *dobrota* (goodness, kindness), which is said to be a "nenuzhnyi dar"/"unnecessary gift." Although the paternal inheritance is not named outright, the depiction of Dostoevsky in the act of writing implies that this is the paternal legacy: Akhmatova is portraying herself as Dostoevsky's literary heir. The paternal legacy is the antithesis of the maternal: it is the necessary gift, a gift associated with cruelty, to extend the antithesis. Cruelty is a quality that has been associated with Dostoevsky's art since the appearance of N. K. Mikhailovsky's monograph *Zhestokii talant* (*A Cruel Talent*, 1882). It was also a quality ascribed to Akhmatova's lyric talents by N. V. Nedobrovo in his 1915 essay on her poetry: "Akhmatova's very voice, firm, even self-confident, her very calmness in confessing pain and weakness, the very abundance of anguish, poetically refined,—all bear witness, not to tears over life's trivialities, but to a lyrical soul sooner harsh than soft, *cruel* than lachrymose, and clearly masterful rather than downtrodden" (emphasis added).[87] A few lines later Nedobrovo speaks of the poet's "zhestokaia sila" (*S*, 3: 489)/"cruel strength." Akhmatova reread the article in the spring of 1940, and it strongly influenced her identity as a poet.[88] Surely Nedobrovo's repetition of the epithet "cruel" did not escape her attention, nor did the implied link with Dostoevsky.

Akhmatova identifies Dostoevsky as her literary progenitor in other ways as well. First, "Prehistory" is modeled on the poetics of Dostoevsky's novels, recalling their iconography and the role of *Vorgeschichte* in them, as well as the fact that each of them is constructed around a mystery (the Staraia Russa segment). Second, as Roman Timenchik has pointed out, the picture of Dostoevsky engaged in the creative act is metapoetic—it defines Akhmatova's own method in the text.[89] The phrase "Vot on seichas peremeshaet vse"/"Right now he will mix up everything" succinctly expresses Akhmatova's guiding technique in the text—she "mixes up" opposing categories and notions, blending lyric and epic modes, facts and fictions, darkness and light, and blurring the boundaries between past and present, between appearance and reality.

"Prehistory" is Akhmatova's literary genealogy, her exploration of the sources of her poetry. The Pushkinian epigraph excluded, the text names just one poet—Nikolai Nekrasov, whose work epitomizes the turn of Russian poetry toward prose. Allusions abound, by contrast, to nineteenth-century Russian novelists, including Saltykov-Shchedrin, Turgenev, Tolstoy, and above all Dostoevsky. In the early 1920's, several of Akhmatova's commentators pointed out the indebtedness of her poetry to the nineteenth-century Russian novel, but nowhere was it more forcefully expressed than in Osip Mandelstam's "Letter on Russian Poetry" (1922):

Akhmatova brought into Russian lyric poetry the whole immense complexity and richness of the nineteenth-century Russian novel. Akhmatova would not exist, were it not for Tolstoy and *Anna Karenina*, Turgenev and *A Nest of Gentlefolk*, all of Dostoevsky, and in part even Leskov. Akhmatova's genesis [*genezis*] lies wholly in Russian prose, not poetry. Her poetic form, sharp and unique, she developed with a backward glance at psychological prose.[90]

"Prehistory" was clearly inspired by these words. Mandelstam's use of the non-Slavic *genezis* finds its Slavic counterpart—*bytie*—in Akhmatova's circumlocution "prostilis' s nebyt'em"/"bid farewell to nonbeing." Even the dominant role of Dostoevsky in the poem, with just cursory references to *Anna Karenina* and Turgenev, is anticipated here. By locating her origins in the tradition of the nineteenth-century Russian novel, Akhmatova is appropriating as her own that tradition and the moral authority that it commands.

It is in this sense that the regenerative, revitalizing potential of the creation myth is fully exploited by Akhmatova in "Prehistory."

This new myth of origins proclaims a new source of authority for the poet, one suited to the inimical age in which she found herself: not that of a classically inspired muse, as in "At that time," but that of the preeminent nineteenth-century novelist. In "Prehistory" Dostoevsky exemplifies the tragic and supreme role of the writer in Russian society: despite being persecuted, threatened with death, and deprived of freedom, he writes, judging his age and transcending it in his art.

Chapter 4

The Poet's Lot in
Poem Without a Hero

Оттого, что мы все пойдем
По Таганцевке, по Есенинке
Иль большим Маяковским путем...

Because we will all go
Down Tagantsev Street, down Esenin Street,
Or by the grand Mayakovsky route. . . .
—Anna Akhmatova, 1930–32

    Без палача и плахи
Поэту на земле не быть.

    Without the executioner and the block
The poet cannot exist on earth.
—Anna Akhmatova, 1935

"Reshka" ("Tails"), the metapoetic second part of *Poem Without a Hero*, opens with a satirical account of the reaction of the poet's editor to Part One, the opaque "Deviat'sot trinadtsatyi god" ("Nineteen Hundred Thirteen"). The disgruntled editor bluntly expresses his dissatisfaction in a speech that, as Tat'iana Tsiv'ian has observed, accentuates the distinctive characteristics of Akhmatova's "Petersburg Tale":[1]

    ...«Там три темы сразу!
   Дочитав последнюю фразу,
    Не поймешь, кто в кого влюблен.

   Кто, когда, и зачем встречался,
    Кто погиб, и кто жив остался,
     И кто автор, и кто герой,—
  И к чему нам сегодня эти

Рассуждения о поэте
 И каких-то призраков рой».

 . . . "There are three themes at once there!
 Having read the last sentence,
   You won't understand who's in love with whom,

Who met whom, and when, and why,
 Who perished, and who remained alive,
   And who's the author, and who's the hero,—
And what good to us today are these
 Ratiocinations about the poet
   And a swarm of some sort of ghosts."

The tale's great complexity, comically understated in the editor's complaint that it treats "three themes at once," engenders such confusion that the editor comprehends nothing at all, from critical turns in the plot—who survives and who dies—to the crucial distinction between author and hero. The editor's failure to understand reflects the blurring of fundamental categories and distinctions throughout Part One: not only are the boundaries between the dramatis personae obscured (as underscored in the editor's repetition of the pronoun "who" seven times), but past, present, and future are intermingled, as are different states of consciousness— memory, dream, and waking.

The editor's speech is modeled on a passage from the beginning of Pushkin's 1828 poem "Poet i tolpa" ("The Poet and the Crowd"), in which the "uninitiated" (*neposviashchennyi*) and "dull" (*tupoi*) crowd listens "uncomprehendingly" (*bessmyslenno*) to the poet's playing upon his lyre and then asks:

«Зачем так звучно он поет?
Напрасно ухо поражая,
К какой он цели нас ведет?
О чем бренчит? Чему нас учит?
Зачем сердца волнует, мучит,
Как своенравный чародей?
Как ветер, песнь его свободна,
Зато как ветер и бесплодна:
Какая польза нам от ней?»[2]

"Why does he sing so sonorously?
Striking the ear in vain,
To what goal does he lead us?
About what does he strum? What does he teach us?
Why does he trouble, torment hearts
Like a capricious wizard?
Like the wind, his song is free,
But, like the wind, it is fruitless, too:
What use is it to us?"

Just as in the editor's speech in "Tails," a cascade of interrogatives culminates by calling into question the usefulness of the poet's creation: compare Akhmatova's "I k chemu nam segodnia eti"/"And what good to us today are these" with Pushkin's "Kakaia pol'za nam ot nei?"/"What use is it to us?" These Pushkinian allusions not only mark the editor as a representative of the obtuse crowd, they recall what follows in "The Poet and the Crowd"—the poet's scornful denunciation of the crowd for its preoccupation with utility.

The last two lines of the editor's speech pithily define "Nineteen Hundred Thirteen" as "Rassuzhdeniia o poete/I kakikh-to prizrakov roi"/"Ratiocinations about the poet/And a swarm of some sort of ghosts." This formulation puts what drives the dramatic action of Part One—the author's visitation by a band of ghosts from 1913—on a par with the text's "ratiocinations about the poet." The two are inextricably linked, for while the "swarm of . . . ghosts" sets in motion the plot of Akhmatova's Petersburg tale, that plot serves as a framework for exploring the role and fate of the poet in postrevolutionary Russia. This theme occupies a central place in the later poetry, as confirmed in a fragment from the poet's autobiographical prose: "Itak, pozdniaia A[khmatova] . . . perekhodit na razdum'ia o roli i sud'be poeta."/"Thus, the later A[khmatova] . . . switches to meditations on the role and fate of the poet."[3] The phrase "razdum'ia o roli i sud'be poeta"/"meditations on the role and fate of the poet" strongly echoes the editor's "Rassuzhdeniia o poete"/"Ratiocinations about the poet," although the stylistic coloration differs: *razdum'ia* is a neutral literary word, while *rassuzhdeniia* is in this context a colloquial word with somewhat pejorative connotations, expressing the editor's negative valuation. The problem of the role and fate of the poet dominates Akhmatova's later work, but nowhere is it explored as fully and in such complexity as in *Poem Without a Hero*.

Shades of Poets in "Nineteen Hundred Thirteen"

Part One of *Poem Without a Hero* abounds in direct and enciphered references to poets. Virtually all of the chief dramatis personae are poets. The sole exception is the "heroine," but even she is called the "dvoinik"/"double" of a poet—the authorial persona herself: "Ty—odin iz moikh dvoinikov" (*S*, 2: 114, line 304)/"You are one of my doubles." At the beginning of "Tails," the author identifies the three chief poets featured in "Nineteen Hundred Thirteen":

> «Там их трое—
> Главный был наряжен верстою,
> А другой как демон одет,—
> Чтоб они столетьям достались,
> Их стихи за них постарались...
> Третий прожил лишь двадцать лет.
>
> И мне жалко его.»
> (*S*, 2: 123, lines 13–19)

> "There are three of them there—
> The main one was dressed up as a milepost,
> And another was dressed as a demon,—
> That they would be inherited by the centuries,
> Their poems made sure for them . . .
> The third lived just twenty years,
>
> And I feel sorry for him."

The first poet, the "main one," appears in chapter 1 "dressed up as a striped milepost" ("Polosatoi nariazhen verstoi" [*S*, 2: 107, line 107]) and "covered crudely with motley paint" ("Razmalevan pestro i grubo" [line 108]). The latter phrase evokes the ethos of the

Futurists, recalling their penchant for shocking outfits replete with bizarrely patterned grease paint. The portrait of this poet incorporates a series of unmistakable references to Mayakovsky and his poetry,[4] but likewise contains allusions to Velimir Khlebnikov's work.[5] Akhmatova herself commented on this persona in a 1959 fragment devoted to *Poem Without a Hero*: "The Demon was always Blok, the Milepost [*Verstovoi Stolb*] was the Poet in general [*Poet voobshche*], Poet with a capital letter (something like Mayakovsky)."[6] Akhmatova emphasizes the symbolic role of this Mayakovsky-like "Poet in general," and his motley Futurist attire oxymoronically masks his ancient origins, revealed in this description of him: "rovesnik Mamvriiskogo duba,/Vekovoi sobesednik luny" (*S*, 2: 108, line 110)/"coeval of the oak of Mamre,/Age-old interlocutor of the moon." Himself a creator and writer of "iron laws," the "Poet in general" never errs: "I ni v chem ne povinen: ni v etom/Ni v drugom i ni v tret'em . . . /Poetam/Voobshche[7] ne pristali grekhi" (*S*, 2: 108, lines 110–11)/"And he is not guilty of anything: not of this,/Not of that, nor the other thing . . . /Sins/Generally do not become poets." The other key attribute ascribed to the "Poet in general" is impatience:

> Существо это странного нрава,
> Он не ждет, чтоб подагра и слава
> Впопыхах усадили его
> В юбилейные пышные кресла,
> А несет по цветущему вереску,
> По пустыням свое торжество.[8]

> This being has a strange nature,
> He won't wait for gout and glory
> Hastily to seat him
> In luxurious jubilee armchairs
> But carries across the blooming heather,
> Across the deserts his triumph.

The poet's impatience is expressed in his early departure from society, suggesting his alienation from his contemporaries; on another level, however, that departure is symbolic of the poet's untimely death. The passage recalls the premature deaths of Khlebnikov[9] of an illness at the age of 37 in 1922, of Esenin, who hanged himself in 1925 at the age of 30, and of Mayakovsky, who shot himself five years later at the age of 37.

The second of the three poets featured in Part One is described in "Tails" as "kak demon odet"/"dressed like a demon," a phrase harking back to the oxymoronic description of him in chapter 2 as "Demon sam s ulybkoi Tamary" (*S*, 2: 113, line 269)/"The Demon himself with the smile of Tamara." [10] Modeled on Alexander Blok, he makes a fleeting appearance in chapter 1 of "Nineteen Hundred Thirteen," is described at length in chapter 2, and briefly reappears to escort the heroine home just before the abrupt denouement in chapter 4. As V. N. Toporov has shown in his study *Akhmatova and Blok*, the portrait of this persona (*S*, 2: 113–14, lines 265–86) interweaves a series of allusions to Blok's poetry, the most marked of which is the phrase "bez litsa i nazvaniia"/"without face or name," a conflation of two quotations from Blok that underscores the poet's devilish nature. [11]

Both the Futuristically garbed "Poet in general" and the Demon poet die prematurely (Blok died in 1921 at the age of 40), yet both win immortality through their poetry. It is this that sets them apart from the third poet, a low-ranking officer who commits suicide at the age of twenty and is fated to be "naveki zabyt"/"forever forgotten" (*S*, 2: 119, line 411). The death of this young poet is first presaged in the funereal tones of the first and second dedications, especially in this passage from the latter:

> Кто-то маленький жить собрался,
> Зеленел, пушился, старался
> Завтра в новом блеснуть плаще.
> > (*S*, 2: 102, lines 10–13)

> Someone little got ready to live,
> Sprouted green, fluffed himself up, and tried
> To shine tomorrow in a new cloak.

These lines place "Nineteen Hundred Thirteen" in the tradition of Petersburg narratives of the "little man" crushed by historical and social forces, a tradition initiated by Pushkin in *The Bronze Horse-*

man (the protagonist Evgenii's ill-fated plans for a peaceful domestic life with his Parasha are recalled in the first line above), continued in Gogol's "Shinel'" ("The Overcoat") (the phrase "novyi plashch"/"new cloak" recalls the new overcoat responsible for Akakii Akakievich's demise; later Akhmatova's protagonist is said to be wearing a *shinel'* [*S*, 2: 111, line 213]), and recast a century later by Osip Mandelstam in his 1928 novella *Egipetskaia marka* (*The Egyptian Stamp*) to depict the overwhelming forces impinging on the individual in the postrevolutionary age. *Poem Without a Hero* owes much to *The Egyptian Stamp*: not only does its title allude to Mandelstam's novella,[12] both texts comment on their own writing, and the bounds are blurred in both between the authorial persona and the hero/heroine. These links with other Petersburg narratives foretell the untimely death of Akhmatova's young poet long before he takes his place on the stage of *Poem Without a Hero* at the very end of chapter 1.[13] The beginning of chapter 4 proclaims the imminence of the denouement in the detail of the "nevidimykh zvon kopyt" (*S*, 2: 119, line 407)/"ringing of invisible hooves," which Zhirmunskii has identified as an allusion to Pushkin's description of the hapless Evgenii being pursued by the Bronze Horseman.[14] For all the similarities linking the young poet to Evgenii, Akakii, and other Petersburg protagonists, one thing sets him apart: they are crushed by forces larger than themselves, forces against which they are powerless, but he destroys himself.

The suicide is announced in chapter 4, when the protagonist repeats with just a few small changes the farewell speech recited at the end of chapter 1. The authorial persona then terms his death "bessmyslennaia"/"meaningless"[15] and immediately afterward describes his death in terms commenting on that epithet:

Не в проклятых Мазурских болотах,
　　Не на синих Карпатских высотах...
　　　　Он—на твой порог!
　　　　　Поперек...
Да простит тебя Бог!

　　　Сколько гибелей шло к поэту,
　　　Глупый мальчик: он выбрал эту,—

> Первых он не стерпел обид,
> Он не знал, на каком пороге
> Он стоит и какой дороги
> Перед ним откроется вид...

Not in the accursed Masurian bogs,
  Not in the blue Carpathian heights . . .
    He—[has fallen] on your threshold!
      Crosswise . . .
And may God forgive you!

> *How many deaths were coming toward the poet,*
> *The silly boy: he chose this one,—*
> *He could not bear the first wrongs,*
> *He did not know on what threshold*
> *He was standing and what road's*
> *View was to open before him . . .*

The repetition of the word "porog"/"threshold" marks its pivotal importance here: the cornet killed himself on his beloved's threshold, unaware of the metaphorical threshold on which he was standing—the end of one historical era and the beginning of a new one—the "Nastoiashchii Dvadtsatyi Vek" (*S*, 2: 118, line 384)/ "Real Twentieth Century," whose ominous approach is described in a passage in chapter 3 predicting both war and revolution.[16] What defines the new age is the abundance of possible deaths it held for the protagonist: "*Skol'ko gibelei shlo k poetu*"/"*How many deaths were coming toward the poet.*" The neutral word for death in Russian is *smert'*; *gibel'* specifically denotes an untimely, violent death. Two such deaths are named in the first two lines cited above: the Masurian Lakes and Carpathian Mountains were the sites of two terrible battles between the Russians and the Austro-Hungarians in 1914–15. Many more possible deaths, however, are hinted at in the mention of the "view" of a "road" ("vid" "dorogi") that had been about to open before him, a "view" that opens before the reader only at the very end of *Poem Without a Hero.*

One other death coming toward the protagonist is alluded to in Part One through a prominent feature of his depiction: though the main prototype for him is Vsevolod Kniazev, a young poet who committed suicide in 1913, numerous unmistakable references to Osip Mandelstam are incorporated into his portrait.[17] *Poem Without a Hero* begins by blending the images of Kniazev and Mandelstam in the "First Dedication." [18] Inscribed "To the Memory of Vs. K.," the poem commemorates Kniazev's death in its closing references to "khvoia mogil'naia" (lines 11–12)/"graveside evergreen branches" and Chopin's "Marche funèbre" (lines 14–15). At the same time, the poem bears the date of the anniversary of Mandelstam's death, December 27, 1940 (the official date of his death is December 27, 1938), so that the funereal imagery simultaneously recalls his death somewhere in Siberia's prison camps and his burial in an unmarked grave. The most important link between the poet-protagonist and Mandelstam is established in chapter 1, at the end of the former's farewell speech to his beloved:

Слышу шепот: «Прощай! Пора!
Я оставлю тебя живою,
Но ты будешь *моей* вдовою,
Ты—Голубка, солнце, сестра!»
На площадке две слитые тени...
После—лестницы плоской ступени,
Вопль: «Не надо!»—и в отдаленье
Чистый голос:
     «Я к смерти готов».

I hear a whisper: "Farewell! It's time!
I shall leave you alive
But you will be *my* widow,
You—My Dearest, sun, sister!"
Two merged shadows are on the landing . . .
After that, the steps of the low stairs,
A cry: "Don't!"—and in the distance
A clear voice:
     "I am ready for death."

In context, the last sentence reads as the protagonist's declaration of his readiness to commit suicide. In fact, the words are Mandelstam's, as Akhmatova herself revealed in her memoirs of the poet, "Listki iz dnevnika" ("Sheets from a Diary," 1962):

Несмотря на то, что время было сравнительно вегетарианское, тень неблагополучия и обреченности лежала на этом доме. Мы шли по Пречистенке (февраль 1934 г.), о чем говорили—не помню. Свернули на Гоголевский бульвар, и Осип сказал: «Я к смерти готов». Вот уже 28 лет я вспоминаю эту минуту, когда проезжаю мимо этого места. (*S*, 2: 179)

Despite the fact that the times were relatively vegetarian, the shadow of trouble and doom lay on that household. We were walking along Prechistenka[19] (February 1934), what we were talking about I don't remember. We turned onto Gogol Boulevard, and Osip said, "I am ready for death." I have been recollecting that moment for 28 years now, whenever I go by that place.

It is not simply a matter of Akhmatova attributing Mandelstam's words to her protagonist. As Nadezhda Mandelstam writes in her memoirs, "the voice of Mandelstam himself and his own authentic words sound for one brief moment in the *Poem*: 'I am ready for death.'"[20] The phrase "i v otdalen'i"/"and in the distance" heightens the ambiguity, for it may be interpreted both spatially—as an indication that the protagonist has distanced himself from the door of his beloved—and temporally—as designating Mandelstam's 1934 utterance.[21]

Mandelstam's was another of the deaths coming toward the "cornet of the dragoons" in the Real Twentieth Century. Like the cornet, Mandelstam consciously chose to die, but while the young officer was propelled toward suicide by a wounded ego—"Pervykh on ne sterpel obid"/"He could not bear the first wrongs"—[22] Mandelstam's choice was inseparable from his understanding of the poet's role in society. In her memoirs of Mandelstam, Akhmatova recounts one of their conversations about poetry that bears directly on this issue:

Осип Эмильевич, который очень болезненно переносил то, что сейчас называют культом личности, сказал мне: «Стихи сейчас должны быть гражданскими», и прочел «Под собой мы не чуем».

(S, 2: 181)

Osip Emil'evich, who very painfully bore what is now called the cult of personality, said to me, "Now poems must be civic," and he recited, "We do not feel beneath us."

What Mandelstam meant by "civic" is evident from the poem he recited to Akhmatova—"My zhivem, pod soboiu ne chuia strany"/ "We live, not sensing the country beneath us." Written in November 1933, it denounces Stalin and his subordinates for their lawless and bloody rule: "Kak podkovy kuet za ukazom ukaz—/Komy v pakh, komu v lob, komu v brov', komu v glaz"[23]/"Like horseshoes he forges edict after edict—/Some get it in the groin, some in the forehead, some in the brow, some in the eye." To compose such a "civic poem" was a crime, and as the words "I am ready for death" indicate, Mandelstam was fully aware of the penalty. What is more, he seemed set on bringing the poem to the attention of the authorities, for he recited it not only to trusted friends but willingly to a wider circle of acquaintances.[24] When he was arrested in May 1934, it was because of his poems, as Akhmatova's eyewitness account of the search of his room makes clear:

Искали стихи, ходили по выброшенным из сундучка рукописям. Мы все сидели в одной комнате. Было очень тихо. За стеной, у Кирсанова, играла гавайская гитара. Следователь при мне нашел «Волка» и показал Осипу Эмильевичу. Он молча кивнул. Прощаясь, он поцеловал меня. Его увели в 7 утра.

(S, 2: 181–82)

They were searching for poems, walking across the manuscripts that had been thrown from a little chest. We all sat in one room. It was very quiet. On the other side of the wall, at Kirsanov's, a Hawaiian guitar was playing. In my presence the investigator found "The Wolf" and showed it to Osip Emil'evich. He nodded silently. Taking his leave, he kissed me. He was led away at 7 A.M.

"The Wolf" is "Za gremuchuiu doblest' griadushchikh vekov" (1931)/"For the thunderous valor of future centuries," in which

Mandelstam envisions his own journey to Siberia. The beginning of Akhmatova's last sentence—"Ego uveli"/"He was led away"—alludes to this very poem, and specifically to its last stanza, which begins "Uvedi menia v noch', gde techet Enisei"[25]/"Lead me away into the night, where the Enisei flows."[26] This poem and others predict Mandelstam's arrest and journey to the prison camps, and they led to his arrest and exile in 1934 and ultimately to his death.

In *Poem Without a Hero*, the sentence "I am ready for death" recalls both Mandelstam's belief in the poet's sacred duty to write civic verse, to protest against tyranny, and his death for that belief—a selfless death, the antithesis of the one chosen by the young protagonist of *Poem Without a Hero*—a "civic death," as Akhmatova writes elsewhere:

> Торжествами гражданской смерти,
> Я по горло сыта, поверьте,
> Вижу их что ни ночь во сне.[27]

> I have had more than enough, believe me,
> Of the solemnities of civic death,
> I see them most every night in my dreams.

Under Stalin, civic poems had as their most probable consequence a civic death—another of the deaths that the protagonist of *Poem Without a Hero* avoided.

Over the Threshold: Figures of Repression in "Tails"

The word *reshka* denotes "tails" in the sense of the reverse of a coin; Part One is retrospectively identified with "heads," which in Russian is *orel*—literally, "eagle," a reference to the principal design on prerevolutionary Russian coins—the double-headed eagle, emblem of the Russian empire. The identification is highly appropriate, for 1913 was one of the last years of the empire; Part Two, by contrast, is associated with the postrevolutionary era. The implied switch between Parts One and Two from "heads" to "tails" is in itself a reversal, suggesting a change in fortune from better to worse. The word *reshka* also calls to mind its synonym *reshetka*, now obsolete in the sense of "tails," but not in its primary meaning of "grating," that is, a network of bars set in at a window or door. This meaning of *reshetka* is highly relevant here, for in Russian the phrase *za reshetkoi* means "behind bars" or "in prison." The seemingly innocuous title "Reshka" thus conceals a comment on the repressive nature of postrevolutionary Russia.[28]

"Tails" represents much more than a metapoetic "intermezzo" in *Poem Without a Hero*. To be sure, the role of the metapoetic in it is very large: it comments on the opaqueness of Part One, on the poetics and the very origins of *Poem Without a Hero* as a whole, as well as describing in detail the author's experience of writing it. The latter points up a crucial difference between Parts One and Two: in the former, the author figures as one of the dramatis personae, while in "Tails" she emerges as the author of Part One. The opening exchange between the poet and her editor underscores that shift in roles: the main conflict is now not between characters in a tale written by the poet but between the poet and society.

"Tails" is supplied with three epigraphs, the last of which bears directly on this issue (*S*, 2: 122):

> ...жасминный куст,
> где Данте шел и воздух пуст.
> Н. К.

> . . . a jasmine bush,
> where Dante walked and the air is empty.
> N. K.

N. K. is Nikolai Kliuev (1887–1937), the peasant poet who perished in Siberia a year before Mandelstam's death. The epigraph is taken from Kliuev's vitriolic long poem "Ia gnevaius' na vas i gorestno braniu" ("I am wroth at you and sorrowfully curse you," 1932–33), also known as "Khuliteli iskusstva" ("The Defamers of Art").[29] In it Kliuev execrates the Soviet authorities for their mistreatment of him. The first ten lines of the text are representative of the tone of the whole:

Я гневаюсь на вас и горестно браню,
Что десять лет певучему коню,
Узда алмазная, из золота копыта,
Попона же созвучьями расшита,
Вы не дали и пригоршни овса
И не пускали в луг, где пьяная роса
Свежила б лебедю надломленные крылья.
Не волчья пасть, ни дыба, ни копылья
Не знали пытки вероломней
Пегасу русскому в каменоломне.[30]

I am wroth at you and sorrowfully curse you,
Because for ten years to the singing horse,
With bridle of diamonds, hoof of gold,
And saddlecloth embroidered with consonances,
You did not give even a handful of oats
And did not let him into the meadow, where the drunken dew
Would have cooled the swan's broken wings.
Not the wolf's maw, nor the rack, nor the rods,
Have known a torture more perfidious
Than that endured by the Russian Pegasus in a quarry.

Kliuev pictures himself both as a swan, a traditional symbol for the poet, and as a singing horse—the winged Pegasus, identified with poets since he created Mount Helicon's Hippocrene fountain—the spring of poetic inspiration—by stamping his hoof. Both the swan and the horse have been abused: the swan cannot fly because its wings have been broken; the horse, which has been starved and tortured, is held captive in a quarry. The use of a quotation from this poem as an epigraph indirectly establishes as one of the chief concerns of "Tails" the persecution of Russian poets by the state after the revolution.

Just as significant to "Tails" is the special role "The Defamers of Art" played in Kliuev's fate, as Akhmatova attests in her memoirs of Mandelstam, just a paragraph after quoting the latter's words, "I am ready for death":

Осип читал мне на память отрывки стихотворения Н. Клюева «Хулители искусства»—причину гибели несчастного Николая Ал-

ексеевича. Я своими глазами видела у Варвары Клычковой за-
явление Клюева (из лагеря о помиловании): «Я, осужденный за мое
стихотворение "Хулители искусства» и за безумные строки моих
черновиков». Оттуда я взяла два стиха как эпиграф—«Решка».
(*S*, 2: 180)

Osip recited to me from memory fragments of N. Kliuev's poem "The
Defamers of Art"—the cause of the death of the unfortunate Nikolai Alekseevich. At Varvara Klychkova's I saw with my own eyes Kliuev's petition
(from prison camp for mercy): "I, convicted for my poem 'The Defamers
of Art' and for the insane lines of my rough drafts." I took two lines from
there as an epigraph to "Tails."

Kliuev was arrested in 1933 for disseminating "kulak propaganda"—poems criticizing collectivization—and other anti-Soviet
poems, including "The Defamers of Art"; he was interrogated,
convicted, and sent into exile in Siberia.[31] He died there in 1937,
but for years nothing certain was known about the circumstances
of his death. According to one account, he died of a heart attack
while being returned to Moscow for the review of his case; another
version had it that he was arbitrarily executed. The truth came to
light in early 1989: on June 5, 1937, Kliuev was rearrested and
after four months in prison he was executed by a firing squad.[32]
The epigraph thus synecdochically points not just to the persecution of the Russian poet but to the arrest, imprisonment, and death
of the poet (*gibel' poeta*) at the hands of the state.

"Tails" focuses on the fate not of Kliuev but of the poet alluded
to in the epigraph proper—an inexact quotation from a lyrical
digression in Kliuev's philippic:

Ахматова—жасминный куст,
Обложенный асфальтом серым,
Тропу утратила ль к пещерам,
Где Данте шел и воздух густ...[33]

Akhmatova is a jasmine bush,
Laid round with gray asphalt,
Has she lost the path to the caves
Where Dante walked and the air is thick . . .

In linking Akhmatova's name with Dante's, the digression associates her with Dante's hell: the word *peshchery* (caves) is redolent of the underworld. By omitting the two middle lines, the epigraph to "Tails" transplants Kliuev's "jasmine bush"—the main part of his metaphor for Akhmatova—from some indeterminate setting to Dante's inferno, recalling the important role of Dantesque imagery in Akhmatova's *Requiem*. There is a direct reference to *Requiem* at the end of the prose remarks prefacing "Tails": "V pechnoi trube voet veter, i v etom voe mozhno ugadat' ochen' gluboko i ochen' umelo spriatannye obryvki Rekviema" [34]/"The wind howls in the stovepipe, and in this howl can be divined very deeply and very skillfully hidden scraps of Requiem." This sentence foregrounds the presence of concealed references to *Requiem*—and the Ezhov terror—in "Tails." The epigraph is one such reference, and it is "skillfully hidden" indeed, for the symbolism of the jasmine bush is masked through the ellipsis used by Akhmatova in the first line.

Concealment figures here on several levels: the significance of the epigraph is obscured through the elision of Akhmatova's name; fragments of *Requiem* are hidden in "Tails," but even the fact of their concealment is withheld in some versions of the text. Later on in "Tails," the author admits to employing "simpaticheskie chernila"/"sympathetic ink" and "zerkal'noe pis'mo"/"mirror writing" (*S*, 2: 126)—means of concealment both—asserting that she had no other choice: "I drugoi mne dorogi netu"/"And there is no other road for me." This bespeaks external compulsion, alluding to the suppression of free speech in Stalin's Russia.[35]

A different kind of concealment is pictured in the eighth stanza, which conjures up another aspect of the sociohistorical context:

VIII

Карнавальной полночью римской
И не пахнет. Напев Херувимской
У закрытых церквей дрожит.
В дверь мою никто не стучится,
Только зеркало зеркалу снится,
Тишина тишину сторожит.

(*S*, 2: 124)

VIII

Of a Roman carnival midnight
There's no scent. The melody of the Cherubic hymn
Trembles near closed churches.
No one knocks at my door,
The mirror dreams only of the mirror,
Silence keeps watch over silence.

Here the interiors of churches are hidden from view. The phrase "zakrytye tserkvi"/"closed churches" is akin to the parenthetical mention of Optina in "Prehistory," for it conjures up the suppression of religion after the revolution—the destruction and desecration of churches, their conversion into warehouses and museums of atheism. The "Napev Kheruvimskoi"/"melody of the Cherubic hymn" refers to a hymn from the Russian Orthodox liturgy that begins "Izhe kheruvimy taino obrazuiushche . . ."/"We who mysteriously represent the Cherubim . . ."; sung when the doors to the altar are opened, revealing the holy of holies, the hymn proclaims the setting aside of earthly cares and heralds the approach of the high point of the service—Communion.[36] In Akhmatova's stanza, the divine liturgy has been expelled from the sanctuaries; the Cherubic hymn "drozhit"/"trembles" outside, recalling the divine mysteries from which the faithful have been excluded and the earthly cares from which there is no respite.

The eighth stanza marks the transition to a lyrical digression on the fate of the author and her poetry and does so by foregrounding the themes of repression and silence. The latter is introduced reflexively in the final line of the stanza—"Tishina tishinu storozhit"/"Silence keeps watch over silence." This emphasis on silence sharply departs from the preceding stanzas' account of the author's "visitation" by the *poema*, where references to thunderous music and raucous noise predominate.[37] The twin themes of repression and silence dominate the next five stanzas of "Tails":[38]

IX

И со мною моя «Седьмая»,[39]
Полумертвая и немая,

Рот ее сведен и открыт,
Словно рот трагической маски,
Но он черной замазан краской
И сухою землей набит.

X

....
....

....

И проходят десятилетья:
Пытки, ссылки и казни—петь я,
Вы же видите, не могу.

XI

И особенно, если снится
То, что с нами должно случиться:
Смерть повсюду—город в огне,
И Ташкент в цвету подвенечном...
Скоро там о верном и вечном
Ветр азийский расскажет мне.[40]

XII

....
....
....
....
....
....

XIII

Я ль растаю в казенном гимне?
Не дари, не дари, не дари мне
Диадему с мертвого лба.
Скоро мне нужна будет лира,
Но Софокла уже, не Шекспира.
На пороге стоит—Судьба.

IX

And with me is my "Seventh,"
Half-dead and mute,

Its mouth is contorted and open,
Like the mouth of a tragic mask,
But it is smeared with black paint
And stuffed with dry earth.

    X

. . . .
. . . .
. . . .

And the decades pass by:
Torture, exile, and executions—sing,
As you see, I cannot.

    XI

And especially, if I dream of
What will happen to us:
Death all around—the city in flames,
And Tashkent in wedding blossom,
Soon the Asian wind will tell me there
About the faithful and the eternal.

    XII

. . . .
. . . .
. . . .
. . . .
. . . .
. . . .

    XIII

Will I melt in an official hymn?
Do not give, do not give, do not give me
The diadem from a dead brow.
Soon I will need a lyre,
But that of Sophocles, not Shakespeare.
On the threshold stands Fate.

The ninth stanza conjures up some of Akhmatova's poetry, ambiguously identified as her "Sed'maia" ("Seventh"). In her edition
of the text, Jeanne Rude glosses this as a reference either to Akh-

matova's seventh book of poems or to the seventh elegy in *The Northern Elegies* cycle.[41] Akhmatova's seventh collection, contain-ing poems written between 1936 and 1946, was entitled "Nechet" ("Odd"), from the numerical pair *chet* (even) and *nechet* (odd); accepted for publication in 1946, it was printed, bound, and then destroyed following the August 14, 1946, Resolution of the Central Committee.[42] Later, beginning with *The Flight of Time* 1965, "Sed'maia kniga" ("The Seventh Book") becomes the heading not only for the poems of the destroyed collection but for all subse-quent poems as well.[43] The successful publication of "The Seventh Book" in *The Flight of Time* weighs strongly against reading the ninth stanza's "Seventh" as a reference to it.

Until recently, the seventh Northern Elegy was the most impor-tant lacuna in Akhmatova's corpus.[44] Viktor Zhirmunskii noted in his commentary to *Stikhotvoreniia i poemy* that the poet's archives contained several unfinished drafts of the elegy (*SP*, 506), but he published none of them, apparently for reasons of censorship. He did, however, describe the place of the elegy in the cycle: *The Northern Elegies* treat events extending chronologically from the eve of the author's birth ("Prehistory") to the very end of her life; the seventh, conceived of as a kind of epilogue to the cycle, focused on the period "after 1946" (*SP*, 507)—a transparent reference to the aftermath of the August 14, 1946, Resolution. Zhirmunskii slipped another detail about the elegy into his notes on the unfin-ished play *Prolog* (*Prologue*): "The unfinished 'Seventh Elegy' was evidently connected with the theme of the trial" (*SP*, 510). This was confirmed by Lidiia Chukovskaia in a brief article called "Polu-mertvaia i nemaia" ("Half-Dead and Mute," 1976) (the title quotes the ninth stanza's second line); according to Chukovskaia, Akh-matova read her a draft of the elegy on May 28, 1965, saying that she planned to call it "Posledniaia rech' podsudimoi" ("The Last Speech of the Accused"), a title situating the persona's discourse in the context of her own trial.[45]

Chukovskaia goes on to call the elegy an "elegy on silence," a designation recalling the epithet "nemaia"/"mute" from stanza IX, and she asserts that it is the referent of the ninth stanza's "Seventh."[46] The elegy is indeed dominated by the theme of silence, as its first eleven lines show:

> А я молчу, я тридцать лет молчу.[47]
> Молчание арктическими льдами
> Стоит вокруг бессчетными ночами,
> Оно идет гасить мою свечу.
> Так мертвые молчат, но то понятно
> И менее ужасно. . . . .
>
> Мое молчанье слышится повсюду,
> Оно судебный наполняет зал,
> И самый гул молвы перекричать
> Оно могло бы, и подобно чуду
> Оно на все кладет свою печать.[48]

> But I am silent, I have been silent for thirty years.
> Silence like arctic ice
> Surrounds me through innumerable nights,
> It is coming to extinguish my candle.
> The dead are silent like this, but that is understandable
> And less terrible. . . . .
>
> My silence is audible everywhere,
> It fills the courtroom,
> And it could outshout
> The very roar of notoriety, and like a wonder
> It puts its imprint on everything.

The elegy opens with a paradox: speech is the persona's medium for proclaiming her own silence, a silence mysteriously unbroken by the poetic utterance, as the present-tense "molchu"/"I am silent" emphasizes.[49] The tropes of paradox and oxymoron dominate the elegy: the persona's silence is audible everywhere (line 7); it can "outshout/The very roar of notoriety" (lines 9–10); although it is likened to "arctic ice" (line 2), it has "burned out the heart" (*vyzhglo serdtse*)[50] of the persona. The silence is also portrayed as an inimical, deathly force ("Tak mertvye molchat" [line 5]/"The dead are silent like this") threatening the very life of the persona ("Ono idet gasit' moiu svechu" / "It is coming to extinguish my candle" [line 4]). In the published version of the elegy, the context of the persona's utterance—her own trial—is only hinted at, notably in the phrase "Ono sudebnyi napolniaet zal" (line 8)/"It fills the courtroom," but also in the persona's identification with Socrates in the allusion to his trial and death sentence: "I razve ia ne vypila tsikutu" (line 17)[51]/"And didn't I drink the hemlock."

The ninth stanza of "Tails" portrays the silencing of this "elegy on silence":

> И со мною моя «Седьмая»,
> Полумертвая и немая,
> Рот ее сведен и открыт,
> Словно рот трагической маски,
> Но он черной замазан краской
> И сухою землей набит.

> And with me is my "Seventh,"
> Half-dead and mute,
> Its mouth is contorted and open,
> Like the mouth of a tragic mask,
> But it is smeared with black paint
> And stuffed with dry earth.

The dominant rhetorical figure here is personification, a trope frequently encountered in Akhmatova's later metapoetry, in which the personified poems are almost invariably in a state of severe privation. All of the personifying attributes ascribed to the "Seventh" bespeak injury, impairment, and destruction; the epithet "nemaia"/ "mute," for instance, deprives the elegy of its capacity for speech. Compare Akhmatova's description of her poems in the last quatrain of "Zastol'naia" ("Table Song," 1955):

> Сплетней изувечены,
> Биты кистенем,
> Мечены, мечены
> Каторжным клеймом.
>
> (S, 3: 71)

Mutilated by gossip,
> Beaten with a bludgeon,
Marked, marked
> With a convict's brand.

The poems of "Table Song" are personified through this cata-
logue of the violence done to them, yet they are not specifically
represented as having human form. The "Seventh," by contrast,
possesses not only an impaired capacity for speech but a mouth
as well—the very icon and instrument of speech. The image of
the mouth dominates the stanza's last four lines, developing and
motivating the theme of muteness. The qualifiers "sveden"/"contorted" and "otkryt"/"open" conjure up a face twisted in a ric-
tus of pain. The compelling simile likening the mouth of the
"Seventh" to that of a tragic mask personifies only in the etymological sense of the word ("person" and its derivatives are from
the Etruscan for "mask"), lending the elegy the traits of inani-
mateness and lifelessness. The last two lines reveal the violence
that has silenced the "Seventh": its mouth has been "smeared
with black paint," blackened in the sense of defamed, denigrated
(compare the Russian *chernit'*, which has the same connotations);
on another level, the image recalls the blacking out of texts by
the censor to render them illegible—a visual analogue of muteness. The mouth has also been packed "with dry earth" (*sukhoiu
zemlei*)—both defiled and obstructed. This vivid image of the
suppression of speech harks back to the end of *Requiem*, where
Akhmatova envisions just such a possibility with regard to herself: "I esli zazhmut moi izmuchennyi rot" (*S, 2: 369*)/"And if
they stop my tortured mouth."

The mouth of the poet's "Seventh" has been both tortured
and stopped. The theme of torture, obliquely introduced into
"Tails" through the Kliuev epigraph, resounds in the second half
of the tenth stanza: "I prokhodiat desiatilet'ia:/Pytki, ssylki i
kazni"/"And the decades go by:/Tortures, exiles, and executions." [52] The first half of the tenth stanza was omitted from the
final version of the *poema*, but it evokes a specific scene of torture:

Враг пытал: А ну, расскажи-ка,
Но ни слова, ни стона, ни крика
Не услышать ее врагу.[53]

The enemy tortured: Well now, tell me,
But not a word, not a moan, not a cry
Could her enemy hear.

The victim, as signaled in the feminine gender of the possessive pronoun, is the preceding stanza's "Seventh." The scene evoked is based on one of the master plots of Stalinist literature and folklore: a communist girl is captured by the (Nazi) enemy and tortured mercilessly but heroically maintains her silence, dying a martyr to the cause. Variations on this plot were featured constantly in the literature of World War II and even made their way into folklore (for instance, the well-known ditty "Vragi partizanku poimali"/"The enemies captured a partisan girl"). In the omitted lines of the tenth stanza, Akhmatova depicts the martyring of her "Seventh" at the hands of Stalin's secret police; silence under torture is normally a sign of courage and heroism, but here it reflects the main theme of the "Seventh," as well as the elegy's forced silencing.

Akhmatova omitted the first three lines of the tenth and the entire twelfth stanza from the final version of the *poema*, marking the missing lines with ellipses to foreground their absence.[54] The omitted lines extend the muteness of the "Seventh" to the poet herself, implying that she, too, has been forcibly silenced.[55] The last half of the tenth stanza motivates the poet's silence:

И проходят десятилетья:
Пытки, ссылки и казни—петь я,
Вы же видите, не могу.

(S, 2: 124)

And the decades go by:
Tortures, exiles, and executions—sing,
As you see, I cannot.

The poet's professed inability to "sing" in the face of "Tortures, exiles, and executions" is manifested not only in the missing lines, but also in the second line's fitful rhythm and the knotty syntax of the last two lines.[56]

In a footnote to the omitted twelfth stanza, Akhmatova gives a very different explanation for the elided lines:

Пропущенные строфы—подражание Пушкину. См. «Об Евгении Онегине»: «Смиренно сознаюсь также, что в Дон Жуане есть две выпущенные строфы», писал Пушкин.

The omitted stanzas are in imitation of Pushkin. See "On *Eugene Onegin*": "I humbly confess likewise that there are two omitted stanzas in *Don Juan*," wrote Pushkin.

The note motivates the omitted lines in purely literary terms, suggesting that they are simply a part of the literary play pervading the *poema*. In Lidiia Chukovskaia's view, "the reference to Pushkin . . . is not only yet another instance of mystification but a reliable screen as well."[57] This is very true: Pushkin's sacrosanct status in Soviet culture ensured that this reference to his practice would lend an incontrovertible authority to Akhmatova's own omission of lines.

Nevertheless, Akhmatova's "imitation of Pushkin" is relatively limited, and those limitations demand close scrutiny. The imitation does not, in the first place, extend to the compositional role of the omitted stanzas. Ironically, in the number of stanzas omitted Akhmatova mimics Byron more closely than Pushkin: "Tails" has one and a half omitted stanzas, as compared to almost twenty-five in *Eugene Onegin*.[58] The omitted lines do not play a salient role in the composition of *Poem Without a Hero* as a whole because they occur within the space of three consecutive stanzas in "Tails"; in *Eugene Onegin*, by contrast, the omitted stanzas are scattered throughout, making omission itself, as Iurii Tynianov observed, one of Pushkin's key compositional devices.[59] Furthermore, in her imitation of Pushkin's defense of the omitted stanzas, Akhmatova diverges from him in several respects. Pushkin's defense was not incorporated into *Eugene Onegin* proper, whereas Akhmatova makes it a part of *Poem Without a Hero*.[60] Even more important, Pushkin's defense of the omitted stanzas is not limited to the sen-

tence quoted, as the word *takzhe* (likewise) signals in the quotation; in fact, Akhmatova excludes most of Pushkin's remarks,
which are adduced below in full:

The omitted stanzas have repeatedly given cause for censure. That there
are strophes in *Eugene Onegin* that I could not or did not want to print is
nothing to wonder at. Once omitted, however, they break the continuity
[*preryvaiut sviaz'*] of the story, and therefore the place where they were
supposed to be is marked. It would be better to replace these stanzas with
others or to correct and fuse together the ones I preserved. But sorry, I am
too lazy for that. I humbly confess likewise that there are two omitted
strophes in *Don Juan*.[61]

Literary imitation, it turns out, is but the last of several reasons
Pushkin gives for the omitted stanzas. Following as it does a
tongue-in-cheek confession of authorial laziness,[62] the reference to
Don Juan rings highly ironic. Pushkin's irony doubtless appealed
to Akhmatova, who infuses his words with new irony by citing
them in the context of two stanzas portraying the suppression of
her work and the silencing of her voice. The chief reason mentioned
by Pushkin for omitting stanzas from his novel—that he "could not
or did not want" to publish them—is not directly quoted by Akhmatova, but clearly her intent is to allude to it: Pushkin's "there
were stanzas that I could not . . . print" smacks of censorship and
suppression, much like Akhmatova's "pet' ia/. . . ne mogu"/"I cannot . . . sing."[63]

Which stanzas of *Eugene Onegin* did Pushkin actually omit because of censorship? M. L. Gofman's painstaking examination of
the extant drafts of the novel did not yield a single example of such
an omission: in certain instances the strophes in question had never
existed, making their omission fictitious; in other cases they were
deemed unsuitable for publication because they were unfinished or
because they did not satisfy the poet in some way.[64] Almost six
decades after the publication of Gofman's study, however, Iurii Lotman identified one stanza omitted by Pushkin for reasons of censorship: the thirty-eighth stanza of chapter 6,[65] which comes in the
middle of a lyrical digression prompted when young Lensky is

killed by Onegin in a duel. The digression explores the question of what "udel"/"lot" had awaited Lensky, the same question Akhmatova raises about her protagonist at the end of Part One. The thirty-seventh stanza of chapter 6 imagines as Lensky's future the glorious career of a renowned poet; the thirty-ninth, by contrast, conjures up the comically prosaic life of a staid, gouty landowner. The omitted thirty-eighth envisions another possibility—the career of a military leader:

Исполня жизнь свою отравой,
Не сделав многого добра,
Увы, он мог бессмертной славой
Газет наполнить нумера.
Уча людей, мороча братий
При громе плесков иль проклятий,
Он совершить мог грозный путь,
Дабы последний раз дохнуть
В виду торжественных трофеев,
Как наш Кутузов иль Нельсон,
Иль в ссылке, как Наполеон,
Иль быть повешен, как Рылеев.[66]

Having imbued his life with venom,
and not having done much good,
alas, he might have with undying fame
the issues of newspapers filled.
Teaching men, gulling brethren,
to the thunder of plaudits or of curses,
a grim course he might have achieved,
so as to breathe his last
in sight of solemn trophies
like our Kutuzov, or like Nelson,
or like Napoleon, in exile,
or on the gallows, like Rîleev . . . [67]

Pushkin envisages three different fates Lensky might have met as a military leader: he might have died revered as a national hero, "like our Kutuzov, or like Nelson," or else in defeat and disgrace—"like Napoleon, in exile." Finally, he might have been executed as a traitor: "Il' byt' poveshen, kak Ryleev"/"Or have been hanged, like Ryleev" (translation mine). Of the four historical figures named, the only one to whom Lensky bears any resemblance is Kondratii Ryleev, a leader of the 1825 Decembrist uprising who was hanged in 1826. Like Lensky, Ryleev was not only a romantic poet but, in Nabokov's words, "a completely mediocre" one as well.[68] "The mention of Ryleev," Lotman writes, "made the strophe unprintable, and P[ushkin] threw it out, doubling up the number of the next strophe."[69]

Akhmatova was more than familiar with this omitted stanza and its reference to Ryleev: she refers to it in the late essay "Pushkin i nevskoe vzmor'e" ("Pushkin and the Neva Seacoast," 1963), quoting the stanza's final line in proof of Pushkin's devotion to the Decembrists:

Transitions, shifts from plane to plane, are organic to *Onegin*: irony accompanies Lensky almost to the last hour of his life, but Pushkin mourns him with incredible strength and sorrow, and returns to this in the seventh chapter. In a strophe of 1826 not included in the sixth chapter, he presents him as a possible participant in the uprising on Senate Square: "Or [he could] have been hanged, like Ryleev."[70]

There are some striking similarities between this description of Pushkin's attitude toward Lensky in *Eugene Onegin* and the author's attitude toward the protagonist in *Poem Without a Hero*. Not only does irony dominate his portrayal in Part One, but specific details link him to Lensky, especially the circumstances surrounding his death: like Lensky, he dies for love, is betrayed by his beloved, and is forgotten after his death. Furthermore, Akhmatova borrows from Pushkin the theme of what possible deaths had awaited the poet. Finally, she highlights the parallel between Lensky and her poet-protagonist at the very beginning of the fourth stanza of "Tails" in the words "I mne zhalko ego"/"And I feel sorry for him"—a phrase Roman Timenchik has identified as an echo of the beginning of Pushkin's chapter 6, stanza 36: "Druz'ia moi, vam zhal' poeta"/"My friends, you feel sorry for the poet."[71]

In the passage quoted above from "Pushkin and the Neva Sea-coast," Akhmatova argues that Lensky's death had a special significance for Pushkin because he associated it with Ryleev's execution and the Decembrists' fate as a whole. Lotman concurs with Akhmatova on this point: "The sixth chapter was written in 1826, during the investigation of the Decembrists' case, and was finished after their sentencing and execution. The heavy atmosphere of these months is reflected in its generally gloomy and tragic tone." [72] In the same way, the arrests, sentencings, and executions of the postrevolutionary decades left their imprint on Akhmatova's treatment of her protagonist's death.

In the thirty-eighth stanza of chapter 6, Ryleev's hanging is paired with a mention of Napoleon's exile, and the latter could be read as a veiled reference to the fate of those Decembrists sent to work in the mines of Siberia; compare the famous line from the last strophe of *Eugene Onegin* that serves as one of the epigraphs to *Poem Without a Hero*: "Inykh uzh net, a te daleche" [73]/"Some are no longer, while others are far away"—a patent reference to the executed and the exiled Decembrists. [74] "Tails" features the same pairing in the tenth stanza's "ssylki, kazni"/"exiles, executions": the third component of the series—"pytki"/"tortures"—finds no counterpart in Pushkin's thirty-eighth stanza, a measure of the relative humaneness of the prerevolutionary legal system.

Akhmatova's singling out of Ryleev in the Pushkin essay raises one final question: the poet-protagonist is Lensky's counterpart, but who is Ryleev's? Ryleev's Real-Twentieth-Century counterpart, in his fate although not in his truly great poetic talent, is Nikolai Gumilev, executed in August 1921 for allegedly participating in a conspiracy to overthrow the Bolsheviks. [75] Just as Lensky's premature death may have kept him from sharing Ryleev's death, Gumilev's was another of the possible fates the poet-protagonist of Akhmatova's Petersburg tale denied himself by committing suicide. The contrast between Gumilev's execution and the protagonist's suicide is paralleled in the first epigraph to this chapter, a fragment dating from the early 1930's that juxtaposes Gumilev's end with the suicides of Esenin and Mayakovsky, asserting that either execution, suicide, or compromise leading inevitably to suicide awaits all Russian poets.

The latter option is directly addressed in the thirteenth stanza of "Tails":

> Я ль растаю в казенном гимне?
> Не дари, не дари, не дари мне
> Диадему с мертвого лба.
> Скоро мне нужна будет лира,
> Но Софокла уже, не Шекспира.
> На пороге стоит—Судьба.

> Will *I* melt in an official hymn?
> Do not give, do not give, do not give me
> The diadem from a dead brow.
> Soon I will need a lyre,
> But that of Sophocles, not Shakespeare.
> On the threshold stands Fate.

The first three lines conjure up another role played by poets in the Real Twentieth Century—that of the official poet, a poet in the service of the state; the "kazennyi gimn"/"official hymn"—the antithesis of Mandelstam's "grazhdanskie stikhi"/"civic poems"—was the main genre of civic poetry sanctioned under Socialist Realism. "Diademu s mertvogo lba"/"The diadem from a dead brow" refers metonymically to some deceased poet who not only produced such "official hymns" but enjoyed the status of official poet laureate. This cluster of traits pointedly recalls the fate of Vladimir Mayakovsky, who committed suicide in 1930.[76] After the revolution Mayakovsky proclaimed himself its singer and devoted his talents to serving the new Soviet state, but his avant-garde propaganda was largely derided as utterly useless nonsense by ideologically minded critics, and first and foremost by Lenin. Mayakovsky was canonized by Stalin as Soviet poet laureate only posthumously, in 1935, a fact alluded to in the phrasing "Diademu s *mertvogo* lba"/"The diadem from a *dead* brow" (emphasis added).[77]

The opening lines of the stanza call to mind a passage from Mayakovsky's "Vo ves' golos" ("At the Top of My Voice") in which the poet's turn from lyric poetry to propaganda is retrospectively described as violence against himself and his art: "No ia/sebia/smi-rial,/stanovias'/na gorlo/sobstvennoi pesne"[78]/"But I/subdued/myself, / stepping/on the throat/of my own song." Akhmatova's use of the verb *rastaiat'* similarly bespeaks self-silencing, for it denotes melting or dissolving, suggesting the complete disappearance of the lyric "I"; in Russian it also designates the disappearance or dying out of sounds. Akhmatova emphatically distances herself from Mayakovsky's self-destructive self-silencing through the incantatory repetition of the negative. At the same time, the very mention of the "official hymn" recalls Akhmatova's one foray into the genre—the cycle *Glory to Peace* (1950), written ostensibly to glorify Stalin but in fact to save the life of her son. Fear, not tender emotion (another of the connotations of the verb *rastaiat'* is *priiti v umilenie* [to enter a state of tender emotion]), governed the cycle's creation.[79]

The consequences of the poet's refusal to sing an "official hymn" are envisaged in the last half of the stanza, which announces an impending reorientation in the poet's writing from Shakespeare to Sophocles, as well as the imminence of her own violent death, symbolized in the figure of a personified Fate on her threshold.[80] Akhmatova's poetry abounds in allusions to Shakespeare's tragedies, but none is more important to *Poem Without a Hero* than *Macbeth* with its theme of ineradicable guilt.[81] There are several references to tragedy in Part One—most notably, the authorial persona's declaration "Ia zhe rol' rokovogo khora/Na sebia soglasna priniat'" (S, 2: 114, lines 291–92)/"I agree to take on/The role of the fateful chorus." Akhmatova's Petersburg tale, however, lacks a protagonist of heroic stature, and its plot is not the stuff of tragedy, as attested when the protagonist's fate is called the "naigorchaishaia drama" (S, 2: 109, line 148)/"bitterest drama": in Russian the word *drama* metaphorically means a misfortune or calamity, but literally it denotes a play of serious—but not heroic—content. Tragedy's emblem, the tragic mask, is situated beyond the bounds of the Petersburg tale of 1913 in "Tails," marking the Real Twentieth Century as the age of tragedy. Whereas Shakespeare's tragedies are psychological in nature, the dramatic action in Sophocles' plays is determined by fate (*moira*), which dictates the sudden reversals in characters' lives, particularly their violent deaths. The prediction of Akhmatova's violent death in the last line of the stanza promotes the authorial persona from the tragic chorus in Part One's drama to a leading figure in the Real Twentieth Century's tragedy.

Two full strophes of "Tails" omitted by Akhmatova from the final version of *Poem Without a Hero* for censorship reasons recast the classical concept of tragedy to portray the fate of the Russian people after the revolution:

Xa

Ты спроси у моих современниц,
Каторжанок, стопятниц, пленниц,
И тебе порасскажем мы,
Как в беспамятном жили страхе,
Как растили детей для плахи,
Для застенка и для тюрьмы.

Xb

Посинелые стиснув губы,
Обезумевшие Гекубы
И Кассандры из Чухломы,
Загремим мы безмолвным хором,
(Мы, увенчанные позором):
«По ту сторону ада—мы».[82]

Xa

Just ask my female contemporaries,
Convicts, one-hundred-and-fivers,[83] captives,
And we will tell you
How we lived in oblivious fear,
How we raised our children for the executioner's block,
For the torture chamber, and for prison.

Xb

Having pressed shut our dark blue lips,
Insane Hecubas
And Cassandras from Chukhloma,

We will thunder in a speechless chorus,
(We—crowned with disgrace):
"Beyond hell are we!"

Here are the "skillfully hidden" fragments of *Requiem* mentioned in the prose remarks prefacing "Tails." The strophes are saturated with references to *Requiem*'s imagery, themes, and style: the women's "Posinelye . . . guby"/"dark blue lips," for example, are a variation on the "golubye guby"/"blue lips" of the woman described in "Instead of a Foreword" and share the same connotations.[84] The women's "bespamiatnyi strakh"/"oblivious fear" recalls the collective portrait drawn in the first part of *Requiem*'s "Epilogue," a portrait framed by both *strakh* (fear) and *ispug* (fright; *S, 1: 368–69*); the epithet *bespamiatnyi* (oblivious), furthermore, harks back to the deployment of the theme of forgetfulness in *Requiem*, as, for example, in a line from the seventh poem "The Sentence"—"Nado pamiat' do kontsa ubit'" (*S, 1: 365*)/"I must kill my memory to the end"—and even more graphically in the ninth numbered poem "Uzhe bezumie krylom" (*S, 1: 367*)/"Already the wing of madness," which treats the persona's surrender to madness as a gradual but inexorable forgetting of all that is dear to her. Finally, the second strophe's participle *obezumevshie* (who have gone insane) recalls these lines from the "Introduction" to *Requiem*: "obezumev ot muki,/Shli uzhe osuzhdennykh polki" (*S, 1: 363*)/"having gone insane from the torment,/Regiments of those already convicted marched."

While the "Dedication" of *Requiem* speaks for the women who stood with Akhmatova in Leningrad's prison lines, the "we" of these strophes embraces the poet's female "contemporaries," all of whom have been deprived of freedom (the word "plennitsy"/"captives" is a synonym for "nevol'nye," the epithet describing the poet's addressees in *Requiem* at the end of the Dedication), some by being sentenced to hard labor ("katorzhanki"), others by being exiled ("stopiatnitsy"/"one-hundred-and-fivers"); compare the allusion to exile and the camps in the "Dedication": "Chto im chuditsia v sibirskoi v'iuge"/"What appears to them in the Siberian blizzard."

The women, termed "Insane Hecubas and Cassandras from Chukhloma," are likened to Hecuba, queen of Troy, featured in Euripides' eponymous tragedy, and her daughter, the prophetess Cassandra, one of the protagonists of Aeschylus's *Agamemnon*; both Hecuba and Cassandra figure in Euripides' *Trojan Women*.[85] All three tragedies are set after the sack of Troy, when the Greeks have enslaved everyone they have not killed. In *Hecuba*, the queen of Troy first sees her daughter Polyxena sacrificed by the Greeks to the shade of Achilles; then her son Polydorus is murdered. Mad with grief, Hecuba wreaks a horrible vengeance, enticing her son's murderer into her tent, then killing his two sons and blinding him. In *Agamemnon*, Cassandra is brought to Argos as Agamemnon's slave; she not only foresees the murder of both Agamemnon and herself, she is privy to all the past crimes of the house of Atreus: "The blood-stained hands of them that smite their kin—/The strangling noose, and, spattered o'er/With human blood, the reeking floor."[86] These crimes have their counterparts in Akhmatova's portrayal of the Ezhov terror: compare "Pod krovavymi sapogami" (S, 1: 363)/"Under the bloodied boots" from the "Introduction" to *Requiem*, as well as the related phrase "okrovavlennyi pol" (S, 3: 72)/"the bloodied floor," from a poem of the late 1940's.[87] The stench of blood detected by Cassandra is that of the children of the house; compare the end of stanza Xa: "Kak rastili detei dlia plakhi"/"How we raised our children for the executioner's block." The plundering of the homeland, the murder of loved ones, enslavement, and exile all link the fate of the women of Russia with the fates of Hecuba and Cassandra. In Akhmatova, the names of Hecuba and Cassandra figure in what could be termed an oxymoronic metaphor, as noble vehicles for a common tenor: the women imaged as these tragic heroines are not of royal blood but are ordinary Russian women, and they hail not from the capital city but from Chukhloma, a name symbolizing any small forgotten provincial town. The jarring use of the names of these heroines in the plural serves to convey both the intensity of the Russian women's suffering and the magnitude of the national tragedy.

In an echo of the "rokovoi khor"/"fateful chorus" of Part One, these modern-day Hecubas and Cassandras form with the author a new tragic chorus, made up not of observers but of main participants in the tragedy.[88] The women's mouths are shut, but still they are not silent. The striking oxymoron in which stanza Xb culminates—"Zagremim my bezmolvnym khorom,/. . . . ./'Po tu storonu ada my!' "/"We will thunder in a speechless chorus,/. . . . ./ 'Beyond hell are we!' "—conflates the notions of speechlessness (*bezmolvie*) and its antithesis—thunderous speech. This paradox transcends human logic to triumph over the logic-bound authorities: the whole nation has been silenced, Akhmatova's mouth has been stopped, the women's lips are pressed shut, but still their speechlessness roars, miraculously overcoming the force used against them, for no force can silence silence.

The Road to Siberia

One more glimpse at the poet's fate in the Real Twentieth Century comes in the Epilogue's nightmarish vision of imprisonment, interrogation, and death:

А за проволокой колючей,
В самом сердце тайги дремучей—
Я не знаю, который год—
Ставший горстью лагерной пыли,
Ставший сказкой из страшной были,
Мой двойник на допрос идет.
А потом он идет с допроса,
Двум посланцам Девки безносой
Суждено охранять его.
И я слышу даже отсюда—
Неужели это не чудо!—
Звуки голоса своего:
   За тебя я заплатила

                Чистоганом,

Ровно десять лет ходила

                Под наганом,

   Ни налево, ни направо

                Не глядела

А за мной худая слава

Шелестела.

(*S*, 2: 130–31)

And beyond the barbed wire,
In the very heart of the dense taiga—
I don't know what year it is—,
Having become a handful of camp dust,
Having become a legend from a terrible true story,
My double goes to an interrogation.
And then it comes from the interrogation,
With two envoys of the noseless Wench
Destined to guard it.
And I hear even from here—
Isn't it a miracle!—
The sounds of my voice:
  For you I paid

                      In cash,

For exactly ten years I walked

                      Under a revolver,

    Not to the left or the right

                      Did I look

While behind me ill fame

                      Rustled.

The barbed wire and the taiga delineate the deathly, infernal world of Siberia's prison camps. The presence of the author's double recalls her double from Part One ("Columbine of the 1910's" [*S*, 2: 114]), but while the latter mirrors the poet's self on the eve of World War I, the double evoked in the Epilogue has met a fate typical of the Real Twentieth Century, a fate that Akhmatova herself escaped. The double was sent to Siberia "for" Akhmatova ("Za tebia"), recalling those who were arrested and imprisoned to punish the poet: her son Lev Gumilev, whose release from the camps was secured in 1956, and Nikolai Punin, who perished in the camps in 1953. On another level, this picture of the camps complements the allusions to Mandelstam's death contained in the First Dedication and in Part One, particularly the statement "I am ready for death."[89] The fourth line's "Stavshii gorst'iu lagernoi pyli"/"Having become a handful of camp dust" conjures up very literally the fate met by Mandelstam, and with it the fate of all those who perished in Siberia.

The beginning of the Epilogue is devoted to the fate of Peter's city (nowhere in the *poema* does Akhmatova refer to it as Leningrad) during World War II—its complete destruction by the Germans,[90] a destruction that is portrayed as the death of a living being. The last lines of the Epilogue point away from Petersburg, circling back toward the vision of the camps:

И открылась мне та дорога,
По которой ушло так много,
По которой сына везли,
И был долог путь погребальный
Средь торжественной и хрустальной
Тишины
Сибирской земли.
От того, что сделалось прахом,
Обуянная смертным страхом
И отмщения зная срок,
Опустивши глаза сухие
И ломая руки, Россия
Предо мною шла на восток.

And before me opened that road
Along which so many had departed,
Along which my son was conveyed,
And the funereal way was long
Amidst the solemn and crystal
Silence
Of the Siberian land.
Away from what had turned into ashes,
Seized by mortal fear,
And knowing the hour of vengeance,
Having lowered her dry eyes
And wringing her hands, Russia
Went before me to the East.

Poem Without a Hero culminates in this revelation of the very prospect mentioned at the end of Part One—namely, of the road that was to "open" before the protagonist: "On ne znal . . . /. . . kakoi dorogi/Pered nim otkroetsia vid . . ." (S, 2: 120)/"He did not know . . . /. . . what road's/View was to open before him. . . ." This road is the road to Siberia, to the camps, as confirmed in the third line's mention of Akhmatova's son; it is the road of loss, of bereavement, as underscored in the epithet *pogrebal'nyi* (funereal), as well as in the line "Po kotoroi ushlo tak mnogo"/"Along which so many had departed."[91] The silence reigning over the Siberian land ("Tishiny/Sibirskoi zemli"/"Silence/Of the Siberian land") has the same connotations of the silence figuring in the ninth and tenth stanzas of "Tails": it bespeaks suffering, violence, and death—the deaths of Mandelstam, of Kliuev, of Punin, the deaths of millions of nameless people.

Poem Without a Hero closes with the image of a personified Russia mournfully moving along the road to Siberia, traveling away from the ashes of Petersburg ("Ot togo, chto sdelalos' prakhom"/"Away from what had turned into ashes") toward the dust of the camps (*lagernaia pyl'*). The line "I otmshcheniia znaia srok"/"And knowing the hour of vengeance" predicts an end to the mournful retreat in the form of a future vengeance, a highly ambiguous vengeance, surely to be wrought not only against the invaders who destroyed Peter's city but also against those responsible for the camps of Siberia.

Chapter 5

The Poet's Transfigurations
in *The Sweetbrier Blooms*

Рукописи не горят.
Manuscripts do not burn.
—Mikhail Bulgakov, *The Master
and Margarita*

All manner of thing shall be well
When . . .
. . . the fire and the rose are one.
—T. S. Eliot, "Little Gidding"

T he lyrical cycle *Shipovnik tsvetet* (*The Sweetbrier Blooms*)
consists of fourteen poems written over an eighteen-year
period (1946–64). The sequence of events that gave rise to the cycle
is well-known.[1] In November 1945 and January 1946, Akhmatova
was visited by Isaiah Berlin at her home in Leningrad, and these
meetings prompted the writing of the short lyrical cycle called *Cinque*. Akhmatova later came to view those encounters with the foreigner Berlin in the xenophobic atmosphere of Stalin's rule as the
cause of the Central Committee Resolution of August 14, 1946,
which not only launched a virulent campaign against her and her
poetry but led to the rearrest of Lev Gumilev and Nikolai Punin in
1949.[2] When the persecution of Akhmatova began to abate with
Stalin's death in 1953, Punin had already perished in the camps;
Gumilev's release was secured in May 1956. In the same year, just
a few months after Gumilev's release, Berlin returned to the Soviet
Union, but Akhmatova refused to meet with him for fear of the
consequences, whence the crucial motif of the *nevstrecha* (nonmeeting) in *The Sweetbrier Blooms*.[3] The arrival of a foreigner, the
poet's fateful meeting with him, his departure, and its ruinous con-

sequences for the poet, the "nonmeeting" many years later—all of these events figure in the *Sweetbrier* poems, yet as the title of one of them—"V razbitom zerkale" ("In a Shattered Mirror")—indicates, they are presented in a confused way, with constantly shifting spatial and temporal perspectives that recall those of Part One of *Poem Without a Hero*.

The cycle has much in common with *Poem Without a Hero*, from its large size and the many years over which it was written, to the radical changes in its composition during that time, to the publication of several different versions of it, to the presence of a number of poems closely related to it at its periphery.[4] The most profound link between the two works lies in the fact that the prototype for the *poema*'s "Gost' iz budushchego"/"Guest from the future" is the addressee of the *Sweetbrier* cycle; the cycle revolves around the poet's encounter with that individual and its ruinous consequences for her. As was argued in the preceding chapter, the story of the author's fate told in "Tails" is civic in nature, reflecting the *poema*'s larger concern with the fate of the Russian poet in the Real Twentieth Century. In the *Sweetbrier* cycle, the fate of the lyrical persona proper is the primary focus, and what shapes that fate is love. As in *Poem Without a Hero*, the lyrical persona's fate is inextricably bound up with that of her poetry.

The prominence of the theme of love in *The Sweetbrier Blooms* recalls Akhmatova's early lyrics, where the theme predominates. In the early period, however, Akhmatova did not create formal cycles of poems addressed to a single individual; poems addressing the same individual were dispersed among other unrelated lyrics, and the addressee's identity was masked in various ways. Crucial to the individual poems of the *Sweetbrier* cycle, by contrast, is their interrelatedness, for the lyrical events figuring in them are part and parcel of a single story, and their imagery constitutes a unified whole.

As in all the later poetry, the role of literary allusions and quotations is very large, but what sets *The Sweetbrier Blooms* apart is the nature and role of the intertextual element in it: the cycle does not simply quote phrases and refer to lines and passages from other works; it alludes to whole narratives, and specifically to the plots of illustrious love stories. The lyrical persona's fate is illuminated through the mediation of these other tales, the most important of which is that of Dido and Aeneas.

Dido and the Burned Notebook

Written in 1962, after the poems preceding it in the cycle, the untitled eleventh text of *The Sweetbrier Blooms* was initially conceived of as an epilogue to the cycle: when first published in 1962, it bore the title "Govorit Didona (Sonet-epilog)"/"Dido Speaks (Sonnet-Epilogue)." Later, when two more poems were added to the cycle, the title was dropped.[5] The poem's references to the story of Dido and Aeneas constitute an overarching framework for the cycle as a whole:

> Против воли я твой, царица,
> берег покинул.
> > «Энеида», песнь 6

Не пугайся—я еще похожей
Нас теперь изобразить могу.
Призрак ты—иль человек прохожий,
Тень твою зачем-то берегу.

Был недолго ты моим Энеем,—
Я тогда отделалась костром.
Друг о друге мы молчать умеем.
И забыл ты мой проклятый дом.

Ты забыл те, в ужасе и муке,
Сквозь огонь протянутые руки
И надежды окаянной весть.

Ты не знаешь, что тебе простили...
Создан Рим, плывут стада флотилий,
И победы славословит лесть.

> (*SP*, 243)

> Against my will, O queen, I
> abandoned thy shore.
> > —*Aeneid*, Book VI

Don't be afraid—I can now depict
Us with a still greater likeness.

Whether you are an apparition—or a wayfarer,
I preserve for some reason your shade.

Not long were you my Aeneas,—
I got off easy then—by the pyre.
We know how to keep silent about one another.
And you forgot my accursed house.

You forgot those arms stretched out
In horror and in torment through the fire,
And the news of damned hope.

You know not what you've been forgiven ...
Rome has been founded, flocks of flotillas sail,
And flattery extols victories.

The persona recapitulates the story of her relations with the addressee through the prism of Virgil's tale of Dido and Aeneas, as signaled in the poem's epigraph—a line from Book VI of the *Aeneid* in Afanasii Fet's translation.[6] The main part of Aeneas and Dido's story is narrated in Book IV of the *Aeneid*: Aeneas, in flight from the ruins of Troy, is shipwrecked on the shores of Carthage, where he is given shelter by Queen Dido. Through Venus's intervention, Dido falls in love with Aeneas and offers to share her kingdom with him. The gods once more intervene, telling Aeneas that he is destined to found Italy and must leave Carthage at once. Dido implores Aeneas to stay, but he secretly sets sail, prompting her suicide. She is cremated on a great funeral pyre, the flames of which are seen by Aeneas, now far out at sea, at the beginning of Book V.

The epigraph to "Don't be afraid" is drawn from Book VI of the *Aeneid*, which relates Aeneas's encounter with Dido's shade in the underworld. Aeneas first asks Dido if he was the cause of her death (Book VI, line 458), but immediately justifies his departure in the words chosen by Akhmatova as her epigraph, adding that he was compelled to obey the will of the gods.[7] Aeneas then begs Dido to speak to him, but her fury is unmitigated by his entreaties, and she flees without uttering a single word, administering what T. S. Eliot has called "perhaps the most telling snub in all poetry":[8]

illa solo fixos oculos aversa tenebat
nec magis incepto voltum sermone movetur,
quam si dura silex aut stet Marpesia cautes.
tandem corripuit sese atque inimica refugit
in nemus umbriferum.

(Book VI, lines 469–73)

She turning away, kept her looks fixed on the ground and no more changes her countenance as he essays to speak than if she were set in hard flint or Marpesian rock. At length she flung herself away and, still his foe, fled back to the shady grove.[9]

Aeneas's speech to Dido's shade is answered in the *Aeneid* only by silence. In "Don't be afraid," Akhmatova presents Dido's belated verbal response to Aeneas. Her speech is set long after the meeting with Aeneas in Hades, as the final tercet indicates: not only has Aeneas's divine mission—the founding of Rome—been accomplished, but the Roman empire has been built, as signaled in the phrase "plyvut stada flotilii"/"flocks of flotillas sail."

"Don't be afraid" is an epilogue to the *Aeneid*'s story of Dido and Aeneas, an ending that takes the form of a complex polemic with Virgil. The polemic first makes itself felt in the phrase "Ten' tvoiu zachem-to beregu" (line 4)/"I preserve for some reason your shade," which pointedly harks back to Aeneas's words in the epigraph: "Protiv voli ia tvoi, tsaritsa, bereg pokinul"/"Against my will, O queen, I abandoned thy shore." The basic grammatical structure of these two sentences is identical, and they are closely linked by the homonymic rhyme "*beregu*" and "*bereg* pokin*ul*" (*beregu* means "I preserve" and *bereg* means "shore"). The grammatical and phonological parallelism belies the profound semantic difference between these utterances: Aeneas forsakes Dido by abandoning her shore, while Dido preserves Aeneas's shade, demonstrating her faithfulness to him.

Dido's monologue in "Don't be afraid" begins epigrammatically with an ironically understated recapitulation of the story of her relations with Aeneas: "Byl nedolgo ty moim Eneem,—/Ia togda otdelalas' kostrom" (lines 5–6)/"Not long were you my Aeneas,—/I then got off easy—by the pyre." The second line dismisses Dido's suicide, a direct consequence of Aeneas's departure, as an insignificant ill. A few lines later, however, the text circles back to the same subject, recollecting Dido's agony with great pathos:

Ты забыл те, в ужасе и в муке,
Сквозь огонь протянутые руки
И надежды окаянной весть.

You forgot those arms stretched out
In horror and in torment through the fire,
And the news of damned hope.

Her suffering is conveyed in the emblematic gesture of her arms reaching out in vain through the flames for deliverance. This tragic gesture is cast in a complex *zvukovoi zhest* (sound gesture)—a Russian Formalist term connoting, as Victor Erlich puts it, "an approximate analogy between the articulatory activity underlying a given sound-repetition—the process involved in producing a speech-sound—and a physical gesture." [10] In "Don't be afraid," the sound gesture mirrors the physical gesture described through a quadruple repetition of the rounded *u* (oo): "te, v *ú*zhase i v m*ú*ke,/Skvoz' ogon' protian*u*tye r*ú*ki." To produce the *u* sound in Russian, the lips must be "stretched," so this is literally a gesture of extending the outer articulatory organs, the lips, in a phonokinetic metaphor of sorts. On another level, the gesture is embodied in the figure of enjambment: the demonstrative adjective "te"/"those" is separated from its noun "ruki"/"arms" by fourteen syllables and separated by the very "ogon'"/"fire" through which the arms stretch, forming a syntactical correlative of the image evoked.

The phrase "news of damned hope" (line 11) refers to the news of Aeneas's departure from Carthage, yet Aeneas is not explicitly criticized for leaving. He is chastised instead for forgetting Dido after his departure, as underscored in the repetition of the phrase "you forgot" in lines 8–9. Here Akhmatova's polemic with Virgil emerges in full force. Nowhere in the *Aeneid* is Aeneas's forgetting of Dido mentioned. After their brief meeting in the Mourning Fields, however, Aeneas never again in the course of the *Aeneid* refers to Dido. Neither, incidentally, does Virgil. In "Don't be afraid," silence is thematized in the mention of a reciprocal silence on the part of Dido and Aeneas: "Drug o druge my molchat' umeem" (line 7)/"We know how to keep silent about each other." This line ironically recalls Dido's stony silence throughout the encounter with Aeneas in the underworld—an eloquent measure of the intensity of her feelings for Aeneas. Aeneas's silence about Dido in the last half of the *Aeneid* has, in Akhmatova's reading, a very different significance: it attests to his forgetting her.

Though Aeneas forgets, "Don't be afraid" as a whole testifies to Dido's supreme faithfulness to him, as well as to the workings of a memory powerful enough to transcend the Lethean oblivion of death. Of the many artistic treatments of Dido over the centuries, one in particular foregrounds the theme of memory—Henry Purcell's 1689 opera *Dido and Aeneas*. In the heroine's final aria, the mortally wounded Dido repeats again and again: "Remember me, remember me, do not forget my fate." In Purcell, these words are addressed not to Aeneas but to Dido's sister Anna, in whose arms she dies, and they clearly underlie and motivate the posthumous complaint of Akhmatova's Dido to her Aeneas: "I zabyl ty moi prokliatyi dom./Ty zabyl ... "/"And you forgot my accursed house./You forgot...."[11]

Dido's fate is forgotten in the second half of the *Aeneid*, where both Virgil and his hero appear to be held in the thrall of Aeneas's destiny. The last six books of the *Aeneid* focus on the battles waged by Aeneas for the site of the future Rome, the founding and rise of which are alluded to in Akhmatova's final lines: "Sozdan Rim, plyvut stada flotilii,/I pobedy slavoslovit lest'"/"Rome has been founded, flocks of flotillas sail,/And flattery extols victories." Although the narrative of the *Aeneid* breaks off even before Rome's founding, Virgil's text does predict the future glories of the Roman empire in the eighth book's description of the shield made for Aeneas by Vulcan. Modeled on Achilles' shield in the *Iliad*, this weapon foretells the history of Rome, portraying "the glory and destiny of [Aeneas's] heirs," including events from Virgil's own lifetime. Of paramount importance to "Don't be afraid" is the scene on the shield depicting the battle at Actium (31 B.C.), where Octavian defeated Mark Antony: "in medio classis aeratas, Actia bella" (line 675)/"In the centre [could be seen] the brazen ships with Actium's battle." [12] Presiding over the scene is Augustus Caesar, standing "on the high quarter-deck of his ship." [13] The battle at Actium was just one victory for Augustus, yet Akhmatova's use of the plural tense ("flattery praises victories") is motivated by the paean to Augustus that concludes the shield passage in Book VIII: it envisages his triumphal return to the capital and the tribute paid him by the many peoples vanquished by Rome. The adulatory spirit of this passage is alluded to in Akhmatova's last line, which implicitly criticizes Virgil for courting Augustus's favor in the *Aeneid*. Book VIII presents the reign of Augustus as the ultimate justification for all of Aeneas's actions, including his abandonment of Dido. Akhmatova's epilogue to the *Aeneid* confutes this view: Aeneas's historical feat pales before its human costs—Dido's suffering and death.

Although Akhmatova polemicizes with Virgil in her text, several fine threads link the lyrical persona of "Don't be afraid" with Virgil, pointing to a partial identification with him on Akhmatova's part. The persona is, like Virgil, a poet, who consciously selects Virgil's story of Dido and Aeneas as a vehicle for portraying her relations with her addressee, as the opening lines of the text state explicitly: "ia eshche pokhozhei/Nas teper' izobrazit' mogu"/"I can now depict/Us with a still greater likeness." A Dantesque allusion in the third line of the text—"Prizrak ty—il' chelovek prokhozhii"/"Whether you are an apparition—or a wayfarer"—establishes yet another link between Akhmatova and Virgil. M. B. Meilakh and V. N. Toporov have identified in these lines a reference to the first canto of the *Inferno*, and specifically to Dante's meeting with the shade of Virgil:[14]

> Quando vidi costui nel gran diserto,
> "*Miserere* di me," gridai a lui,
> "qual che tu sii, od ombra od omo certo!"
> Rispuosemi: "Non omo, omo già fui. . . ."
> (lines 64–67)[15]

When I saw him in that vast desert,
　I cried to him, "Have pity on me
　whatever you are, shade or living man!"
"No, not a living man, though once I was. . . ."[16]

Like the Dantesque allusions in *Requiem*, the reference to these lines in "Don't be afraid" situates the persona in the world of the dead.[17] In two key respects, however, the allusion aligns Dante not with Akhmatova but with her addressee: Akhmatova's addressee, like Dante in the underworld, is both an "omo certo" and a "chelovek prokhozhii," a "wayfarer" journeying through the realm of the dead. Akhmatova herself, however, is identified with Dante's addressee, Virgil, who is no longer a living person—an "omo certo"—but a shade.[18]

Another resonant detail linking Akhmatova and Virgil is Dante's description of the appearance of Virgil's shade in the lines immediately preceding those quoted above:

Mentre ch'i' rovinava in basso loco,
　dinanzi a li occhi mi si fu offerto
　chi per lungo silenzio parea fioco.
　　　　(lines 61–63)

While I was running down to the depth
　there appeared to me one
　who seemed faint through long silence.[19]

In "Don't be afraid," Dido's voice similarly speaks "through long silence"—a silence that began with her death and continued through her meeting with Aeneas in the underworld. In *The Sweetbrier Blooms* as a whole, Akhmatova, too, speaks "through long silence"—a silence lasting ten years, from 1946 to 1956—from shortly after her visitor's departure until the "nonmeeting" with him ten years later.[20] This temporal gap is inscribed in the cycle through the dates borne by its texts: the second and third poems of the cycle—"Naiavu" ("Awake") and "Vo sne" ("Asleep")—were both written in 1946, but the rest of the poems date from 1956 or later.[21] The continuation of Virgil's speech in the *Inferno* reinforces the parallel between him and Akhmatova:

Poeta fui, e cantai di quel giusto
   figliuol d'Anchise che venne di Troia,
   poi che 'l superbo Iliön fu combusto.
                 (lines 73–75)

I was a poet, and sang of that just
   son of Anchises who came from Troy
   after proud Ilium was burned.[22]

Virgil's words "Poeta fui"/"I was a poet" are expressive of Akhmatova's experience after the event caused, in her view, by her meeting with the foreigner—the Central Committee Resolution of August 14, 1946. The following octet from the cycle *Cherepki* (*Shards*), written in the late 1940's or early 1950's, describes what she suffered:

Вы меня как убитого зверя
На кровавый подымете крюк,
Чтоб хихикая и не веря
Иноземцы бродили вокруг
И писали в почтенных газетах,
Что мой дар несравненный угас,
Что была я поэтом в поэтах,
Но мой пробил тринадцатый час.
                (*S*, 3: 74)[23]

You will raise me up, like a killed beast
On a bloody hook,
So that giggling and incredulous
Foreigners will circle around
And write in respected newspapers
That my incomparable gift has died out,
That I was a poet among poets,
But my thirteenth hour struck.

The text conjures up the public display and humiliation of the silenced poet; the simile "like a killed beast/On a bloody hook" bespeaks the brutality and violence that silenced her. The destruction of the poet is underscored in the last two lines of the text, the first of which strongly echoes Virgil's "Poeta fui."[24]

Both "Don't be afraid" and *The Sweetbrier Blooms* as a whole suppress explicit references to Akhmatova's persecution by the authorities and treat the poet's predicament obliquely, using imagery deriving in large part from the *Aeneid*. Akhmatova borrows from Virgil, for instance, the motif of the fatal gifts brought by the foreigner. In the *Aeneid*, Aeneas's gifts to Dido are delivered by Cupid in the guise of Aeneas's son; Cupid also secretly gives Dido a present from Venus—an ardent love for Aeneas.[25] The motif of the ruinous gift dominates the second half of the cycle's ninth poem, "In a Shattered Mirror" (1956):

> Ты отдал мне не тот подарок,
> Который издалека вез.
> Казался он пустой забавой
> В тот вечер огненный тебе.
> И стал он медленной отравой
> В моей загадочной судьбе.
> И он всех бед моих предтеча,—
> Не будем вспоминать о нем!...
>
> > (*SP*, 241)

> You gave me not the gift
> Which you had brought from afar.
> It seemed an empty trifle
> To you on that fiery evening.
> And it became a slow poison
> In my mysterious fate.
> And it was the precursor of all my woes—
> We shall not recall it! . . . [26]

Though "In a Shattered Mirror" refrains from naming the gift, its pernicious nature is encoded in the description of the persona's meeting with the foreigner given in the first stanza:

> Непоправимые слова
> Я слушала в тот вечер звездный,
> И закружилась голова,
> Как над пылающею бездной.
> И гибель выла у дверей,
> И ухал черный сад, как филин,

И город, смертно обессилен,
Был Трои в этот час древней.

(*SP*, 242)

Irremediable words
I listened to that starry night,
And my head spun round
As over a flaming abyss.
And ruin howled at the door,
And the black garden hooted like an owl,
And the city, mortally weakened,
Was at that hour more ancient than Troy.

The image of the "flaming abyss," the ominous, funereal howls and calls, the animated *gibel'* (ruin) located on the threshold, and the comparison of the city to Troy—all these details portend imminent destruction. From the "flaming abyss" of the first strophe to the second strophe's phrase "v tot vecher ognennyi"/"on that fiery evening" (line 14), fire imagery is omnipresent, recalling Virgil's use of the same in his rendering of Dido's passion for Aeneas. "In a Shattered Mirror" seems particularly indebted to Virgil's account of Dido and Aeneas's first union: "fulsere ignes et conscius Aether conubiis, summoque ululurunt vertice Nymphae. ille dies primus leti primusque malorum causa fuit" (Book IV, lines 167–70)/"fires flashed in Heaven, the witness to their bridal, and on the mountaintop screamed the Nymphs. That day was the first day of death, that first the cause of woe" (Virgil, 1: 441). There are three points of affinity here with "In a Shattered Mirror": the motifs of celestial fires and ominous screaming, as well as the notion of the meeting as the first "cause of woe," which is echoed in Akhmatova's "I on vsekh bed moikh predtecha"/"And it was the precursor of all my woes."

The version of Dido's death presented in "Don't be afraid" diverges from Virgil's account in one crucial respect. According to Virgil, Dido orders everything associated with Aeneas to be placed on a funeral pyre. She then ascends the pyre, picks up a Trojan sword given her by Aeneas, and impales herself on it. The flames from the pyre, which was lit only after her death, were intended by her to convey to the departing Aeneas the news of her death. "Don't be afraid" excludes any mention of the sword and self-impalement, conjuring up instead a scene of self-immolation: "Ia togda otdelalas' kostrom."/"I then got off easy—by the pyre."

Elsewhere in *The Sweetbrier Blooms* fire serves as the agent of the destruction of poems, as proclaimed in the cycle's subtitle, *Iz sozhzhennoi tetradi (From a Burned Notebook)*, which paradoxically identifies the poems of the cycle as having survived an all-consuming fire.[27] The untitled poem prefacing the cycle, dated December 24, 1961, sets the tone by establishing a link between fire and poetry:

> Вместо праздничного поздравленья
> Этот ветер, жесткий и сухой,
> Принесет вам только запах тленья,
> Привкус дыма и стихотворенья,
> Что моей написаны рукой.
>
> (SP, 237)

> Instead of a festive greeting
> This wind, harsh and sere,
> Will bring you only the smell of moldering,
> The flavor of smoke, and poems
> Written by my hand.

The first two things borne by the wind—"zapakh tlen'ia"/"the smell of moldering" and "privkus dyma"/"the flavor of smoke"—bespeak destruction: *tlen'e* and *dym* are indices, in Peirce's terminology, of death and fire, but the latter is emphasized, since *tlen'e* denotes both "moldering" and "smoldering" in Russian. The third thing carried by the wind—"poems"—is not present in a reduced form, as a smell or a taste, or as an index of something else. On the contrary, the substantiality of the poems is underscored in the persona's assertion that they were "written by [her] hand."

As Marcia Rose Satin first noted, the phrase "privkus dyma"/"flavor of smoke" is a quotation from a poem Osip Mandelstam dedicated to Akhmatova in May 1931, the first two lines of which are quoted here:

Сохрани мою речь навсегда за привкус несчастья и дыма,
За смолу кругового терпенья, за совестный деготь труда.[28]

Preserve my speech forever for its flavor of misfortune and smoke,
For the pitch of its all-around patience, for its conscientious tar of
   labor.

Akhmatova quotes Mandelstam's "privkus . . . dyma" and recalls
his "moiu rech'" in her "moei . . . rukoi"; her phrase "zapakh
tlen'ia" paronomastically rhymes with Mandelstam's "*Za* smolu
. . . *terpen'ia*." By quoting Mandelstam, Akhmatova fulfills his bidding and perpetuates his speech, identifying her poetry with his and
implying that it, too, bears the "zapakh neschast'ia"/"flavor of
misfortune."

In Mandelstam's text, the phrase "privkus . . . dyma"/"flavor of
. . . smoke" is in part motivated by the second line's references to
"pitch" and "tar," but there is no direct reference to fire in his text.
The same is true of Akhmatova's "Instead of a festive greeting," but
not of the text immediately following it, the first numbered poem
of the cycle. Written in 1961, it evokes the poet's burning of her
own poems:

Сожженная тетрадь

Уже красуется на книжной полке
Твоя благополучная сестра,
И над тобою звездных стай осколки,
И под тобою угольки костра.
Как ты молила, как ты жить хотела,
Как ты боялась едкого огня!
Но вдруг твое затрепетало тело,
А голос, улетая, клял меня.
И сразу все зашелестели сосны
И отразились в недрах лунных вод.
А вкруг костра священнейшие весны
Уже вели надгробный хоровод.

(*SP*, 238)

The Burned Notebook

Your fortunate sister
Already graces the bookshelf,

But above you are the shards of starry flocks,
And beneath you are the embers of the fire.
How you begged, how you wanted to live,
How you feared the consuming fire!
But suddenly your body trembled
And your voice, flying away, was cursing me.
And instantly all the pines began to rustle
And were reflected in the depths of lunar waters.
And round the fire the most sacred springs
Were already leading the funereal round dance.

The dominant trope here is personification: the notebook figures as the persona's addressee (it is referred to solely in the second-person singular), and one of the poet's published books of poetry is called the notebook's "blagopoluchnaia sestra"/"fortunate sister," a personifying metaphor. Furthermore, a series of human traits, emotions, and actions are imputed to the notebook (lines 5–6), including the desire to live ("kak ty zhit' khotela"/"how you wanted to live"). The personification reaches its apogee in the attribution to the notebook of the dualistic, distinctively human traits of body and voice.

The significance of Akhmatova's recourse to personification is revealed when "The Burned Notebook" is compared with Pushkin's lyric "Sozhzhennoe pis'mo" ("The Burned Letter," 1825), which evokes a similar scene of burning. As the rhyming titles suggest, Akhmatova's text is closely modeled on Pushkin's:[29]

Сожженное письмо

Прощай, письмо любви! прощай: она велела.
Как долго медлил я! Как долго не хотела
Рука предать огню все радости мои!...
Готов я; ничему душа моя не внемлет.
Но полно, час настал. Гори, письмо любви.
Уж пламя жадное листы твои приемлет...
Минуту... Вспыхнули! пылают—легкий дым,
Виясь, теряется с молением моим.
. . . .
Свершилось! Темные свернулися листы;
На легком пепле их заветные черты

Белеют... Грудь моя стеснилась. Пепел милый,
Отрада бедная в судьбе моей унылой,
Останься век со мной на горестной груди...[30]

The Burned Letter

Farewell, love letter! farewell: she ordered it.
How long I have tarried! How long my hand has not wanted
To commit to fire all my joys! . . .
But enough, the hour has come. Burn, love letter.
I am ready; my soul apprehends nothing.
Now the greedy flame receives your sheets . . .
Wait a minute! . . . They catch fire, they blaze; the light smoke,
Winding, is lost with my prayer.

. . . .

It is done! The dark sheets have curled;
On the light ashes their cherished lines
Show white . . . My breast is heavy. Dear ashes,
Poor comfort in my gloomy fate,
Remain with me evermore on my sorrowful breast . . .

Not only does Akhmatova recall Pushkin's title, metrical scheme (Pushkin's is Alexandrine, Akhmatova's iambic pentameter), and the general scene he evokes, she echoes his lexicon and syntax as well. Compare, for example, Pushkin's "*Kak dolgo* medlil ia! *Kak dolgo* ne *khotela*/Ruka predat' *ogniu* vse radosti moi! . . ." with Akhmatova's "*Kak ty* molila, *kak ty* zhit' *khotela*,/*Kak ty* boialas' edkogo *ognia*!" Akhmatova not only echoes Pushkin's lexicon and adopts his exclamatory intonation, she intensifies his use of anaphora. She follows Pushkin's lead in personifying the burned object by addressing it in the second-person singular. In "The Burned Letter," all emotions and actions described belong to the persona. In "The Burned Notebook," by contrast, not only is the notebook ascribed emotions and actions, they are in part the very actions and emotions of Pushkin's persona: the prayer ("molen'e") of Pushkin's persona, for example, is uttered by Akhmatova's notebook ("kak ty molila").[31] The outcomes of the fires in the two poems are also radically different. Pushkin's persona finds solace in the ashes remaining from the fire: the phrase "bednaia ot*rada*" ("poor comfort") underscores their continuity with the original letter, bearer of the persona's "*rado*sti"/"joys." "The Burned Notebook" mentions no ashes, implying that none are left to console the poet. The material *telo* (body) of the notebook is destroyed, and the *golos* (voice) flees from the fire, cursing the persona, not consoling her.[32]

The absence of ashes that is only implied in "The Burned Notebook" figures explicitly in the fourth poem of the cycle *Cinque*. Wondering what memento of their meeting to leave the addressee, the persona proposes: "Posviashchenie sozhzhennoi dramy/Ot kotoroi i pepla net" (*SP*, 237)/"The dedication of a burned drama/ From which not even ashes remain." The reference is to the tragedy *Enūma elish*, written by the poet in Tashkent and burned by her on June 11, 1944, after her return to Leningrad.[33] Burned literary texts abound in the later poetry, making the destruction of poetry by fire one of the period's chief metapoetic themes. The theme reflects the circumstances of the poet's life from the late 1930's until well after Stalin's death in 1953. During those years Akhmatova burned her archives at least three times: first, after the arrest of Lev Gumilev and Nikolai Punin during the Ezhov terror; next, upon her return to Leningrad from Tashkent in 1944; and finally, in 1949, after Gumilev and Punin were rearrested.[34] In addition to the archives, the burning of poems became in the same years an integral part of the poet's everyday life. Her certainty that she was under constant surveillance by the secret police and that her room was bugged and was being regularly searched in her absence gave rise to the following custom during Lidiia Chukovskaia's visits to Akhmatova in 1939 and 1940:

Suddenly in the midst of a conversation she would fall silent, and having indicated the ceiling and walls to me with her eyes, she would take a scrap of paper and a pencil, then would loudly say something very mundane: "Would you like some tea?" or, "You've grown so tan"; and then she would cover the scrap with a quick script and pass it to me. I would read through the poems and, on memorizing them, would silently return them to her. "Autumn is so early this year," Anna Andreevna would say, and, striking a match, she would burn the paper over an ashtray.

It was a ritual: the hands, the match, the ashtray—a beautiful and sorrowful ritual.[35]

This "sorrowful ritual" is commemorated in a poem written for the ashtray, "Zastol'naia" ("Table Song," 1955), the last quatrain of which was quoted in chapter 4 above. Here it is in full:

Застольная

Под узорной скатертью
    Не видать стола.
Я стихам не матерью—
    Мачехой была.
Эх, бумага белая,
    Строчек ровный ряд!
Сколько раз глядела я,
    Как они горят.
Сплетней изувечены,
    Биты кистенем,
Мечены, мечены
    Каторжным клеймом.

        (*S*, 3: 71)

Table Song

Under the patterned tablecloth
    The table can't be seen.
To my poems I have been not a mother
    But a stepmother.
Oh, white paper,
    Even row of lines!
How many times I have watched
    Them burn.
Maimed by gossip,
    Beaten with a bludgeon,
Marked, marked
    With a convict's brand.

"Table Song" mimics the parallelisms, diction, and rhythms of Russian folk poetry.[36] The persona's confession that she has been not a mother to her poems but a stepmother—a metaphor that personifies the poems—draws on one of the commonest motifs in Russian folklore, that of the evil stepmother who brings suffering and perdition to her stepchildren. The personification of the poems intensifies in the last four lines of the text through the motifs of mutilation, beating, and penal servitude (*katorga*), all of which bespeak disfiguration through violence. In other texts from the same period, Akhmatova depicts her own fate in precisely the same terms as that of her poems in "Table Song." In "Liubovnaia" ("Love Song"), she describes herself as a convict: "Ne zhalei menia,/Katorzhanochku" (*S*, 3: 72)/"Do not pity me,/A poor little convict." The line "Spletnei izuvecheny"/"Maimed by gossip" recalls a different kind of verbal abuse to which the poet was subjected, named in the following lines of the lyric "Vse ushli i nikto ne vernulsia"/"Everyone left and no one returned": "Obkormili menia klevetoiu,/Opoili otravoi menia" (*S*, 3: 73)/"They fed me with slander,/Gave me poison to drink." Finally, "Beaten with a bludgeon" brings to mind a compelling image from the cycle *Cherepki* (*Shards*), written in the late 1940's and early 1950's: "Muzu zasekli moiu" (*S*, 3: 74)/"they flogged my Muse to death."

The many parallels between "The Burned Notebook" and "Don't be afraid" similarly emphasize the oneness of the fates of the poet and her poems.[37] The two texts are very closely linked: the words *koster* (bonfire, pyre) and *ogon'* (fire) figure in both; the notebook shares Dido's feminine gender, and both Dido and the notebook beg—in vain—to be saved from the flames. Finally, in both poems fire is not all-consuming, for a voice survives it: in "Don't be afraid" Dido's speech as a whole constitutes that voice, while "The Burned Notebook" portrays the flight of the voice from the fire: "A golos, uletaia, klial menia"/"And your voice, flying away, cursed me." This cursing recalls Virgil's account of Dido's last minutes, when she utters a series of vengeful curses against Aeneas.[38] "Don't be afraid," by contrast, focuses not on Aeneas's responsibility for Dido's death but on his betrayal of her memory; the tone is reproachful, not vengeful.

The burning of poetry is one of the chief metapoetic themes of the later period, and its concomitant is the imperishability of the poetic word. The subtitle of *The Sweetbrier Blooms—From a Burned Notebook*—establishes the cycle's poems as having survived the very fire portrayed in "The Burned Notebook." The notebook has been burned, but paradoxically its poems appear on the page of the printed book, testifying to their indestructibility.[39] The poems' imperishability is strongly suggested in the mysterious, "almost magical"[40] last four lines of "The Burned Notebook":

> И сразу все зашелестели сосны
> И отразились в недрах лунных вод.
> А вкруг костра священнейшие весны
> Уже вели надгробный хоровод.

> And instantly all the pines began to rustle
> And were reflected in the depths of lunar waters.
> And round the fire the most sacred springs
> Were already leading the funereal round dance.

The rustling of trees is usually attendant to the creative act in Akhmatova. In the lyric "Oni letiat, oni uzhe v doroge" ("They are flying, they are already on their way," 1916), for example, "zhidkie berezy"/"scrawny birches" "sukho shelestiat" (*SP*, 89–90)/"dryly rustle," signaling the onset of creative inspiration. In "The Burned Notebook," the rustling of the pines accompanies the words' return whence they came.[41] The second line quoted above strongly recalls lines 3–4 of Mandelstam's "Preserve my speech," to which Akhmatova refers in "Instead of a festive greeting":

> Сохрани мою речь навсегда за привкус несчастья и дыма,
> За смолу кругового терпенья, за совестный деготь труда.
> Так вода в новгородских колодцах должна быть черна и
>   сладима,
> Чтобы в ней к Рождеству отразилась семью плавниками
>   звезда.[42]

> Preserve my speech forever for its flavor of misfortune and smoke,
> For the pitch of its all-around patience, for its conscientious tar of
>   labor.
> Thus the water in Novgorod wells must be black and sweet,
> For the seven-finned star to be reflected in it by Christmas.

Akhmatova's "I otrazilis' v nedrakh lunnykh vod" shares with Mandelstam's third and fourth lines the image of reflection (the past tense of the verb *otrazit'sia* is used in both texts) in water (the word *voda* appears in both); in both instances, celestial light is reflected in the water (in Akhmatova's text, the moon is reflected, while Mandelstam's predicts the reflection of the star); and finally, in both texts, heavenly light is reflected in *deep* water (compare Mandelstam's "v novgorodskikh kolodtsakh" with Akhmatova's "v nedrakh lunnykh vod").

The last two lines of "The Burned Notebook" echo the final two lines of a poem Akhmatova addressed to N. V. Nedobrovo, "Esli pleshchetsia lunnaia zhut'" ("If the moon's horror splashes," October 1, 1928), which conjure up the grave of Nedobrovo: "A zastyvshii navek khorovod/Nadmogil'nykh tvoikh kiparisov" (*SP,* 185)/"But the round dance, frozen forever,/Of your graveside cypresses." In "The Burned Notebook," the round-dance motif is retained, but stasis gives way to movement in the circling of the dance. The funereal "graveside cypresses," associated with the underworld and immortality, are replaced in the round dance by "sviashchenneishie vesny"/"the most sacred springs." This is an allusion to Stravinsky's ballet *Vesna sviashchennaia,* known in English as *The Rite of Spring,* which portrays pagan rites ensuring the renewal of life in the spring. The unusual employment of the plural number compresses the eternal turn of the seasons into a single vertiginous image, a circular movement without end that is a powerful intimation of immortality.

Under the Sweetbrier

The epigraph of *The Sweetbrier Blooms*—"And thou art distant in Humanity"—is drawn from John Keats's narrative poem "Isabella, or The Pot of Basil" (1819), and it points to yet another network of intertextual relations operating in the cycle.[43] Keats tells how Isabella, the daughter of a rich Florentine merchant family, falls in love with Lorenzo, a poor laborer for her family. They spend blissful days and nights together, until Isabella's brothers learn of the affair. Intent on a profitable match for their sister, they lure Lorenzo away from the city and murder him, burying his corpse in a desolate spot. Isabella pines for him for months, until at last Lorenzo's ghost appears and tells her of his violent death, bidding her:

> Go, shed one tear upon my heather-bloom,
> And it shall comfort me within the tomb.
>
> I am a shadow now, alas! alas!
>   Upon the skirts of human nature dwelling
> Alone: I chant alone the holy mass,
>   While little sounds of life are round me knelling,
> And glossy bees at noon do fieldward pass,
>   And many a chapel bell the hour is telling,
> Paining me through: those sounds grow strange to me,
> And thou art distant in Humanity.[44]

Isabella hurries in secret to the burial place, unearths the badly decomposed corpse, severs the head, and takes it home. There she bathes it in her tears and then

> She wrapp'd it up; and for its tomb did choose
>   A garden-pot, wherein she laid it by,
> And covered it with mould, and o'er it set
> Sweet Basil, which her tears kept ever wet.[45]

Isabella devotes herself to tending the pot of basil, which flourishes under her care. Her brothers, alarmed by her behavior, steal the pot and unearth Lorenzo's head; horrified by the evidence of their crime, they flee the city, and Isabella dies mourning the loss of her pot. In Keats, "And thou art distant in Humanity" contrasts the realm of the living with that of the dead: Lorenzo's ghost addresses an Isabella still "in Humanity." The roles are reversed in *The Sweet-brier Blooms*: the same line locates Akhmatova's addressee in the realm of the living while situating the poet in the realm of the dead.[46]

In one of his digressions, Keats links the fate of Lorenzo and Isabella with Dido's:

> But for the general award of love,
>   The little sweet doth kill much bitterness;
> Though Dido silent is in under-grove,

And Isabella's was a great distress,
Though young Lorenzo in warm Indian clove
 Was not embalm'd, this truth is not the less—
Even bees, the little almsmen of spring bowers,
Know there is richest juice in poison-flowers.[47]

There are some important parallels between the two stories. In both
the lovers are tragically separated, and one of the lovers meets a
violent death; both feature an encounter between the survivor and
the ghost of the loved one. The narratives diverge, however, in several key respects. In Keats, Isabella is the embodiment of faithfulness to her beloved: separated from Lorenzo, she pines away, and
upon learning of his death, she devotes herself to mourning his
death and caring for his remains. In the *Aeneid*, Aeneas betrays
Dido by setting sail from Carthage, but Dido by no means epitomizes faithfulness. Her love for Aeneas is predicated on forgetting—forgetting the memory of a deceased loved one. The roots of
it lie in her prehistory. Dido was originally married to Sychaeus,
the richest man in the kingdom of Tyre. Pygmalion, the king of Tyre
and the brother of Dido, quarrels with Sychaeus:

> . . . ille Sychaeum
> impius ante aras atque auri caecus amore
> clam ferro incautum superat, securus amorum
> germanae; factumque diu celavit et aegram
> multa malus simulans vana spe lusit amantem.
> ipsa sed in somnis inhumati venit imago
> coniugis; ora modis attollens pallida miris
> crudelis aras traiectaque pectora ferro
> nudavit, caecumque domus scelus omne retexit.
>   (Book I, lines 348–56)

The king, impiously before the altars and blinded by lust of gold, strikes
down Sychaeus by stealthy blow unawares, careless of his sister's love;
and for long he hid the deed, and by many a pretence cunningly cheated
the lovesick bride with empty hope. But in her sleep came the very ghost
of her unburied husband; raising his face pale in wondrous wise, he laid
bare the cruel altars and his breast pierced with steel, unveiling all the
secret horror of the house.[48]

The evil brother's murder of his sister's beloved, the concealment of the crime, the lack of a proper burial, the revelation of the crime by the ghost of the beloved—all these elements are likewise present in Keats's narrative poem. When Dido learns of her brother's crime, she flees Tyre with the stolen riches and founds Carthage. At the beginning of the *Aeneid*'s fourth book, Dido confesses that since Sychaeus's death Aeneas alone has stirred her heart ("adgnosco veteris vestigia flammae" [Book IV, line 23]./"I recognize the traces of the olden flame"[49]), but she swears to remain faithful to Sychaeus, a vow that is soon broken. On the eve of Aeneas's departure, one of the omens of death Dido apprehends is the sound of Sychaeus's voice coming from the chapel devoted to his memory: "hinc exaudiri voces et verba vocantis visa viri, nox cum terras obscura teneret (Book IV, lines 460–61)"/"Thence she heard, it seemed, sounds and speech as of her husband calling, whenever darkling night held the world."[50] Soon afterward she herself bemoans her betrayal of Sychaeus: "non servata fides cineri promissa Sychaeo" (Book IV, line 552)/"The faith vowed to the ashes of Sychaeus I have not kept!"[51] The conclusion of the story of Dido and Sychaeus comes in Book VI, for when Dido flees Aeneas in the underworld, she returns to the grove where the faithful Sychaeus awaits her.[52]

Despite the prominence of Dido's betrayal of Sychaeus's memory in the *Aeneid*, Akhmatova excludes any reference to it from "Don't be afraid." Essential to *The Sweetbrier Blooms* is the unwavering faithfulness of the woman after separation, hence the appeal of Keats's "Isabella." In Akhmatova's epilogue to Virgil's story, Dido epitomizes (posthumous) remembrance, and Aeneas, forgetting. The cycle's untitled twelfth poem, which immediately follows "Don't be afraid" and was also written in 1962, develops the bitterly ironic tone of the sonnet's final tercet, and through a Dantesque allusion it comments on the relations between the poet and her addressee. It begins with the stanza:

Ты стихи мои требуешь прямо...
Как-нибудь проживешь и без них.

Пусть в крови не осталось и грамма,
Не впитавшего горечи их.

(SP, 243)

You demand my poems outright . . .
Somehow you will manage without them, too.
Granted that not even a gram remains in the blood
That has not imbibed their bitterness.

The poem was originally supplied with an epigraph from the *Purgatorio*, Canto 30; the words express Dante's reaction to the appearance of Beatrice:

> "Men che dramma
> di sangue m'è rimaso che non tremi:
> conosco i segni de l'antica fiamma."
> (lines 46–48)

"Not a drop of blood is left in me that does not tremble;
I know the tokens of the ancient flame."[53]

In their article on Akhmatova and Dante, Meilakh and Toporov observe that Dante's "conosco i segni de l'antica fiamma" is an "exact translation of the words of Dido—'adgnosco veteris vestigia flammae' (*Aeneid*, Book IV, line 23)—with which she announces to [her sister] Anna the beginning of her love for Aeneas."[54] Meilakh and Toporov then comment on the formal relationship between the lines of Virgil, Dante, and Akhmatova:

It is extremely interesting that the lines "Pust' v krovi ne ostalos' i gramma,/Ne vpitavshego gorechi ikh" not only are a paraphrase of Dante's terza rima, but also preserve Dante's rhyme, which goes back to Virgil's line, just as Dante himself here gives a translation of his teacher's verse. The theme of the "return of love's flame" . . . was real for all three poets, although in different ways.[55]

In Akhmatova's text, the theme of the return of love's flame is completely transfigured; instead of traces of the "ancient flame," bitterness pervades the poet's blood, a bitterness stemming from disappointed love, as implied in the wording of the caustic denial of the addressee's request for poems. As for the semantic import of the

Dantesque allusion, what is most relevant to *The Sweetbrier Blooms* is the context of the original utterance: Dante is announcing the appearance of Beatrice, who replaces Virgil as his guide. Beatrice's first action is to castigate Dante for betraying her memory, for forgetting her after her death:

> "Quando di carne a spirito era salita,
>   e bellezza e virtù cresciuta m'era,
>   fu' io a lui men cara e men gradita;
> e volse i passi suoi per via non vera,
>   imagini di ben seguendo false,
>   che nulla promission rendono intera.
> Né l'impetrare ispirazion mi valse,
>   con le quali e in sogno e altrimenti
>   lo rivocali; sì poco a lui ne calse!"
>
> (lines 127–35)

"When from flesh to spirit I had ascended, and beauty and virtue were increased in me, I was less dear and less pleasing to him and he turned his steps along a way not true, following false images of good, which pay no promise in full. Nor did it avail me to obtain inspirations with which, both in dream and otherwise, I called him back, so little did he heed them."[56]

Like Beatrice, the persona of Akhmatova's cycle belongs to the world of the spirit. Although separated from her addressee, she sends him various communications "both in dream and otherwise." To be sure, the cycle as a whole is addressed to him, but she also calls him, as enacted in *Cinque*'s "No zhivogo i naiavu,/Slyshish' ty, kak tebia zovu" (*SP*, 236)/"But alive and awake,/You hear me calling you"; her poems are carried to him by the wind ("Instead of a festive greeting"); and her shade haunts him ("Ten' prizraka tebia i den' i noch' trevozhit" [*SP*, 241]/"The shade of a phantom troubles you both day and night"). The addressee does not heed these signs, much like Dante, who confesses his guilt in Canto 31 of the *Purgatorio*:

> "Le presenti cose
>   col falso lor piacer volser miei passi,
>   tosto che 'l vostro viso si nascose."
>
> (lines 34–36)

"The present things, with their false pleasure, turned my steps aside, as soon as your countenance was hidden."[57]

Dante forgets Beatrice after her death, just as Aeneas forgets Dido in the *Aeneid* and the addressee forgets the persona in "Don't be afraid."

Keats's story of Isabella and Lorenzo is even more relevant to the theme of faithfulness and remembrance even after death in *The Sweetbrier Blooms*. The two characters are not mentioned by name in the cycle, but their story motivates the most important image in the cycle—the sweetbrier (*shipovnik*) itself. The key to the sweetbrier's significance lies in the fifth poem's epigraph, a quatrain that at one point served as the epigraph to the cycle as a whole:[58]

Несказанные речи
Я больше не твержу,
Но в память той невстречи
Шиповник посажу.

(SP, 239)

Unspoken speeches
I no longer repeat,
But in memory of that nonmeeting
I will plant a sweetbrier.

Shipovnik denotes a genus of wild roses; among its varieties are the dog rose (*sobachii shipovnik*; *Rosa canina*) and the sweetbrier or eglantine (*rzhavchinnyi shipovnik*; *Rosa eglanteria*). The word "sweetbrier" is preferred in the translation because not only is it true to the etymology of the original (*ship* means "thorn"), it also recalls its prototype—Isabella's "Sweet Basil." The sweetbrier is to serve as a remembrance, a motif that first sounds in the fourth poem of *Cinque*, in which the persona recalls her meeting with the addressee ("nashei vstrechi gorchaishii den'"), wondering what to give him as a memento: "Chto tebe na pamiat' ostavit'?"/"What memento should I leave you?" The rest of the text enumerates possible mementos, all of them highly elusive and insubstantial, such as the persona's shade, the already mentioned "dedication of a burned drama," and the "slyshimyi ele-ele/Zvon berezovykh ugolkov"/"barely audible ringing of birch coals" (*SP*, 237). The relation between event and remembrance is reversed in the quatrain-epigraph: the event—the nonmeeting—is spectral, and the object commemorating it will be real.

There is a threefold correspondence between the quatrain-epigraph and Keats's "Isabella": first, the action of planting; next, what is planted is sweet-smelling yet common; and finally, the action is motivated by the desire to commemorate. The parallel with "Isabella" is extended in "Pervaia pesenka" ("First Little Song," 1956), the fourth poem of *The Sweetbrier Blooms*, which adumbrates the insubstantialities and negativities of the non-meeting:

Таинственной невстречи
Пустынны торжества,
Несказанные речи,
Безмолвные слова.
Нескрещенные взгляды
Не знают, где им лечь.
И только слезы рады,
Что можно долго течь.
Шиповник Подмосковья,
Увы! при чем-то тут...
И это все любовью
Бессмертной назовут.

(SP, 239)

Empty are the solemnities
Of the mysterious nonmeeting.
Unuttered speeches,
Silent words.
Glances that have not met
Know not where to alight.
And only tears are glad
That they can flow a long time.
The sweetbrier of Moscow's environs
Alas! is somehow relevant here . . .
And all this will be called
Immortal love.

The long-flowing tears, mentioned just before the sweetbrier, recall the abundant tears shed by Isabella over her pot of basil. Isabella's weeping is an insistent refrain in Keats, as the following examples—all taken from the last lines of their stanzas—demonstrate: "and still she kissed and wept"; "Sweet Basil, which her tears kept ever wet"; "And moisten'd it with tears unto the core"; and "Beside her Basil, weeping through her hair." [59]

The sweetbrier image recurs in the cycle's untitled seventh poem, which evokes a walk taken by the persona on the outskirts of Moscow:

> Я шла, как в глубине морской...
> Шиповник так благоухал,
> Что даже превратился в слово.
> (SP, 241)

> I walked as if in the depths of the sea . . .
> The sweetbrier smelled so sweet
> That it even turned into speech.

Accentuating the fragrance of the sweetbrier, these lines hark back to Keats's description of the extraordinary aroma of Isabella's basil:

> And so she ever fed it with thin tears,
>   Whence thick, and green, and beautiful it grew,
> So that it smelt more balmy than its peers
>   Of Basil-tufts in Florence; for it drew
> Nurture besides, and life, from human fears,
>   From the fast mouldering head there shut from view:
> So that the jewel, safely casketed,
> Came forth, and in perfumed leafits spread.
> (LIV)

Transfiguration is central to the symbolism of Keats's basil: Lorenzo's "fast mouldering head," repulsive and malodorous, the very emblem of death, is transformed into a fragrant, "thick, and green, and beautiful" plant—an emblem of life. Like Keats's basil, Akhmatova's sweetbrier is bound up with transfiguration: the real sweetbrier to be planted by the persona will commemorate the "mysterious nonmeeting" with her addressee, a nonmeeting characterized by all that could not happen during it—by emotions and desires that could be neither expressed nor acted on. The rose is of course an age-old symbol of love—"immortal love," as the "First Little Song" has it—and Akhmatova's choice of the common sweetbrier, a poor relation of the sublime yet timeworn rose, revitalizes the symbolism. Beyond this, however, the sweetbrier itself is transfigured: "Shipovnik tak blagoukhal,/Chto dazhe prevratilsia v slovo" (*SP*, 241)/"The sweetbrier smelled so sweet/That it even turned into speech." The transformation of the wild rose into speech, into poetry, into art, ensures its immortality and is accomplished through an allusion to Shakespeare's immortal speech—"a rose by any other name" (*Romeo and Juliet*, 2.2).

The motif of concealment is crucial to Keats's evocation of the flourishing basil:

> . . . for it drew
> Nurture besides, and life, from human fears,
> From the fast mouldering head there *shut from view*:
> So that the jewel, *safely casketed*,
> Came forth, and in perfumed leafits spread.
> (Emphasis added.)

The basil is nourished not only by the "mouldering head" of Lorenzo, but also by "human fears," a phrase that, as John Sobolewski has noted, doubtless had a special resonance for Akhmatova, recalling the fear pervading Russian society in the postwar years of Stalin's rule.[60] More specifically, the sweetbrier conceals, and at the same time feeds on, the poet's fears for her loved ones in the aftermath of her meeting with the foreigner; it was fear of the consequences that turned the desired meeting in 1956 into a nonmeeting.

The question of concealment is even more relevant to Akhmatova's sweetbrier than to Keats's Sweet Basil, since from ancient times the rose has been an emblem of secrecy and silence, as in the Latin expression *sub rosa*. As featured in the title of the cycle, the sweetbrier engages yet another network of intertextual echoes. The word *shipovnik* (sweetbrier) occurs just once in all of Pushkin's poetry, and it appears with the predicate "tsvetet." The source is *Eugene Onegin*, chapter 7, stanza 6:

Меж гор, лежащих полукругом,
Пойдем туда, где ручеек,
Виясь, бежит зеленым лугом
К реке сквозь липовый лесок.
Там соловей, весны любовник,
Всю ночь поет; цветет шиповник,
И слышен говор ключевой,—
Там виден камень гробовой
В тени двух сосен устарелых.
Пришельцу надпись говорит:
«Владимир Ленский здесь лежит,
Погибший рано смертью смелых,
В такой-то год, таких-то лет.
Покойся, юноша-поэт!»[61]

Amidst the hills, down in that valley,
let's go where, winding all the time
across green meadows, dilly-dally,
a brook flows through a grove of lime.
There sings the nightingale, spring's lover,
the wild rose blooms, and in the covert
the source's chattering voice is heard;
and there a tombstone says its word
where two old pinetrees stand united:
"This is Vladimir Lensky's grave
who early died as die the brave"—
the headpiece thus indited—
the year, his age, then, "may your rest,
young poet, be forever blest!"[62]

In Pushkin, the sweetbrier blooms by Lensky's grave, a grave visited at first by two girls, but now forgotten:

Но ныне ... памятник унылый
Забыт. К нему привычный след
Заглох. Венка на ветви нет;
                              (stanza 7)

Today . . . the sad memorial's lonely,
forgot. Its trodden path is now
choked up. There's no wreath on the bough.[63]

The blooming sweetbrier is nature's adornment of Lensky's grave, which is untended and has been abandoned, as the absence of a wreath and the overgrown path eloquently attest. Lensky's memory has been forgotten by his beloved, the unfaithful Olga:

Мой бедный Ленский! изнывая,
Не долго плакала она,
Увы, невеста молодая
Своей печали неверна.
Другой увлек ее вниманье,
Другой успел ее страданье
Любовной лестью усыпить...

(stanza 10)

Poor Lensky! Set aside for weeping,
or pining, Olga's hours were brief.
Alas for him! there was no keeping
his sweetheart faithful to her grief.
Another had the skill to ravish
her thoughts away, knew how to lavish
sweet words by which her pain was banned . . . [64]

Olga's betrayal of Lensky is epigrammatically expressed in the second line, which, translated literally, reads "Not long did she weep." This phrase distinguishes her both from the faithful Isabella, whose tears for Lorenzo flow continuously, and from the persona of *The Sweetbrier Blooms*, who says: "I tol'ko slezy rady/Chto mozhno dolgo tech'" (*SP*, 239)/"And only tears are glad/That they can flow a long time."

In *Eugene Onegin*, the blooming sweetbrier is associated with Lensky's death—the death of a poet.[65] Chapter 4 explored a different allusion to Lensky's death in the omitted lines of "Tails," an allusion hinting at Nikolai Gumilev's execution for treason, and more broadly at the killing of poets by the state. In *The Sweetbrier Blooms*, the allusion to Lensky establishes a parallel between Lensky's fate and that of the poet-persona; both meet violent ends, and in both cases the beloved is implicated in the poet's death: in *Eugene Onegin*, Olga is entranced by Onegin's attentions, leading to the fatal duel, while in Akhmatova's cycle, the foreigner's visit brings about the poet's ruin. In *The Sweetbrier Blooms*, the blooming sweetbrier is identified with the poet's posthumous fate, and specifically with the beloved's betrayal of the poet's memory.

The same concern dominates Akhmatova's essay on Pushkin's *Stone Guest*, an essay completed in 1947, the year after the Central Committee resolution attacking her: in it, remarkably, both "Lensky's grave" and "Olga's betrayal" are invoked.[66] The essay explores the theme of *zagrobnaia revnost'* (posthumous jealousy) in Pushkin, shrewdly equating it with its anagram *zagrobnaia vernost'* (posthumous faithfulness). The Commander's vengeance from beyond the grave in *The Stone Guest* is contrasted with Lensky's betrayal by Olga in *Eugene Onegin*:

Pushkin touches on the theme of posthumous jealousy in the seventh chapter of *Onegin* in connection with Lensky's grave and Olga's betrayal.

По крайней мере, из могилы
Не вышла в сей печальный день
Его ревнующая тень.
И в поздний час, Гимену милый,
Не испугали молодых
Следы явлений гробовых...

At least out of the grave
there did not rise on that sad day
his jealous shade,
and at the late hour dear to Hymen,
no traces of sepulchral visitations
frightened the newlyweds.[67]

says Pushkin, as if with disappointment, and he searches for a plot wherein an enraged and jealous shade could appear. For this he changes the plot of Don Juan, and makes the Commander not the father of Doña Anna, but her husband.[68]

The lines of verse quoted here are a variant ending to stanza 11 from the drafts of *Eugene Onegin*. Pushkin laid Lensky's *rev-nuiushchaia ten'* (jealous shade) to rest in the drafts of *Onegin*, but almost a century and a half later Akhmatova summons it forth in her essay on *The Stone Guest*. Particularly germane to *The Sweet-brier Blooms* is the disappointment that Akhmatova attributes to Pushkin, betraying her own disappointment at the failure of Len-sky's shade to appear and avenge his betrayal. Her sense of justice was similarly offended by the silence of Dido's shade in Book VI of the *Aeneid*, for in "Don't be afraid" Dido's "enraged and jealous shade" not only reappears but breaks her silence and chastises the forgetful Aeneas, demonstrating her own posthumous faithfulness to him.

Virgil's Dido and Aeneas, Keats's Lorenzo and Isabella, Pushkin's Lensky and Olga, Dante and Beatrice of the *Purgatorio*—elements of all these love stories inform and shape the one told in *The Sweet-brier Blooms*. Although the imagery of death dominates the ren-dering of the poet's situation, in every instance it is counterbalanced by images of transcendence, regeneration, and immortality. In "Don't be afraid," Dido's death on the pyre and her silence in the underworld are overcome through speech alone. In "The Burned Notebook," the voice of the poems escapes destruction, and the promise of resurrection is borne out in the presence of these poems *From a Burned Notebook* on the printed page. Finally, the bloom-ing sweetbrier, transplanted from Lensky's forgotten grave, is recast into a powerful symbol of transcendence: commemorating the *nev-strecha* (nonmeeting), it attests to the poet's triumph over death, oblivion, and betrayal through memory and poetry.

Chapter 6

The Design of Memory

The power of the memory is prodigious,
my God. It is a vast, immeasurable
sanctuary.
—Saint Augustine, *Confessions*

Few are those who retain sufficient
memory.
—Plato, *Phaedrus*

"Est' tri epokhi u vospominanii" ("Memories have three epochs"), the sixth elegy of *The Northern Elegies*,[1] is unique among the poems of that cycle for its impersonality. In contrast to the other elegies, it does not feature the first-person singular voice. The circumstances of its writing are well known. The elegy was composed in Leningrad on February 5, 1945, some eight months after the poet's return from Tashkent. The city's destruction was a source of profound grief to Akhmatova, but she also met with a great disappointment in her personal life: her anticipated reunion with Vladimir Georgievich Garshin did not occur. Garshin, who had seen Akhmatova through the worst years of the Ezhov terror, had remained in Leningrad during the siege; the two had corresponded while separated, and Garshin had proposed marriage to Akhmatova. Upon her return to Leningrad, she learned that he had secretly married someone else during her absence.[2]

Akhmatova responded to Garshin's betrayal in the following poem, dated January 13, 1945:

... А человек, который для меня
Теперь никто, а был моей заботой
И утешеньем самых горьких лет,—

Уже бредет как призрак по окрайнам,
По закоулкам и задворкам жизни,
Тяжелый, одурманенный безумьем,
С оскалом волчьим...
                    Боже, Боже, Боже!
Как пред Тобой я тяжко согрешила!
Оставь мне жалость хоть...
                              (*S*, 1: 282)

. . . And the person who to me
Is now nobody, but was my care
And consolation during the bitterest years,—
Wanders like a phantom through the outskirts,
Through the dark alleys and backwoods of life,
Heavy, stupefied by insanity,
With the bared teeth of a wolf . . .
                    O God, O God, O God!
How gravely I have sinned before You!
Leave me pity at least . . .

The poet has been betrayed by her beloved, as in "Don't be afraid" from *The Sweetbrier Blooms*, but this lyric suppresses any direct mention of that betrayal (to be sure, it hints at it in the phrase "S oskalom volch'im"/"With the bared teeth of a wolf") and refrains from directly addressing the beloved; the poem is instead couched as a prayer of repentance (*pokaianie*). The portrait of the beloved evoked in the first seven lines measures the extent of the loss suffered by the persona, apparently in punishment for her sins: her former "care" (*zabota*) is now "nobody" (*nikto*) to her, pointing up the loss of her love for him; her former "consolation" has gone mad and become a threat to others. The harshness of the portrait suggests that the persona has even been deprived of pity, hence her final plea.

This prayer of repentance is closely related to "Memories have three epochs," written less than a month later. The elegy takes the form of a meditation on the relationship between remembering and forgetting. The memories in question are memories of love, and it is precisely their loss that the poem traces. The 43-line text is a veritable treatise on memory, which plays a crucial role in the later poetry,[3] as the preceding chapters have demonstrated: the poet recovers the distant past from oblivion in "Prehistory" and *Poem Without a Hero* and records for posterity the recent past in *Requiem*. In *The Sweetbrier Blooms*, memory is the means by which the poet triumphs over the forces of death and destruction. "Memories have three epochs" diverges from these texts by linking memory inextricably with oblivion, which is precisely what memory combats in the other texts studied here. The elegy is also particularly valuable for its metapoetic nature: not only does it explore the interrelationship of memory and forgetting, it defines the relationship between memory and poetry.

> Есть три эпохи у воспоминаний.
> И первая—как бы вчерашний день.
> Душа под сводом их благословенным,
> И тело в их блаженствует тени.
> Еще не замер смех, струятся слезы,   5
> Пятно чернил не стерто со стола,—
> И, как печать на сердце, поцелуй,
> Единственный, прощальный, незабвенный...
> Но это продолжается недолго...
> Уже не свод над головой, а где-то   10
> В глухом предместье дом уединенный,
> Где холодно зимой, а летом жарко,
> Где есть паук, и пыль на всем лежит,
> Где истлевают пламенные письма,
> Исподтишка меняются портреты,   15
> Куда как на могилу ходят люди,
> А возвратившись, моют руки мылом,
> И стряхивают беглую слезинку
> С усталых век—и тяжело вздыхают...
> Но тикают часы, весна сменяет   20
> Одна другую, розовеет небо,
> Меняются названья городов,
> И нет уже свидетелей событий,
> И не с кем плакать, не с кем вспоминать.
> И медленно от нас уходят тени,   25
> Которых мы уже не призываем,
> Возврат которых был бы страшен нам.

И, раз проснувшись, видим, что забыли
Мы даже путь в тот дом уединенный,
И, задыхаясь от стыда и гнева,   30
Бежим туда, но (как во сне бывает)
Там всё другое: люди, вещи, стены,
И нас никто не знает—мы чужие.
Мы не туда попали... Боже мой!
И вот когда горчайшее приходит: 35
Мы сознаем, что не могли б вместить
То прошлое в границы нашей жизни,
И нам оно почти что так же чуждо,
Как нашему соседу по квартире,
Что тех, кто умер, мы бы не узнали,   40
А те, с кем нам разлуку Бог послал,
Прекрасно обошлись без нас—и даже
Всё к лучшему...

Memories have three epochs.
And the first seems like yesterday.
The soul rests under their blessed vault,
And the body is blissful in their shade.
Laughter has not yet died down, tears are streaming,   5
The inkspot has not been wiped from the table,
And, like a seal on the heart, a farewell kiss—
The only one, the unforgettable . . .
But this continues not for long . . .
There is no longer a vault overhead, but somewhere   10
In a remote suburb an isolated house,
Where it's cold in winter and hot in summer,
Where there's a spider, and dust covers all,
Where ardent letters are moldering
And portraits are changing surreptitiously,   15
Where people go as to a grave,
And on returning, wash their hands with soap,
And brush a fleeting tear
From weary lids, and sigh heavily . . .
But the clock ticks, one spring replaces   20
Another, the sky grows roseate,
The names of cities change,
And the witnesses of events are no more,

And there is no one to cry with, no one to recollect with.
And slowly from us depart the shades   25
Whom we no longer summon,
Whose return would be terrible to us.
And, once upon awakening, we see that we've forgotten
Even the path back to that isolated house,
And choking with shame and anger   30
We run there, but (as it happens in dreams)
Everything there is different: the people, the things, the walls,
And no one knows us—we are strangers.
We've landed in the wrong place . . . My God!
And this is when the bitterest comes: 35
We realize that we couldn't have fit
That past into the boundaries of our life,
And that it is almost as alien to us
As to our communal-apartment neighbor,
That we wouldn't recognize those who died,   40
And that those from whom God separated us
Have managed beautifully without us—and even
That it's all for the best . . .

A Myth of Memory
and Forgetting

The elegy's gnomic first line sets the stage for an exploration of the
effect of time on memories. The word *epokha* (epoch) commonly
designates a sharply defined period of history initiated through a
radical break with the past. The phrase "tri epokhi"/"three epochs" accordingly portends radical change and disjunction.[4] The
memories are imaged as a three-dimensional space—a metaphor
for memory—that radically changes as the elegy unfolds; remembering, in turn, figures as a visit to the locus of memory.[5] Akhmatova's casting of memory in terms of a three-dimensional, enclosed
space is constant throughout her work, although the specific characteristics of the space vary. Among her other tropes for memory
are "khoromy pamiati"/"the mansion of memory"; "terema [pa-
miati]"/"the tower chambers [of memory]"; and the well-known

"podval pamiati"/"cellar of memory," from the poem of the same title.[6] Such imagery is hardly specific to Akhmatova. Saint Augustine, for instance, deploys a variety of spatial metaphors as figures for memory in Book X of his *Confessions*, as the following quotation demonstrates: "The next stage is memory, which is like a great field or a spacious palace, a storehouse for countless images of all kinds." He likewise speaks of the "vast cloisters," the "great treasure-house," the "wide plains" and "innumerable caverns" of memory.[7]

In the first epoch, the memories are portrayed as all-enveloping, all-encompassing:

> И первая—как бы вчерашний день.
> Душа под сводом их благословенным,
> И тело в их блаженствует тени.
> Еще не замер смех, струятся слезы,
> Пятно чернил не стерто со стола,—
> И, как печать на сердце, поцелуй,
> Единственный, прощальный, незабвенный...

> And the first seems like yesterday.
> The soul is under their blessed vault,
> And the body is blissful in their shade.
> Laughter has not yet died down, tears are streaming,
> The inkspot has not been wiped from the table,
> And, like a seal on the heart, a farewell kiss—
> Singular, unforgettable . . .

The spaciousness of the locus of memories is remarkable: the word *svod* (vault) conjures up a high, overarching, sky-like ceiling, while the phrase "v ikh teni"/"in their shade" evokes overspreading trees. The loftiness of the vault is mirrored in the elevated diction of these lines. Alliteration, paronomasia, and syntactical inversion figure prominently, and Church Slavic loans—indicators of the high style—abound, as underscored in the near rhyme of two of them—*blagoslovénnym* (blessed) and *nezabvénnyi* (unforgettable). The former is pointedly echoed in another word of Church Slavic origin, *blazhenstvuet* (is blissful), and together the two lend sublime, paradisiacal connotations to remembering in the first epoch.

The remembering subject is immersed, body and soul, in the memories, which are a source of both joy (*smekh*) and sorrow (*slezy*).[8] The memories—traces of the past—are still fresh (they are "like yesterday"), and the emotions attached to them flow freely. The last two lines of the passage reveal the origin of the memories: the phrase "farewell kiss" ("potselui / . . . proshchal'nyi") conjures up the subject's moment of parting from a loved one. The elegy lingers over the kiss, assigning it three weighty epithets; even more important, the kiss is summoned up in the present tense, emblematizing the love that will prevail during separation. This notion is reinforced in the simile comparing the kiss to a "pechat' na serdtse"/"seal on the heart," for a seal ensures the authenticity and inviolateness of the contents of whatever it marks. The actual making of the memories—their imprinting on the mind—is suggested in the images of the inkspot, seal, and kiss. The inkspot and the seal point to the inscription or imprinting of images on the mind; the kiss, itself a kind of impression, is the image that is being recollected. The symbolic unity of the images of the inkspot, seal, and kiss is underscored by the paronomastic relation between them: *piatno chernil/pechat' na serdtse/potselui.*[9]

The epithet *nezabvennyi* (unforgettable) closes the evocation of the first epoch of memories, and along with its near rhyme it names the epoch: this is the blessed age of nonoblivion, of absolute memory. Remembering in the first epoch makes the past present: the passage contains two past-tense verbs, but both are negated and so serve to express the nonpast. The first epoch is the Edenic age of memory—memory before the fall into linear time. The blissfulness attached to remembering in the first epoch, the harmony between body and soul, the unity between self and other—all these elements conjure up paradise. This paradisiacal realm is coterminous with that of poetry, as evidenced in the inkspot on the table: the scene evoked is one of writing. Poetry is likewise implied in the elevated, markedly poetic diction of the passage, manifested on every level of the text—lexical, syntactic, phonological, and semantic.

The onset of change is abruptly announced in a line heralding the end of the first epoch: "No eto prodolzhaetsia nedolgo . . ."

(line 9)/"But this continues not for long. . . ." The verb *prodol-zhat'sia* (to continue) signifies duration, persistence in time—the essence of remembering in the first epoch—but it is immediately negated in the etymologically related adverb *nedolgo* (not for long). In the first epoch, the negative expresses continuity with the past and the absence of change (*ne zamer, ne sterto, ne-zabvennyi*), but here it foretells the disruption of that continuity,[10] a disruption borne out in the second epoch of memories (lines 10–19):

Уже не свод над головой, а где-то
В глухом предместье дом уединенный,
Где холодно зимой, а летом жарко,
Где есть паук, и пыль на всем лежит,
Где истлевают пламенные письма,
Исподтишка меняются портреты,
Куда как на могилу ходят люди,
А возвратившись, моют руки мылом,
И стряхивают беглую слезинку
С усталых век—и тяжело вздыхают...

There is no longer a vault overhead, but somewhere
In a remote suburb an isolated house,
Where it's cold in winter and hot in summer,
Where there's a spider, and dust covers all,
Where ardent letters are moldering
And portraits are changing surreptitiously,
Where people go as to a grave,
And on returning, wash their hands with soap,
And brush a fleeting tear
From weary lids, and sigh heavily . . .

The first epoch's "blessed vault" has been superseded by an "uedi-nennyi dom"/"isolated house" of memories. Rather than enveloping the remembering subject, the house has been displaced to a peripheral location, where it stands uninhabited and neglected. Remembering, imaged as a return to the house, is a source not of bliss but of unpleasantness; it occurs only intermittently and is of brief duration.

The prime agent of change in the second epoch is time, whose workings are foregrounded in the reference to the turn of the seasons (line 12). The first epoch is in retrospect revealed to have been seasonless—another indication of its timeless, paradisiacal nature. The second epoch of memories, by contrast, is a post-Edenic epoch, for the fall marked the beginning of time, as Northrop Frye has observed:

> In Adam's situation there is a feeling, which in Christian tradition can be traced back at least to St. Augustine, that time *begins* with the fall; that the fall from liberty into the natural cycle also started the movement of time as we know it. In other tragedies too we can trace the feeling that *nemesis* is deeply involved with the movement of time, whether as the missing of a tide in the affairs of men, as a recognition that the time is out of joint, as a sense that time is the devourer of life.[11]

The second epoch marks the beginning of linear time within the elegy,[12] and the imagery of decay, deterioration, and decomposition attests to the work of the "devourer of life." The sole resident of the house of memories is the spider, a predatory creature symbolically associated with destruction. The omnipresent dust (line 13) bespeaks disintegration, a process that is still going on, as the next line emphasizes: "Gde istlevaiut plamennye pis'ma"/"Where ardent letters are moldering."[13] These letters hark back to the inkspot on the table identifying the first epoch as the age of writing, of poetry; the epithet *plamennyi* (ardent), moreover, reveals them to be love letters, expressions of the very emotion symbolized in the kiss. Their moldering identifies the second epoch with the decomposition of poetry and the disintegration of love.

A different change is described in line 15: "Ispodtishka meniaiutsia portrety"/"And portraits are changing surreptitiously." The line refers to this lyric written by Akhmatova in 1940:

Когда человек умирает,
Изменяются его портреты.
По-другому глаза глядят, а губы
Улыбаются другой улыбкой.
Я заметила это, вернувшись

С похорон одного поэта.
И с тех пор проверяла часто,
И моя догадка подтвердилась.

(*SP*, 197)

When a person dies,
His portraits change.
The eyes gaze differently, and the lips
Smile a different smile.
I noticed that on returning
From the funeral of a certain poet.
And since then I have tested it often,
And my hunch has been confirmed.

On the surface, the octet seems harmless enough, as its publication in the journal *Zvezda* in early 1940 attests.[14] The focus of the poem, however, is death, as proclaimed in the first line; later the funeral of a poet is mentioned, and then the innocuous adverb *chasto* (often) conjures up the deaths of many people. As the date suggests, the poem refers to the victims of the Ezhov terror, although the reference is veiled because as a rule no funerals were given them.[15] There are striking parallels between this poem and the elegy's second epoch. In both the image of portraits changing[16] is succeeded by the motif of return (denoted through the synonymous gerunds "vernuvshis'" and "vozvrativshis'"); in the octet, the return is from a funeral; in the elegy, it is from the isolated house, which is likened to a grave: "Kuda kak na mogilu khodiat liudi,/A vozvrativshis' . . ."/"Where people go as to a grave,/And on returning. . . ." The portraits' presence within the house of memories suggests that they are visual images of the loved one implicated in the kiss and addressed in the "ardent letters."[17] The octet reveals the significance of the portraits' surreptitious changing in the elegy: those pictured in the portraits have died, a notion immediately seconded in the simile comparing the house of memories to a grave.[18]

One other thing changes in the second epoch—the subjective experience of remembering. Most indicative here is the motif of the washing of hands: "A vozvrativshis', moiut ruki mylom"/"And on returning, wash their hands with soap." This act symbolizes the attempt to dissociate the self from the memories, to remove all traces of them. The underlying emotion here is guilt, for the washing of hands has from ancient times been a ritualistic gesture to absolve the self of guilt.[19] The gesture is prominently featured in one of Akhmatova's poems from the 1930's, "Privol'em pakhnet dikii med" ("Wild honey smells of open spaces"):

И напрасно наместник Рима
Мыл руки пред всем народом,
Под зловещие крики черни;
И шотландская королева
Напрасно с узких ладоней
Стирала красные брызги
В душном мраке царского дома...

(SP, 191)

And in vain the Roman governor
Washed his hands before all the people,
Under the ominous cries of the rabble,
And the Scottish queen
In vain rubbed the red splatters
From her narrow palms
In the stifling gloom of the royal house . . .

The repetition of the word *naprasno* (in vain) underscores the ineffectiveness of the gesture. What is particularly jarring in "Memories have three epochs" is the debasement of the symbolic gesture through the complement *mylom* (with soap). Pilate uses water (Matt. 27: 24); Lady Macbeth simply rubs her hands together. The elegy's prosaic twist borders on the grotesque, replacing morality with hygiene.[20]

The guilt is likely owing to the unconscious awareness that forgetting has set in, for forgetting constitutes a betrayal of the loved one. The other emotions expressed (lines 18–19) similarly diverge from those of the first epoch. Instead of bliss and laughter, weariness and heaviness prevail ("s ustalykh vek"/"from weary lids"; "tiazhelo vzdykhaiut"/"sigh heavily"). In contrast to the abundance of tears in the first epoch, the second sees but a single ephemeral tear ("beglaia slezinka"/"fleeting tear"), one that is quickly brushed away[21]—a gesture bespeaking the desire to dissociate the self from the emotions aroused by the memories. The heavy sighing contradicts the kiss sealing the first epoch of memories; that kiss ensures the heart's fullness and integrity (the Russian *potselui* [kiss] derives from the verb *tselovat'*, which etymologically means "to make whole"). The heavy sighing, by contrast, bespeaks an emptying of the self of life itself, in keeping with the biblical verse "Remember that my life is but a breath" (Job 7: 7).[22]

Time encroaches on memory in the second epoch, but the beginning of the next epoch witnesses an ominous quickening in the flow of time (lines 20–27):

> Но тикают часы, весна сменяет
> Одна другую, розовеет небо,
> Меняются названья городов,
> И нет уже свидетелей событий,
> И не с кем плакать, не с кем вспоминать.
> И медленно от нас уходят тени,
> Которых мы уже не призываем,
> Возврат которых был бы страшен нам.

> But the clock ticks, one spring replaces
> Another, the sky grows roseate,
> The names of cities change,
> And the witnesses of events are no more,
> And there is no one to cry with, no one to recollect with.
> And slowly from us depart the shades
> Whom we no longer summon,
> Whose return would be terrible to us.

The first two lines echo Pushkin's description of St. Petersburg's white nights in the *The Bronze Horseman*:

> Одна заря сменить другую
> Спешит, дав ночи полчаса.[23]

> One *zaria* hastens to replace
> Another, giving night just half an hour.

Zaria denotes both "sunrise" and "sunset," and in the speed with which one replaces another, Pushkin underscores the brevity of the sun's absence. Akhmatova mimics Pushkin's strong enjambment to express the turn of the years, not of the days; her conflation of the ticking of seconds with the succession of years similarly conveys a vertiginous acceleration in the pace of time, which brings with it profound changes, as proclaimed in the line "Meniaiutsia nazvan'ia gorodov"/"The names of cities change." The same verb describes the portraits in line 15,[24] and its recurrence here underscores the very different frame of reference: the portraits belong to the subjective domain of memory, but cities are a part of the objective world. The focus has shifted to the context of remembering, to those forces and events which impinge on the individual, threatening not merely the ability to recollect but survival itself. The image of the pinkish sky ("rozoveet nebo," line 21) is fully in keeping with the shift, connoting conflagration and cataclysmic historical events.[25] In view of Akhmatova's reverential, mythopoetic attitude toward the word and the proper name in particular,[26] the renaming of cities is tantamount to altering their very essence and transforming the remembering subject's world beyond recognition, beyond remembering.

The theme of onomastic displacement first arose in Akhmatova's poetry in connection with the renaming of St. Petersburg during World War I. The lyric "Petrograd, 1919" is written from the perspective of those who did not flee the city but stayed behind to preserve it. The closing lines envision a future reversal in the relations between the city and its inhabitants:

Но нам священный град Петра
Невольным памятником будет.
(*SP*, 149)

But the holy city of Peter
Will be an unwitting monument to us.

The phrase "sviashchennyi grad Petra" periphrastically resurrects the original name of the city—*Sankt-Peterburg*—from oblivion, restoring to the city its true identity. In the elegy, the line "The names of cities change" specifically recalls the flurry of renaming that took place after the revolution. No anamnestic act such as that accomplished in "Petrograd, 1919" is possible, for not only is the scope of change much greater, but there are no witnesses left:

> И нет уже свидетелей событий,
> И не с кем плакать, не с кем вспоминать.
>
> And the witnesses of events are no more,
> And there is no one to cry with, no one to recollect with.

The first line here constitutes another veiled allusion to postrevolutionary Russian history: the beginning of it harks back to Pushkin's "Inykh uzh net, a te daleche" [27]/"Some are no more, and others are far away," implying that the witnesses died, very likely by execution, or that they were sent to Siberia. The pairing of the verbs *plakat'* (to weep) and *vspominat'* (to recollect) in the next line comments on the nature of the events themselves: these are the activities of mourners, of those who have suffered losses. The repeated phrase "ne s kem"/"no one with whom" recalls Lermontov's "i nekomu ruku podat' "/"and there is no one's hand to clasp," and even more strongly Mandelstam's echo of Lermontov a hundred years later: "I ne s kem posovetovat'sia mne" [28]/"And there is no one for me to confer with." In Lermontov as in Mandelstam, the negative impersonal construction describes the loneliness of the lyrical persona, his isolation from other people; in the elegy, by contrast, it expresses the common fate, the plight of all survivors, suggesting the destruction of the very fabric of society, the loss of community.

Ironically, it is just at this point that the first-person plural voice suddenly yet unobtrusively appears—"I medlenno *ot nas* ukhodiat teni"/"And slowly *from us* depart the shades" (emphasis added)—and the rest of the elegy is dominated by it. The only other text in *The Northern Elegies* featuring the first-person plural voice is "Prehistory," where it refers to the poet and her generation. In *Requiem's* "Dedication," by contrast, the same voice speaks for Akhmatova and her addressees—the women who stood with her in Leningrad's prison lines. Although the "we" of the sixth elegy refers to the survivors of the cataclysmic events alluded to in line 23, it does not seem to speak for them as a group: instead, it is a limited first-person plural, joining together the poet and her reader by expressing their common experience, implicating the reader in the action traced in the elegy.[29] They are linked not only by their complete isolation (line 24) but also by their failure to continue recollecting—summoning the shades of—the past (lines 25–27). The motivation for this is fear (the shades' return "byl by strashen nam"/ "would be terrible to us"), the roots of which lie in the earlier intimations of guilt. The cessation of anamnesis triggers the departure of the shades ("I medlenno ot nas ukhodiat teni"/"And slowly from us depart the shades"), an image that plays on one of the euphemisms for the dead—*ushedshie* (the departed). Erwin Rohde's discussion of the cult of souls among the ancient Greeks illuminates the significance of this juncture in the elegy:

The continued life of the soul, such as was implied in and guaranteed by the cult of souls, was entirely bound up with the remembrance of the survivors upon earth, and upon the care, the cult, which they might offer to the soul of their departed ancestor. If that memory dies out, if the venerating thoughtfulness of the living ceases, the soul of the departed is at once deprived of the sole element in which it still maintained its shadow of an existence.[30]

Akhmatova's elegy portrays the cult of the souls of loved ones, not of ancestors, but the implications of the cessation of remembrance are the same: the shades are doomed to oblivion, to nonbeing. Their departure is pictured in a way that recalls the very different feelings originally associated with them: "I medlenno ot nas ukhodiat téni"/"And slowly from us depart the shades" harks back to "Telo v ikh blazhenstvuet tení" (line 4)/"The body is blissful in their shade." The departing "shades" are one with the "shade" cast by the memories in the first epoch—all that differentiates them is the placement of the accent—but the bliss they inspired has been replaced by fear.

The next portion of the elegy portrays the consequences of the breaking off of remembrance (lines 28–34):

И, раз проснувшись, видим, что забыли
Мы даже путь в тот дом уединенный,
И, задыхаясь от стыда и гнева,
Бежим туда, но (как во сне бывает)
Там всё другое: люди, вещи, стены,
И нас никто не знает—мы чужие.
Мы не туда попали... Боже мой!

And, once upon awakening, we see that we've forgotten
Even the path back to that isolated house,
And choking with shame and anger
We run there, but (as it happens in dreams)
Everything there is different: the people, the things, the walls,
And no one knows us—we are strangers.
We've landed in the wrong place . . . My God!

The casting of the subjects' realization that they have forgotten in the form of a symbolic awakening reflects the fact that they are no longer oblivious to it. The awakening is, however, only a partial one, as underscored in the parenthetical aside—"(kak vo sne byvaet)"/"(as it happens in dreams"): far from overcoming their amnesia, their attempted return to the isolated house acts it out. Saint Augustine, writing with reference to a forgotten name, makes a subtle distinction between degrees of forgetting that is relevant here: "If the name were completely obliterated from our minds, we could not remember it even if we were prompted. For we do not entirely forget what we remember that we have forgotten. If we had completely forgotten it, we should not even be able to look for what was lost." [31] In "Memories have three epochs," what the subjects "remember to have forgotten" is precisely how to remember, for that is the symbolic import of the metaphorical journey to the isolated house. This awareness prompts the frantic attempt to return to it, for, to paraphrase Saint Augustine, they can look for what they still remember to have forgotten. They do not remember all that they have forgotten, however: they have no recollection whatsoever of the blissful first epoch of memories, and they cannot look for what they have completely forgotten.

A travesty of remembering, the ill-fated return brings them to an unrecognizable, alien interior. Estrangement reaches its apogee through a doubling of the motif of nonrecognition: not only do the subjects recognize nothing ("Tam vse drugoe"/"Everything is different there"), they themselves are not recognized either: "I nas nikto ne znaet—my chuzhie"/"And no one knows us—we are strangers." When it is recalled that this house has been reached through an inner journey into the "caverns of memory," that the house is in fact an "inner chamber" of the mind, the magnitude of the loss suffered becomes apparent: the concomitant of estrangement from the past is alienation from the self.[32] This alienation is succinctly expressed in the phrase "my chuzhie"/"we are strangers," which seems to paraphrase Rimbaud's dictum "je est un autre." [33]

The failure of recognition enacted in the third epoch leaves a void that is filled only by the bitter realizations concluding the elegy (lines 35–43):

И вот когда горчайшее приходит:
Мы сознаем, что не могли б вместить
То прошлое в границы нашей жизни,
И нам оно почти что так же чуждо,
Как нашему соседу по квартире,
Что тех, кто умер, мы бы не узнали,
А те, с кем нам разлуку Бог послал,
Прекрасно обошлись без нас—и даже
Всё к лучшему...

And this is when the bitterest comes:
We realize that we couldn't have fit
That past into the boundaries of our life,
And that it is almost as alien to us
As to our communal-apartment neighbor,
That we wouldn't recognize those who died,
And that those from whom God separated us
Have managed beautifully without us—and even
That it's all for the best . . .

Here alienation and estrangement continue to define the attitude toward the past, but they now also dominate the feelings toward the present. The passage takes the form of a series of rationalizations of aspects of the subjects' present life, beginning with their forgetting of the past: the past simply could not be incorporated "v granitsy nashei zhizni"/"into the boundaries of our life."[34] Those boundaries are delineated in the phrase "nash sosed po kvartire," which designates a neighbor sharing the same communal apartment. The dwelling of the present is thus revealed to be the notorious communal apartment—overcrowded, uncomfortable, and devoid of privacy—where thin walls separate one household's cramped living space from another's. The phrase "my chuzhie" (line 33)/"we are strangers," with its connotations of alienation from the past and from the self, is recalled in line 38 in the etymologically related *chuzhdo* (alien); there is an additional nuance here, however, for *chuzhdo* perfectly captures the essence of communal apartment living: it is life among strangers. The lines containing the reference to the communal apartment gauge the degree of alienation from the self. The personal past is judged to be almost as alien to the self as to one's neighbor, a comparison establishing an equivalence between the self and others, suggesting once again the loss of personal identity.

The motif of nonrecognition resurfaces in the coda with reference to the dead: "tekh, kto umer, my by ne uznali"/"we wouldn't recognize those who died." The reciprocity of nonrecognition in the third epoch is likewise reflected in the coda. The subjects attribute their forgetting of the dead and their alienation from the past to their inability to accommodate that past in their present lives; the subjects themselves, however, have been similarly displaced from the lives of their fellow survivors: "te, s kem nam razluku Bog poslal,/Prekrasno oboshlis' bez nas"/"those from whom God separated us/Have managed beautifully without us." The idiom *oboitis' bez* (to get along without) effectively closes the circle of forgetting: the subjects have forgotten the dead, but they themselves have been excluded from the lives of other survivors.

Just as the subjects become aware of their amnesia in the third epoch, so in the coda they are still conscious of what they have forgotten (the past, the dead), and furthermore they admit to having been forgotten by their fellow survivors. The guilt rooted in their own betrayal of the past and the pain stemming from their betrayal by others in the present are both entirely suppressed. The sole explicit index of these feelings of loss and betrayal is the word *gorchaishee* (the bitterest). The poet's stance is one of merciless irony, which culminates in the cruel *pointe* to the elegy—the vacuous phrase "vse k luchshemu"/"it's all for the best." This simple, prosaic phrase dismisses the loss suffered as irrelevant and insignificant. The very compulsion to suppress and deny the pain, however, measures the enormity of the loss.[35]

Abbie Findlay Potts, in her book *The Elegiac Mode*, has singled out Tennyson's line "Oh! the difference to me!" as emblematic of personal elegiac expression. "This cry," she asserts, "is the index of lyrical elegy."[36] The comparison with the ending of Akhmatova's sixth Northern Elegy is most illuminating, for "the difference to us" is precisely what is suppressed in the elegy's coda, and most pointedly in the cliché "it's all for the best. . . ."[37] The evisceration of the self traced in the elegy precludes any such lyrical expression, and the role of the lyrical is usurped by the ironic.

The abrupt cessation of the elegy in the middle of the verse line realizes the implications of the embrace of forgetfulness, bringing to an end the metapoetic subplot of the elegy. Writing flourishes in the first epoch of memories and molders in the second, but the third epoch—the age of forgetting—sounds the death knell of writing. Given that poetry has its basis in memory and that verse is organized through repetitions and verbal returns, the movement from memory to forgetfulness traced in the elegy predicates the truncation of the text in midline. In a world devoid of memory, there can be no closure, no textual integrity, no return.

The Garden and the House

The depiction of memory in the sixth Northern Elegy exploits two pivotal images in Akhmatova's poetry—the garden and the house.

Each has its own history in her work. While the table lends the first epoch's locus of memories a domestic flavor, the sky-like vault and the shade are both suggestive of a garden. The memory space represents a variation on Akhmatova's *locus amoenus*, most commonly referred to in the early lyrics as a "zelenyi sad"/"green garden." Ernst Robert Curtius defines the classical version of the topos as "a beautiful, natural site" with "a tree (or several trees), a meadow, and a spring or a brook"; it is a place of pleasure, rest, and repose, and it is associated with "various forms of the earthly paradise."[38] The topos appears very early in Akhmatova, most frequently in poems linked with Tsarskoe Selo. The following passage from a 1915 lyric written in Tsarskoe Selo is a good example:

> Я вошла вчера в зеленый рай,
> Где покой для тела и души
> Под шатром тенистых тополей.
>
> (*SP*, 123)

> Yesterday I entered a green paradise,
> Where there is peace for body and soul
> Under the tent of shady poplars.

The presence of shade-giving trees, the attendant peacefulness, and above all the phrase "zelenyi rai"/"green paradise" establish this as an instance of the *locus amoenus*. The first epoch's locus of memories is anticipated here in the references to body (*telo*), soul (*dusha*), and shade (compare "tenistykh" with "v teni"), and while the lyric names paradise (*rai*) outright, the elegy implies it in its diction.[39]

Elsewhere in Akhmatova the garden is explicitly identified with poetry and poetic inspiration, as illustrated in the last quatrain of the 1918 lyric "Noch'iu" ("At Night"):

> Семь дней тому назад,
> Вздохнувши, я прости сказала миру,
> Но душно там, и я пробралась в сад
> Взглянуть на звезды и потрогать лиру.
>
> (*SP*, 146)

> Seven days ago,
> With a sigh I bid the world farewell,
> But it was stifling there, and I made my way into the garden
> To look at the stars and touch the lyre.

In the concluding lines of "Pust' golosa organa snova grianut" ("Let the organ's voices thunder out anew," 1921), the persona similarly takes refuge in the garden:

> А я иду владеть чудесным садом,
> Где шелест трав и восклицанья муз.
> (SP, 171)

> But I go to possess the wondrous garden,
> Where the grasses rustle and the Muses exclaim.

The rustling of vegetation is symbolic of poetic inspiration, as are the Muses' cries. In *Poem Without a Hero*, the garden of the Muses is identified as Tsarskoe Selo: the lyrical digression at the end of the third chapter imagines the poet's return to Tsarskoe Selo:

> *А теперь бы домой скорее*
> *Камероновой Галереей*
> *В ледяной таинственный сад,*
> *Где безмолвствуют водопады,*
> *Где все девять мне будут рады,*
> *Как бывал ты когда-то рад.*
> (S, 2: 118)

> *And now to go home more quickly*
> *Through the Cameron Gallery*
> *To the ice-covered, mysterious garden,*
> *Where the waterfalls are silent,*
> *Where all nine will be glad at my coming,*
> *As you were at one time glad.*

The author's notes to *Poem Without a Hero* gloss the phrase "vse deviat' "/"all nine" as a reference to the nine Muses. In some versions of the *poema*, the digression is entitled "Poslednee vospominanie o Tsarskom Sele" ("The Last Recollection of Tsarskoe Selo"), a reference to Pushkin's Tsarskoe Selo poems,[40] and the digression incorporates numerous allusions to those poems.[41]

A more complicated and enigmatic instance of the *locus amoenus* is found in the 1924 sonnet "Khudozhniku" ("To an Artist"), which is very closely related to "Memories have three epochs":

Мне всё твоя мерещится работа,
Твои благословенные труды:
Лип, навсегда осенних, позолота
И синь сегодня созданной воды.

Подумай, и тончайшая дремота
Уже ведет меня в твои сады,
Где, каждого пугаясь поворота,
В беспамятстве ищу твои следы.

Войду ли я под свод преображенный,
Твоей рукою в небо превращенный,
Чтоб остудился мой постылый жар?...

Там стану я блаженною навеки,
И, раскаленные смежая веки,
Там снова обрету я слезный дар.

(SP, 184)

Your work keeps appearing before me,
Your blessed labors:
The gilt of lindens, forever autumnal,
And the dark blueness of water created today.

Just think, even the slightest drowse
Is already leading me into your gardens,
Where, taking fright at every turn,
I seek your traces in oblivion.

Shall I enter beneath the transfigured vault,
Changed by your hand into the sky,
To cool my dismal fever? . . .

There I shall become blissful forever,
And, closing my inflamed eyelids,
There I shall once more gain the gift of tears.

The convergence of the motifs of trees, water, peacefulness, pleasure, and refuge identifies this as a version of the *locus amoenus*. The diction of the sonnet, like that of the elegy's first epoch, is emphatically poetic and elevated, and the two texts share many words and roots; compare excerpts from the elegy on the left with parallel passages from the sonnet on the right:

Душа *под сводом их благословенным,*	Войду ли я *под свод Твои благословенные* труды
И тело в их *блаженствует* тени.	Там стану я *блаженною навеки*
струятся *слезы*	снова обрету я *слезный дар*

These correspondences show that the elegy's garden paradise and the sonnet's are essentially versions of the same topos. Nevertheless, the status of the locus within these texts differs greatly: in the elegy, the state of bliss is experienced in the present but is short-lived; in the sonnet, by contrast, the suffering persona is outside the paradisiacal realm she conjures up, yet she envisages the future bliss she will enjoy within it, bliss that will last forever (*naveki*).

In its diction and imagery, Akhmatova's treatment of this blessed realm is modeled on Pushkin's Tsarskoe Selo poems.[42] In Pushkin's poetry, the gardens at Tsarskoe Selo are bound up with the thematics of memories, poetic inspiration, and return. In "Vospominaniia v Tsarskom Sele" ("Memories in Tsarskoe Selo," 1814), the poem that first brought Pushkin public acclaim as a poet, the garden of Tsarskoe Selo, which is called an "Elizium polnoshchnyi"/"northern Elysium," figures as a repository of memories impelling the visitor to recall the past.[43] The realms evoked at the beginning of the sonnet and the sixth Northern Elegy are both modeled on Pushkin's 1829 "Memories in Tsarskoe Selo," which begins:

Воспоминаньями смущенный,
Исполнен сладкою тоской,
Сады прекрасные, под сумрак ваш священный
Вхожу с поникшею главой.[44]

Stirred by recollections,
Filled with sweet nostalgia,
O beautiful gardens, into your sacred dusk
I come with bowed head.

The reverential tone and lofty diction of these lines are mirrored in both the sonnet and the elegy; the theme of *vospominaniia* (memories) links this text to the elegy, while the motif of *sady* (gardens) is featured in the sonnet. At the end of the text's second strophe, the gardens of Tsarskoe Selo are called a "predel blagoslovennyi"/ "blessed realm," a euphemism for paradise; the same epithet appears in both the elegy and the sonnet. Finally, Pushkin's persona likens himself to the prodigal son, who, "Uvidev nakonets rodimuiu obitel',/Glavoi ponik i zarydal"[45]/"Having caught sight at last of his native dwelling,/Bowed his head and began to weep." Compare the elegy's "struiat'sia slezy"/"tears are flowing" and the sonnet's "sleznyi dar"/"gift of tears."

The second stanza of Pushkin's text is devoted to the years of separation from the gardens, and the parallel with the prodigal son is extended:

И долго я блуждал, и часто, утомленный,
Раскаяньем горя, предчувствуя беды,
Я думал о тебе, предел благословенный,
    Воображал сии сады.[46]

And long I wandered, and often weary,
Burning with repentance, feeling presentiments of woe,
I thought of thee, O blessed realm,
    I imagined these gardens.

These lines aptly characterize the situation of the speaker in Akhmatova's "To an Artist": separated from the gardens, she thinks of them, imagines them, and dreams of taking refuge in them. In "Memories have three epochs," by contrast, when the "isolated house" replaces the blessed realm of memories, no recollection is retained.

The image of the house stands at the very center of Akhmatova's poetic universe. In the early poems, it figures both as the lyrical persona's abode and as the setting of the lyrical event.[47] One 1914 lyric, "Belyi dom" ("The White House"), written to commemorate the outbreak of World War I, anticipates the role and significance of the house image in Akhmatova's later work. The "white house" of the title actually motivates the lyrical event, figuring as a lost object that the persona strives in vain to recover; its disappearance is symbolic of an irrevocable break with the past.[48] One stanza of "The White House" prefigures the conversion of memory into forgetting in the sixth Northern Elegy, for the loss of the house is associated with amnesia:

Но кто его отодвинул,
В чужие унес города,
Или из памяти вынул
Навсегда дорогу туда...
          (*SP*, 118)

But who moved it aside,
Carried it away to alien cities,
Or removed from my memory
Forever the road leading to it . . .

Compare the elegy's "vidim, chto zabyli/My dazhe put' v tot dom uedinennyi"/"we see that we've forgotten/Even the path back to that isolated house."

The impossibility of returning to the former house becomes a recurrent theme in the later work. It is expressed epigrammatically in a lyric written in 1940:

Один идет прямым путем,
Другой идет по кругу
И ждет возврата в отчий дом,
Ждет прежнюю подругу.
А я иду—за мной беда,
Не прямо и не косо,
А в никуда и никогда,
Как поезда с откоса.
          (*SP*, 244)

One goes by a straight path,
Another goes in a circle

And awaits a return to his father's house,
Awaits his former sweetheart.
But I go—misfortune at my heels—
Not straight and not obliquely,
But into nowhere and into never,
Like trains derailed.

Akhmatova's point of departure here is the traditional metaphor of the road of life (*zhiznennyi put'*). The directionless, meaningless movement of the lyrical persona is contrasted with two other kinds of movement: rectilinear, implying motion toward some goal, and circular, promising a return to the original starting point—the *otchii dom* (father's house), a patent reference to the parable of the prodigal son, that archetypal story of return to the paternal home.

The octet incorporates two salient allusions to the poetry of Nikolai Gumilev. First, it refers to what Akhmatova considered his "first Acmeist piece," "Bludnyi syn" ("The Prodigal Son," 1914), which treats the parable's plot and is dominated by the image of the house.[49] The first line of Gumilev's poem expresses the persona's valuation of his father's house before his departure from it—"Net doma podobnogo etomu domu!"[50]/"There is no house like this house!"; when he returns home, an entire stanza is devoted to the house:

За садом возносятся гордые своды,
Вот дом—это дедов моих пепелище,
Он, кажется, вырос за долгие годы,
Пока я блуждал, то распутник, то нищий.[51]

Beyond the garden the proud vaults ascend,
That is the house—home of my forefathers,
It seems to have grown during the long years
That I roved, now a profligate, now a beggar.

The second allusion to Gumilev comes in the simile likening the persona's movement to that of derailed trains, recalling Gumilev's "Zabludivshiisia tramvai" ("The Streetcar Gone Astray," 1921). In that poem the streetcar carrying the persona jumps its tracks and rushes out of control through space and time, treating the persona to a grotesque—and in retrospect terribly prophetic—vision of his own beheading, followed by a return to the house of Mashen'ka, his "prezhniaia podruga"/"former sweetheart," who is absent and may well be dead.[52] Mashen'ka's house, evoked in the lines "A v pereulke zabor doshchatyi,/Dom v tri okna i seryi gazon . . ."[53]/ "And there is a fence of boards in the lane,/A house with three windows and a gray lawn . . . ," evokes the Tsarskoe Selo residence of the Gorenko family, where the young Anna Gorenko grew up and where she was courted by Gumilev.[54] When the Gorenko family left Tsarskoe Selo in 1905, the 100-year-old house was remodeled and its appearance altered; it was subsequently razed,[55] as witnessed in Akhmatova's 1940 fragment "Moi molodye ruki" ("My young hands"):

> От дома того—ни щепки,
> Та вырублена аллея,
> Давно опочили в музее
> Те шляпы и башмачки.[56]

Of that house not a splinter remains,
That alley of trees has been cut down,
Those hats and little shoes have long since
Passed to their rest in the museum.

The impossibility of returning to the cherished past home is a recurrent theme in her late autobiographical prose. Akhmatova writes, for example, "Liudiam moego pokoleniia ne grozit pechal'-noe vozvrashchenie: nam vozvrashchat'sia nekuda"[57]/"A sad return does not threaten the people of my generation: there is nowhere for us to return." In another autobiographical fragment, Akhmatova lists former dwellings of hers no longer standing: first, the Tsarskoe Selo house of the Gorenkos ("ego uzh davno net"[58]/ "it hasn't existed for a long time"); next, the Crimean dacha near Sevastopol where she spent every summer from the ages of seven to thirteen; and finally, Slepnevo, the estate of Gumilev's mother near Bezhetsk in the Tver' province, where Akhmatova lived intermittently from 1911 to 1917. Of the latter, the poet wrote in later years that there remains "only the word itself under my poems in

White Flock and in *Plantain*."[59] While recording the destruction of these houses, Akhmatova conjures them up in memory, especially the Tsarskoe Selo house, which is vividly evoked in a memoir entitled "Dom Shukhardinoi" ("Shukhardina's House," 1957).[60]

In the later poetry, the house of the present is invariably associated with emptiness and ruin, and the epithet most frequently ascribed to the house is *opustoshennyi* (devastated). The image of the devastated house first appears in a 1921 lyric in the line "Voina, miatezh, opustoshennyi dom"[61]/"War, revolt, the devastated house"; the context suggests that the devastation has been wrought by war and revolution. The image next occurs in the poem "Mnogim" ("To the Many," 1922), in the context of a reference to Gumilev's execution; the house is identified as the persona's own, and the devastation is absolute: "Moi navsegda opustoshennyi dom" (*SP*, 183)/"My forever devastated house."[62] Several decades later, the image of the devastated house became a leitmotif of *The Sweetbrier Blooms*.

Another epithet used to characterize the persona's house in the later lyrics is *opustelyi* (deserted), which is etymologically related to *opustoshennyi*. It figures in the end of "The Sentence," the seventh poem of *Requiem*: "Ia davno predchuvstvovala etot/Svetlyi den' i opustelyi dom" (*S*, 1: 366)/"I had a presentiment long ago of this/Bright day and deserted house." Ostensibly the house is "deserted" because the son has not returned home.[63] At the same time, the phrase "opustelyi dom"/"deserted house" refers to the description of Lensky's death in *Eugene Onegin* (chapter 6, stanza 32):[64]

> Тому назад одно мгновенье
> В сем сердце билось вдохновенье,
> Вражда, надежда и любовь,
> Играла жизнь, кипела кровь,—
> Теперь, как в доме опустелом,
> Все в нем и тихо и темно;
> Замолкло навсегда оно.
> Закрыты ставни, окны мелом
> Забелены. Хозяйки нет.
> А где, бог весть. Пропал и след.[65]

One moment earlier,
this heart had been filled with inspiration,
enmity, hope, and love,
life had sparkled, blood had boiled;
now, as in a deserted house,
all is both still and dark inside;
it has forever fallen silent.
The shutters are closed, the windows whitened
with chalk. The proprietress is gone.
Where to, God knows. The trail is dead.[66]

In "The Sentence" the image of the deserted house has a veiled metaphorical meaning because it carries with it the connotations of its use in *Eugene Onegin*. In Pushkin, the deserted house is a metaphor for the heart of the dead Lensky; in *Requiem*, the house is likewise a figure for a heart—the persona's heart—and the epithet *opustelyi* (deserted) implies that life has abandoned the heart. Compare the opening lines of "The Sentence," which refer to the heart metonymically: "I upalo kamennoe slovo/Na moiu eshche zhivuiu grud' " (*S*, 1: 366)/"And the stone word fell/Upon my still living breast." [67]

The devastated and deserted houses of Akhmatova's later poetry owe their power to the violence they do to the notion of the house as first cosmos, an idea explored by Gaston Bachelard in his *Poetics of Space*. Much of that book is devoted to the image of the house, especially to its role as a vehicle for memories in modern Western literature. The house, Bachelard writes, "is our first universe, a real cosmos in every sense of the word," [68] a protected, domesticated space secure from threatening external forces. A matrix for memories, the image of the house has, according to Bachelard, "become the topography of our intimate being." [69] One of the very few instances in the later lyrics in which a domestic interior is evoked with felicitous connotations is "Prehistory," in which it figures as a recollection of that first cosmos, the childhood home—a home irrevocably lost. The abandoned and plundered houses of Akhmatova's later lyrics no longer protect, and they are devoid of all comfort; in them all of the positive connotations of the house as first cosmos have been negated. These houses emblematize the devastation of "the topography of our intimate being," and nowhere more than in the metaphorical structure of "Memories have three epochs."

In the later lyrics, poetry itself figures as a refuge from suffering, as a protective haven. One of the most striking instances is in a lyric at the periphery of *Poem Without a Hero*, entitled "Eshche odno liricheskoe otstuplenie" ("Yet One More Lyrical Digression," 1943):

> До середины мне видна
> Моя поэма. В ней прохладно,
> Как в доме, где душистый мрак
> И окна заперты от зноя...
>
> $\qquad\qquad$ (*SP*, 220)

> To the middle my *poema*
> Is visible to me. It's cool inside it,
> As in a house, where there is fragrant darkness
> And the windows are locked to keep out the sultry heat . . .

Here the image of the house is endowed with all the connotations of felicity ascribed it by Bachelard. It is cool, giving protection from the sultry heat. It is full of darkness, recalling the shade enveloping the first epoch of memories. The darkness is pleasurable (the epithet "dushistyi"/"fragrant").[70] The poem was written when Akhmatova was living in Tashkent during the evacuation, when sultry heat was a fact of everyday life for her, as was exile. The Epilogue to *Poem Without a Hero* sums up the nature of life in the "homeless," as Alexander Blok called it, twentieth century:[71]

> А веселое слово—дома—
> Никому теперь не знакомо,
> Все в чужое глядят окно.
> Кто в Ташкенте, а кто в Нью-Йорке,
> И изгнания воздух горький—
> Как отравленное вино.
>
> $\qquad\qquad$ (*S*, 2: 131)

And the cheerful phrase *at home*
Is now familiar to no one,
Everyone gazes through someone else's window.
Some are in Tashkent, and others are in New York,
And the bitter air of exile
Is like poisoned wine.

For Akhmatova, displacement and homelessness are the universal conditions of life in the Real Twentieth Century. In this harsh age poetry represents the sole refuge, the only source of comfort. No wonder Akhmatova was so loath to part with, so reluctant to finish, her magnum opus. Its "svod blagoslovennyi"/"blessed vault" sheltered her from 1940 until her death.[72]

➤ Notes

Notes

For full forms of citations, see the Bibliography, pp. 247–63.

Chapter 1

1. Akhmatova, "*Kamennyi gost'* Pushkina," in O *Pushkine*, 89. The first draft of the essay was completed in 1947. The essay itself was eventually published in 1958 with some revisions. Akhmatova made notes for further changes in 1958–59; see O *Pushkine*, 161–71. All translations appearing in this book are mine, except where noted.

2. Ibid., 89–90.

3. Ibid., 90.

4. Ibid., 89.

5. Pushkin, *Eugene Onegin* (trans. Nabokov), 1: 301. Compare Charles Johnston's rhymed translation (Pushkin, *Eugene Onegin*, 225):

> almanacs, journals of reflection,
> where admonitions are pronounced,
> where nowadays I'm soundly trounced,
> but where such hymns in my direction
> were chanted, I remember when—
> *e sempre bene*, gentlemen.

6. Lotman, *Roman A. S. Pushkina "Evgenii Onegin,"* 365–66. See also Nabokov's informative commentary on these lines in his translation: *Eugene Onegin*, 3: 224–27.

7. The resolution said, "Akhmatova is a typical representative of that empty poetry lacking in ideals that is foreign to our people. Her poems are saturated with the spirit of pessimism and degeneration and express the tastes of the old salon poetry frozen in attitudes of bourgeois-aristocratic aestheticism and 'art for art's sake' decadence with no wish to move in step with the people. They will be harmful in the education of our young people and cannot be tolerated in Soviet literature" (quoted in Haight, *Anna Akhmatova*, 143–44). Nataliia Il'ina recently observed that the 1946 resolu-

tion is still being praised for its beneficial role in Soviet literary history in a series of editions of *Russkaia sovetskaia literatura* (last edition 1989), a textbook for secondary school students ("Plody prosveshcheniia, ili Vlast' t'my," p. 7).

8. See Pushkin, *Eugene Onegin* (trans. Nabokov), 3: 227.

9. Mikhail Kuzmin says as much in his introduction to *Evening*, reprinted in Akhmatova, *Sochineniia*, vol. 3, ed. G. P. Struve, N. A. Struve, and B. A. Filippov (Paris: YMCA-Press, 1983), 471–73. Henceforth, references to this edition, as well as to volumes 1 and 2, will appear in the text and in the notes as *S*. For full publication data, see the Bibliography.

10. On the reception of Akhmatova's poetry in the early 1920's, see Haight, *Anna Akhmatova*, 68–74.

11. Ibid., 80.

12. "In 1936 I begin writing again." Akhmatova, *Sochineniia v dvukh tomakh*, ed. V. A. Chernykh (Moscow, 1986), 2: 251. Henceforth this edition will be referred to as *Sochineniia* (Moscow).

What did Akhmatova write in 1936? First and foremost, poems about other poets, including "Poet" ("The Poet"), a tribute to Boris Pasternak; "Voronezh," a poem about Osip Mandelstam in exile; "Dante," which focuses on Dante's relations with Florence; and "Zaklinanie" ("Incantation"), dated April 15, 1936, commemorating the fiftieth anniversary of Nikolai Gumilev's birth. There are also two poems dedicated to Akhmatova's good friend the critic and poet Nikolai Nedobrovo, who died of tuberculosis in 1919; one of them ("Odni gliadiatsia v laskovye vzory" [*Sochineniia* (Moscow), 1: 177]/"Some see themselves reflected in their lover's tender gaze") in its thematization of the persona's guilt anticipates the main impulse behind *Poem Without a Hero*.

13. Quoted in Zhirmunskii, *Tvorchestvo Anny Akhmatovoi*, 25. A fuller version of the notebook entry is given in Akhmatova, *Sochineniia* (Moscow), 2: 251.

14. Tsvetaeva, "Poety s istoriei i poety bez istorii." On Akhmatova, see esp. 433–34.

15. Ibid., 427–39. In his essay "The Keening Muse," Joseph Brodsky echoes Tsvetaeva's idea: "Anna Akhmatova belongs to the category of poets who have neither genealogy nor discernible 'development.' She is the kind of poet that simply 'happens'; that arrives in the world with an already established diction and his/her own unique sensibility. She came fully equipped, and she never resembled anyone" (Brodsky, *Less Than One*, 35).

16. Akhmatova, *Sochineniia* (Moscow), 1: 256. *The Northern Elegies* remained an unfinished cycle at Akhmatova's death; of the seven elegies, only four—the first, fourth, fifth, and sixth—were published in the poet's lifetime. I cite this edition because it prints the elegies in the order envisioned by Akhmatova before her death. See Viktor Zhirmunskii's descrip-

tion of the cycle and its components in Akhmatova, *Stikhotvoreniia i poemy*, 506–8, and compare his ordering of the elegies (pp. 328–34). Henceforth this edition will be referred to as *SP* and references to it will appear in the text.

17. Zhirmunskii, *Tvorchestvo Anny Akhmatovoi*, 26.

18. It formed the very center of Mikhail Kuzmin's essay "O prekrasnoi iasnosti" ("On Beautiful Clarity"), published in *Apollon* in January 1910, just a few months before the first Acmeist manifestoes appeared. Criticizing the vagueness of the Symbolists, Kuzmin called upon writers to adopt a new attitude toward the word: "Love the word, like Flaubert, be economical in your means and spare in words, exact and genuine, and you will find the secret of a marvelous thing—beautiful clarity, which I would name 'Clarism'" (p. 6).

19. For an introduction to Akhmatova's metapoetic utterances, see Timenchik, "Avtometaopisanie."

20. According to Zhirmunskii, the idea for creating the cycle came to Akhmatova relatively late, in 1960 (*SP*, 481).

21. On the provenience and use of this term, see Erlich, *Russian Formalism*, 190, 192–93.

22. To give another example, in Part Two of *Poem Without a Hero*, Akhmatova characterizes her method in the *poema* as, first, writing in "simpaticheskie chernila"/"sympathetic ink," and second, "zerkal'noe pis'mo"/"mirror writing" (*S*, 1: 126).

23. "Bol'shaia ispoved'" was first published in *Den' poezii* (Moscow, 1979), 201–2, and in *Literaturnaia Gruziia*, no. 7 (1979): 91–93. A brief preface to the former by Mikhail Kralin describes the work as a "rough draft, unpolished, [as if] written down on paper for the first time" (p. 201). The text has been reprinted in *S*, 3: 503–6, as well as in *Sochineniia* (Moscow), 1: 377–80.

24. Vinogradov devotes an entire chapter to the subject. See "Nameki, nedomolvki, evfemizmy," *O poezii Anny Akhmatovoi* (*Stilisticheskie nabroski*), reprinted in Vinogradov, *Poetika russkoi literatury*, 444–50. In his 1914 review of Akhmatova's second book of poems, Nikolai Gumilev anticipated Vinogradov's efforts by calling attention to all that is left unsaid in Akhmatova's poems. The comparison he makes between Akhmatova and the Symbolists is of particular interest: "The poetess did not 'invent herself' [*ne 'vydumala sebia'*]; she does not, in order to unite her experiences, place in their center some external fact, she does not resort to something known or comprehensible to herself alone—and herein lies her difference from the Symbolists; but, on the other hand, her themes often are not exhausted within the bounds of a given poem, and much about them seems baseless, because it is not fully shown [*ne dopokazano*]." Gumilev, *Sobr. soch.*, 4: 336.

25. In an article on Akhmatova's poems to Boris Anrep ("Boris Anrep and the Poems of Anna Akhmatova"), Wendy Rosslyn clearly shows how Akhmatova disrupted the order in which the poems to Anrep were written when preparing them for publication in the early collections.

26. Chukovskaia, *Zapiski*, 2: 98. The entry is dated June 30, 1955.

27. Quoted in Toporov, *Akhmatova i Blok*, 96. The same propensity for mystification resounds in Akhmatova's remark to Nikita Struve about the dedication of the late, highly opaque lyric cycle *Polnochnye stikhi* (*Midnight Verses*): "Even such a remarkable connoisseur of poetry as Lidiia Ginzburg has no idea to whom they are dedicated" (Struve, "Vosem' chasov s Annoi Akhmatovoi," *S*, 2: 342).

28. See Gleb Struve's biographical sketch of Gumilev, "N. S. Gumilev. Zhizn' i lichnost'," in Gumilev, *Sobr. soch.*, 1: xxxix–xlii.

29. For the publication history of this text, see *S*, 1: 398. Compare *Sochineniia* (Moscow), 1: 412, which cites this poem's dating in one of the author's lists of her poems in her archives as August 16, 1921. Gumilev was arrested on August 4 and executed between August 23 and 27 (Gumilev, *Sobr. soch.*, 1: xxix, xl).

30. The epithet is Akhmatova's, from her memoir of Mandelstam (*S*, 2: 179).

31. "Prigovor" is published in *SP*, 192, with the correct date but without its title; the same is true of *Sochineniia* (Moscow), 1: 181.

32. The quotation is inexact; in the original, the line reads "I am fire, and air." The sentence, uttered by Cleopatra just before her suicide, continues, "my other elements I give to baser life" (5.2.288).

33. Note also the parallelism between "O, kak malo ostalos'/Ei dela na svete"/"O, how little is left/For her to do on earth" from "Cleopatra" and "U menia segodnia mnogo del"/"Today I have a lot of things to do" from *Requiem*'s "The Sentence."

34. On this aspect of Akhmatova's poetry, see the superb study by Tsiv'ian, "Antichnye geroini—zerkala Akhmatovoi."

35. Tynianov, *Poetika*, 175.

36. Pushkin, *Sobr. soch.*, 1: 10.

37. Akhmatova's use of the word *podtekst* is not to be confused with the specialized meaning attributed to the word—and its English calque, *subtext*—by Kiril Taranovsky and Omry Ronen, who define it as the textual source of a literary citation or allusion. In this book I will use the word *subtext* precisely in the sense of the source text. A theoretical treatment of the problem of the subtext in Mandelstam's work can be found in Omry Ronen, "Leksicheskii povtor, podtekst i smysl v poetike Osipa Mandel'shtama." Also see Taranovsky, *Essays on Mandel'štam*, 1–20, and the preface to Ronen, *An Approach to Mandel'štam*, vii–xx.

38. Osip Mandel'shtam, *Sobr. soch.*, 2: 230–31.

39. Ibid., 368.

40. Timenchik, "Avtometaopisanie," 219–20.

41. See Childers and Crone, "The Mandel'štam Presence."

42. Levin et al., "Russkaia semanticheskaia poetika kak potentsial'naia kul'turnaia paradigma."

43. I am very much indebted to the work of Kiril Taranovsky and Omry Ronen on the role of literary reminiscences in the poetry of Mandelstam in particular, but also in Akhmatova's poetry. Of especial importance are Taranovsky's *Essays on Mandel'štam*, particularly 1–20; Ronen's "Leksicheskii povtor, podtekst i smysl v poetike Osipa Mandel'štama"; "A Beam upon the Axe"; "The Dry River and the Black Ice"; "K istorii akmeisticheskikh tekstov"; and *An Approach to Mandel'štam*.

44. Tat'iana Tsiv'ian singles out *otkrytost'* (open-endedness) as one of the distinctive traits of *Poem Without a Hero* in her "Zametki k deshifrovke 'Poemy bez geroia,'" 257–58.

45. Jerzy Faryno, in "Kod Akhmatovoi," translates this idea into semiotic terms by speaking of Akhmatova's lexicon as a code that can be deciphered only by considering previous usages of its elements.

46. From the poem "Poet i grazhdanin" ("The Poet and the Citizen") in Nekrasov, *Sobr. stikhotvorenii*, 1: 136.

47. For a typology of the kinds of silence in Akhmatova, see Tsiv'ian, "Akhmatova i muzyka," 177–79.

48. See, for instance, Verheul, "Public Themes," 89–90, and Efim Etkind, "Die Unsterblichkeit des Gedächtnisses," 366–67.

49. Pushkin, *Sobr. soch.*, 3: 131.

50. In his typology of quotations in Akhmatova's poetry, Timenchik mentions this kind of allusion that metonymically refers to another segment of the same text. See his "Printsipy tsitirovaniia u Akhmatovoi v sopostavlenii s Blokom," 125.

51. Pushkin, *Sobr. soch.*, 3: 131.

52. This is almost a word-for-word translation from the postscript to "Instead of a Foreword": "I kto-to dazhe sovetuet sdelat' mne poemu bolee poniatnoi" (*S*, 2: 100)/"And someone even advises me to make the poem more comprehensible."

53. Jeanne van der Eng-Liedmeier has written extensively on the theme of reception in Akhmatova's poetry. See her "Reception as a Theme in Akhmatova's Early Poetry" and "Reception as a Theme in Akhmatova's Later Poetry."

54. The most thorough analysis and interpretation of this text to date is by Jerzy Faryno, "'Tainy remesla' Akhmatovoi," 65–70. See also Eng-Liedmeier, "Reception as a Theme in Akhmatova's Later Poetry," 125–27.

55. This literary allusion was first noted by Superfin and Timenchik, "Pis'ma Anny Akhmatovoi k V. Ia. Briusovu," 273.

56. Briusov, *Izbrannye soch.*, 219. Note the parallel between Briusov's "podzemnoe plamia"/"subterranean flame" and Akhmatova's "kholod-noe plamia"/"cold flame."

57. Ibid.

58. Eng-Liedmeier senses in Akhmatova's first stanza "an intimation of a self-portrait in negative form; characteristics such as 'tragic' and 'mysterious' are especially typical of the image that she creates of herself in these years" (Eng-Liedmeier, "Reception as a Theme in Akhmatova's Later Poetry," 126). The reference is to the *tenevoi portret* (shadow portrait), a device Akhmatova borrowed from Pushkin, whereby someone is described by telling what traits someone else does not have so that "in the shadow of one portrait there arises another, unnamed portrait" (Saulenko, "Push-kinskaia traditsiia v 'Poeme bez geroia' Anny Akhmatovoi," 45). For Akhmatova's own use of this term in her Pushkin essays, see Akhmatova, *O Pushkine*, 216.

59. "Remember that you are an actor in a play, the character of which is determined by the Playwright: if He wishes the play to be short, it is short; if long, it is long; if He wishes you to play the part of a beggar, remember to act even this role adroitly. . . . For this is your business, to play admirably the role assigned you; but the selection of that role is Another's" (Epictetus, *Discourses*, 2: 497).

60. The first complete Soviet publication of the final redaction of the poem appeared with an introduction by Andrei Voznesensky in *Den' poezii* (Moscow, 1980), 181.

61. Faryno, "'Tainy remesla' Akhmatovoi," 66. Faryno mentions in passing the parallel with Pasternak's "Hamlet" but does not discuss it (p. 80, n. 42).

62. Mandel'shtam, *Sobr. soch.*, 2: 234.

63. Ibid., 239.   64. Ibid., 240, 237.

65. Ibid., 235, 236.   66. Ibid., 240.

67. Ibid., 239.   68. Ibid., 239.

69. Compare Pasternak's "Hamlet," where the poet is alone, as emblematized in the phrase "Ia odin"/"I am alone," in contrast to the thousand spectators staring at him.

70. Compare the antithetical image from "Voronezh," Akhmatova's 1936 poem about Mandelstam in exile: "A noch' idet/Kotoraia ne vedaet rassveta" (*SP*, 190)/"And the night goes on/That knows no dawn."

71. Mandel'shtam, *Sobr. soch.*, 2: 253.

72. Eng-Liedmeier, "Reception as a Theme in Akhmatova's Later Poetry," 127.

Chapter 2

1. Sam Driver describes *Requiem* as "an amazingly powerful statement which requires no elaboration or 'explanation'" (*Anna Akhmatova*, 125). Unlike *Poem Without a Hero*, *Requiem* has received relatively little critical attention. The most comprehensive study of it to date is Efim Etkind's "Die Unsterblichkeit des Gedächtnisses." Kees Verheul discusses *Requiem* in his "Public Themes," 79–82, 89–90, 93, 98–100, and 105–12. Among others who have written on it are Sam Driver, *Anna Akhmatova*, 125–32; Sharon Leiter, *Akhmatova's Petersburg*, 90–97; and Amanda Haight, *Anna Akhmatova*, 99–108. Two specialized studies of *Requiem* also deserve mention: Milivoe Jovanovich treats the problem of intertextual references in his valuable "K razboru 'chuzhikh golosov'; and an extensive syntactico-metrical analysis is given in Voogd-Stojanova, "Tsezura i slovorazdely." For decades unpublished in the Soviet Union, *Requiem* was long off limits to specialists living within the bounds of the USSR and could be referred to only in passing or obliquely. It is to be hoped that *Requiem*'s recent publication in *Oktiabr'*, no. 3 (1987), and *Neva*, no. 6 (1987), will pave the way for the appearance of serious critical studies of it in the Soviet Union.

2. Jovanovich dates the beginning of Akhmatova's later period "precisely with *Requiem*" ("K razboru 'chuzhikh golosov'," 171). Verheul, by contrast, sees *Requiem* as transitional between Akhmatova's early and later styles ("Public Themes," 112). Although the ten numbered texts of the *poema* do manifest certain features of the early style, as Verheul notes, together they trace a distinct narrative progression from arrest to execution, and this sharply distinguishes them from the early work.

3. Jovanovich's "K razboru 'chuzhikh golosov'" is the only study devoted exclusively to intertextuality in *Requiem*. Particularly useful are his comments on Akhmatova's incorporation of reminiscences—mainly for parodic ends—from Nekrasov's "Russkie zhenshchiny" ("Russian Women"), Lermontov's "Kazach'ia kolybel'naia pesnia" ("Cossack's Lullaby"), and Blok's cycle *Na pole Kulikovom* (*On the Field at Kulikovo*) (pp. 170–71). Verheul discusses in passing some of *Requiem*'s biblical and liturgical subtexts ("Public Themes," 111–12), and Leiter explores the role of some self-reminiscences, Akhmatova's allusions to her own poetry, in the text (*Akhmatova's Petersburg*, 90–97).

4. Akhmatova herself classified *Requiem* as a *poema* (narrative poem). The list of titles she intended to publish in the collection *The Flight of Time* ends with a section called *Poemy*, which was to consist of *The Way of All the Earth*, *Requiem*, and *Poem Without a Hero* (*Pamiati Anny Akhmatovoi*, 29–30). On *Requiem*'s status as a *poema*, see Etkind, "Die Unsterb-

lichkeit des Gedächtnisses," 362–65. Compare Verheul's remarks on the same subject in "Public Themes," 107–8.

5. "Instead of a Foreword" has been widely quoted but has received virtually no commentary. Neither Verheul nor Etkind mentions it in the articles cited above. Among those who quote it without commentary are Leiter (*Akhmatova's Petersburg*, 91–92) and Haight (*Anna Akhmatova*, 99). Driver quotes it and does comment on it, but only by describing the historical context (*Anna Akhmatova*, 125–27). The most detailed comments on the "Dedication" are Etkind's, "Die Unsterblichkeit des Gedächtnisses," 387–88. Compare Verheul, "Public Themes," 80–81.

6. The epithet *strashnye* (terrible), the sole affective epithet in the text, does not belie the narrative's prosaic tone because the phrase "strashnye gody Ezhovshchiny"/"terrible years of the Ezhov terror" is, generally speaking, a fixed expression.

7. Chukovskaia asserts that the image of the "woman with blue lips" originated in her novel *Sof'ia Petrovna*, which she read to Akhmatova in February 1940. See Chukovskaia, *Zapiski*, 2: 305. Jovanovich's recent article on *Requiem* unwittingly proves the strength of the customary formula "s golubymi glazami"/"with blue eyes" by twice erroneously replacing *gubami* (lips) with the word *glazami* (eyes); see "K razboru 'chuzhikh golosov'," 177, n. 7.

8. According to Boris Eikhenbaum, "emotion is conveyed by the description of a gesture or a movement, i.e., precisely as is done in novellas and novels" (*Anna Akhmatova*, 127). Eikhenbaum is pointing to what Osip Mandelstam had described in his 1922 "Pis'mo o russkoi poezii" ("Letter on Russian Poetry") as Akhmatova's indebtedness to the nineteenth-century Russian psychological novel. Compare Mandel'shtam, *Sobr. soch.*, 3: 34.

9. Eikhenbaum writes: "Akhmatova's poetic discourse is as if concentrated on the front plane of articulation and ornamented with a mimicking movement of the lips ('molitvy gub moikh nadmennykh'/'prayers of my haughty lips,' 'dvizhenie chut' vidnoe gub'/'a barely visible movement of the lips'" (*Anna Akhmatova*, 87).

10. The persona describes the name given her at baptism, Anna, as "Sladchaishee dlia gub liudskikh"/"Most sweet for human lips," and remarks on the strangeness of the lips of the *inostranka* (foreigner), a muse figure visiting her (*S*, 1: 191).

11. The first volume of Lidiia Chukovskaia's memoirs of Akhmatova devotes several passages to the faces of the women standing in line. In the entry dated February 22, 1939, Akhmatova is quoted as saying, "I cannot stand to see those eyes. Have you noticed? It is as if they exist separately, separately from the faces" (Chukovskaia, *Zapiski*, 1: 18).

12. "The face of a human being represents the highest spiritual gifts: the forehead represents heavenly love; the eyes—understanding, intelligent contemplation; the ears—understanding and obedience; the nose—the grasping of the good; the cheeks—the grasping of spiritual truths; the mouth—thought and teaching; the lips—spiritual praise" (Dal', *Tolkovyi slovar' zhivago velikorusskago iazyka*, 2: 258).

13. This imagery resurfaces in the collective portrait of the faces of the women who stood in the prison lines given in the first part of the "Epilogue," which commences "Uznala ia, kak opadaiut litsa" (*S*, 1: 368)/"I found out how faces sink in."

14. Akhmatova's early lyrics abound in reported speech, another mark of their indebtedness to the novelistic tradition. Vinogradov devotes a chapter of his study of the early Akhmatova to this feature of her work (*Poetika russkoi literatury*, 451–59). The same volume features a commentary on Vinogradov's study of Akhmatova by R. D. Timenchik and A. P. Chudakov, including these Bakhtin-inspired remarks on the chapter in question that are particularly relevant to *Requiem*: "The 'addressees' and 'dramatis personae' of her poetry bring along into the text fragments and examples of various stylistic systems, 'mixed quotations' from literary and everyday 'styles of speech.' This introduction of various kinds of *chuzhoe slovo* (someone else's word) serves as the chief means of the 'polyphonization' of her lyrics, lending them on the whole a dialogical character" (p. 506). "Instead of a Foreword" and the "Dedication" employ two different types of direct quotations—discourse from everyday life and literary discourse.

15. As Iurii Lotman has written, one may explain a phenomenon by indicating its origins. See his *Struktura khudozhestvennogo teksta*, 260.

16. In her entry for November 10, 1938, Chukovskaia records Akhmatova's account of an episode antithetical to this one: "'A woman standing behind me in line started crying when she heard my last name'" (*Zapiski*, 1: 16). In "Instead of a Foreword," Akhmatova chooses to portray as typical of the 1930's the nonrecognition of her name.

17. Jovanovich, "K razboru 'chuzhikh golosov'," 176–77, n. 6. Jovanovich does not discuss the role of references to the *Inferno* in *Requiem*. Although "The Muse" bears the date 1924, it was in the late 1930's that Dantesque themes and motifs became prominent in Akhmatova's work; compare the obviously related line—"I prosto prodiktovannye strochki" (*S*, 1: 251)/"And the simply dictated lines"—from the 1936 poem "Tvorchestvo" ("Creative Work"); her "Dante" ("On i posle smerti ne vernulsia" [*S*, 1: 236]/"Even after death he did not return") was written in the same year. For an introduction to the role of Dante in Akhmatova's life and works, see Meilakh and Toporov, "Akhmatova i Dante." The article does not comment directly on *Requiem*.

18. Dante, *Divine Comedy*, trans. Singleton, *Inferno*, 1: 310–11, lines 103–5.

19. In Singleton's translation, "as in a callus, all feeling, because of the cold, had departed from my face" (ibid., 354–55, lines 100–102).

20. In Singleton's translation, "I did not die and I did not remain alive: now think for yourself, if you have any wit, what I became, deprived alike of death and life!" (ibid., 362–63, lines 25–27).

21. According to the beginning of *Requiem*'s "Vstuplenie" ("Introduction"), true death brings peace: "Eto bylo, kogda ulybalsia/Tol'ko mertvyi, spokoistviiu rad" (*S*, 1: 363)./"This was when only the dead smiled,/ Glad for the tranquillity." Compare the suppressed tenth and eleventh stanzas of the "Reshka" ("Tails") segment of *Poem Without a Hero*; in the eleventh stanza, the poet and her female contemporaries define their condition through a pun on the notion of the "potustoronnii mir"/"other world": " 'Po tu storonu ada—my!' " (*S*, 3: 116)/" 'Beyond hell are we!' "

22. The first line's brilliant sound orchestration has been well described by Sam Driver: "The close juxtaposition of gutturals suggests a throat constricted by grief. . . . The vowel sounds are carefully ordered in a progression from front to back. The line descends in intonation as in physical articulation" (*Anna Akhmatova*, 155–56, n. 18).

23. Tsvetaeva exploits almost the same resemblance in her *Poema gory* (*Poem of the Mountain*) (*góre/gorá*); cf. the collocation in English poetry "mountains mourn." The phrase "gnutsia gory"/"mountains bend down" appears to realize the apocalyptic prediction of the "glas vopiiushchego v pustyne"/"the voice of one crying in the wilderness" in Isaiah 40: 3–4 that "vsiakaia gora i kholm da poniziatsia"/"every mountain and hill shall be made low."

24. Pushkin, *Sobr. soch.*, 2: 97.

25. Jovanovich notes a somewhat similar line uttered by Clytemnestra in a Russian translation of Euripides' *Iphigenia in Aulis*: "O, tam zapory krepki" ("K razboru 'chuzhikh golosov'," 173). The apparent lack of a series of textual correspondences between the "Dedication" and the translated version of Euripides' tragedy suggests that the parallel is coincidental.

26. The motif of hope is not entirely absent from the "Dedication"; line 15 locates it not within the prison, as in Pushkin's text, but in the distance: "A nadezhda vse poet vdali"/"But hope still sings in the distance." What is portrayed in the fourth stanza of the text dashes even this distant hope. One of Akhmatova's remarks to Chukovskaia recorded in the entry of May 18, 1939, bears on the treatment of the theme of hope in *Requiem*: "Do you know what torture by hope is? After despair, peace sets in, but from hope people go mad" (*Zapiski*, 1: 24). Compare the deployment of imagery relating to madness throughout *Requiem*.

27. In her metrical analysis of the "Dedication," Voogd-Stojanova notes

this violation and comments only that the line is perceived as "contrastive in form" in relation to the rest ("Tsezura i slovorazdely," 318).

28. Pushkin, *Sobr. soch.*, 2: 92.

29. Voogd-Stojanova suggests that the "Dedication" represents a variation on what Kiril Taranovsky has identified as the trochaic pentameter theme initiated in Lermontov's "Vykhozhu odin ia na dorogu"/"I walk out alone onto the road," where "the dynamic motif of the road is juxtaposed to the static motif of life, solitude, and meditations on life and death" ("Tsezura i slovorazdely," 319). In Akhmatova's transformation of this theme, the road leads only to imprisonment and death.

30. Leiter, *Akhmatova's Petersburg*, 92–93, 73–74. See also 61–64 for a discussion of the first occurrence of this imagery in a poem about the beginning of World War I, "Tot avgust, kak zheltoe plamia" (1915; *S*, 1: 194–95)/"That August, like a yellow flame." "To My Fellow Citizens" appears under the title "Petrograd, 1919" with substantial changes in *SP*, 149. See *SP*, 471, and *S*, 1: 398–99, for its publication history.

31. Compare Akhmatova's description of the city to Lidiia Chukovskaia in 1939; confessing that she is fed up with the city, she explains: "Dal', doma—obrazy zastyvshego stradaniia"/"The distance, the houses—images of frozen suffering" (Chukovskaia, *Zapiski*, 1: 21). The final phrase recalls the motif of *otsepenenie* (torpor) from "Instead of a Foreword," as well as the related motif of "okameneloe stradanie"/"petrified suffering" in the central sequence of poems and the "Epilogue."

32. The theme of the suppression of the poet's voice, introduced obliquely into the "Dedication" through the allusions to Pushkin's "In the depths," looms large in *Requiem*, emerging explicitly in the second part of the "Epilogue": "I esli zazhmut moi izmuchennyi rot" (*S*, 1: 369)/"And if they shut my tortured mouth."

33. Compare with line 6 the young Akhmatova's "Zharko veet veter dushnyi" (1910; *S*, 1: 58)/"Hot blows the sultry wind."

34. This conflict is vividly embodied in the sound orchestration of the text: first, the mellifluous paronomasia of line 6—"*veet veter svezhii*"—contrasts with the first line's abrasive "*gorem gnutsia gory*"; similarly, the pleasing near rhyme "svezhii"/"nezhitsia" ("fresh"/"luxuriates") in lines 6–7 finds a jarring third in line 9's "skrezhet"/"gnashing," which recalls the apocalyptic phrase "tam budet plach i skrezhet zubov" (Matt. 8: 12)/ "there shall be weeping and gnashing of teeth," envisaging the suffering of those in hell.

35. My thanks go to Alexander Lehrman for calling my attention to this subtext in the fall of 1986. See Lebedev-Kumach, "Pesnia o rodine," in *Kniga pesen*, 9–10. The lines occur in the third verse, which has since Stalin's death been regularly excised from printings of the song for praising the "Vsenarodnyi Stalinskii Zakon" ("All Peoples' Stalinist Law"). Com-

pare, for instance, Lebedev-Kumach, *Pesni i stikhotvoreniia*, 27–29. Akhmatova's use of Lebedev-Kumach's hacksong as a subtext in the "Dedication" forces one to recall the lines from her 1940 poem "Mne ni k chemu odicheskie rati" ("Odic hosts are of no use to me"): "Kogda b vy znali, iz kakogo sora/Rastut stikhi, ne vedaia styda" (*S*, 1: 251)/"If only you knew from what trash/Poems grow, not knowing any shame."

36. So writes Gleb Struve in his *Russian Literature Under Lenin and Stalin*, 312. Featured in the popular film *Circus* (*Tsirk*), the song was played repeatedly on the radio, and it was "printed in *Pravda, Izvestiia, Komsomol'skaia pravda*, and in a number of newspapers, journals, and collections" (Lebedev-Kumach, *Kniga pesen*, 193).

37. In the rest of *Requiem*, the first-person plural occurs only once, in passing, making its role in the "Dedication" highly marked. It comes toward the end of the "Introduction" in the line "Zvezdy smerti stoiali nad nami" (*S*, 1: 363)/"The stars of death stood above us." "Eto bylo, kogda ulybalsia"/"This was when there smiled" became the "Introduction" of *Requiem* only in 1962, when the first typewritten copy of the *poema* was prepared. See Chukovskaia, *Zapiski*, 2: 473–74. That Akhmatova intended *Requiem* to be at least in part a recasting of the mass song is confirmed in the second part of the "Epilogue," when the theme of the mass song resurfaces. This subject will be discussed in the final section of this chapter.

38. Lebedev-Kumach, *Kniga pesen*, 9–10.

39. Ibid., 9.

40. Ibid., 10. These are the concluding lines of the final stanza.

41. Lebedev-Kumach's "Song of the Motherland" is echoed in other parts of *Requiem* as well. To give but one example, the first stanza's "Starikam—vezde u nas pochet"/"The elderly are esteemed everywhere in our land" is contradicted in the second part of the "Epilogue": "I vyla starukha, kak ranenyi zver'" (*S*, 1: 370) / And an old woman howled like a wounded beast."

42. Compare the fourth numbered text of *Requiem*, where the persona terms herself the "trekhsotaia, s peredacheiu" (*S*, 1: 364)/"three-hundredth [in line] with a parcel."

43. This is yet another instance of the outside world mirroring life within the prison.

44. This design vividly illustrates Akhmatova's fusion in the "Dedication" of lyric and epic elements, of the personal and the national. That the two are conjoined in *Requiem* is a commonplace in the critical literature, although the actual workings of this conjunction have received little attention. Verheul has written that in *Requiem* the "lyrical-autobiographical and the national . . . coincide" ("Public Themes," 108). According to Etkind, "'Requiem' ist ein *episches* Poem, das aus einzelnen *lyrischen* Gedi-

chten aufgebaut ist. Jedes dieser Gedichte ist dem Aufbau nach lyrisch, hat aber eine Tendenz zur Epik" ("Die Unsterblichkeit des Gedächtnisses," 392). See also Chukovskaia's discussion of the tension in *Requiem* between the personal and the national (*Zapiski*, 2: 473–74), and Brodsky's comments on the same subject in Akhmatova's poetry as a whole in "The Keening Muse," *Less Than One*, 34–52, esp. 42–44.

45. The fourth stanza relates an event that occurred regularly in the prison lines, but the terms of its narration—the use of the present tense, the specificity of the details given—lend the event an undeniable singularity. This tension between the iterative and the singular points to the fourth stanza's role as a bridge between the "Dedication" and the central sequence of poems. The first word of the stanza recurs as the title of the seventh poem, "Prigovor" ("The Sentence"), which treats the same event from the perspective of the woman herself. The fourth stanza's last word, "Odna"/"Alone," likewise links the "Dedication" with the central sequence; it recurs in the second numbered poem, "Tikho l'etsia tikhii Don" ("Quiet flows the quiet Don"): "Eta zhenshchina odna" (*S*, 1: 363)/"This woman is alone." The woman is spoken of here in the third person, as in the "Dedication," but the actual point of view is first-person, as revealed in the final couplet: "Muzh v mogile, syn v tiur'me,/Pomolites' obo mne." (*S*, 1: 363)/"Husband's in the grave, son's in prison,/Pray for me."

46. Pushkin, *Sobr. soch.*, 2: 85. In the first volume of her memoirs of Akhmatova, Chukovskaia seems to hint at the importance of allusions to Pushkin in *Requiem* by enciphering references to it as "Pushkin's *Requiem*." For instance, she encodes a reference to the "Dedication" as follows: "Then she read me the newly discovered lines of Pushkin—from his *Requiem*. 'Lunnyi krug'/'The lunar circle.'" See the entry for March 3, 1940, *Zapiski*, 1: 76. There is indeed a *Requiem* in Pushkin: it is Mozart's, and it sounds in the "little tragedy" *Mozart and Salieri*.

47. Pushkin, *Sobr. soch.*, 9: 120. These remarks are contained in a letter to D. M. Shvarts dated December 9, 1824. In his commentary to *Eugene Onegin*, Nabokov argues that Pushkin intentionally encouraged the confusion of Arina Rodionovna "with the generalized nurse [he] gives the Larin girls" and claims that generally Pushkin "romanticized her in his verse." See *Eugene Onegin* (trans. Nabokov), 2: 452. V. F. Khodasevich adduces some concrete textual evidence linking Tat'iana's nanny to Arina Rodionovna in his essay "Iavleniia muzy." He traces the connection between Arina Rodionovna and the poet's many-faced muse, asserting that one of the guises of Pushkin's muse was that of Arina Rodionovna. The essay appears in Khodasevich's *O Pushkine*, 8–38; see esp. 37–38 and 14–20.

48. Lev Gumilev was arrested on March 10, 1937, and was imprisoned in Leningrad until August 17 or 18, 1939. See Haight, *Anna Akhmatova*,

97. Compare Chukovskaia's description of Akhmatova's visit to the prison to see her son on the eve of his transfer to a prison camp in the north; see the entry for August 28, 1939, *Zapiski*, 1: 38–40.

49. Friendship was for Akhmatova an expression of spiritual freedom; she defines it as such in "Nadpis' na knige" ("Inscription on a Book"), dedicated to her old friend Mikhail Lozinskii and written in May 1940, just two months after the "Dedication": "Dushi vysokaia svoboda,/Chto druzhboiu narechena" (*S*, 1: 229)/"The lofty freedom of the soul/That is called friendship."

50. The same notion is conveyed in the second part of the "Epilogue," when the speaker recollects one woman "chto rodimoi ne topchet zemli" (*S*, 1: 369)/"who does not tread on native soil." The question posed in line 23 calls to mind yet another text from the period of Pushkin's exile in which the poet's nanny figures: "Zimnii vecher" (1825) ("Winter Evening") conjures up a snowstorm weathered by the persona and his "dobraia podruzhka"/"kindly dear friend" at Mikhailovskoe.

51. I am indebted here to Stephanie Sandler's discussion of literary dedications in her *Distant Pleasures*, 155–61. To dedicate a work to someone, Sandler writes, is "to say that he or she has in some way made it possible for the lines to be written in the first place" (p. 160).

52. So does the following couplet from the second part of the "Epilogue": "Dlia nikh sotkala ia shirokii pokrov/Iz bednykh, u nikh zhe podslushannykh slov" (*S*, 1: 369)/"For them I have woven a broad shroud/Of poor words overheard from them." Not only did the poet's addressees provide the impulse for the writing of *Requiem*, they unwittingly contributed to the material from which it was woven.

53. I thank Catherine Ciepiela for calling to my attention this parallel between the two texts.

54. Her prayers answer the plea in which the second poem of the central sequence culminates: "Pomolites' obo mne" (*S*, 1: 363)/"Pray for me."

55. The latter text portrays amnesia as a complete obliteration of the individual, a notion demonstrated in the abrupt cessation of first-person discourse with its end and the abrupt shift in the next poem, "Raspiatie" ("The Crucifixion"), to third-person narrative. The ninth poem is constructed as a complex response to a poem by Innokentii Annenskii, "Eshche lilii" ("More Lilies"), which begins: "Kogda pod chernymi krylami"/"When under the black wings" (*Stikhotvoreniia i tragedii*, 183).

56. The nearly identical expression "opadaiut list'ia"/"leaves fall" echoes in the first line's "opadaiut litsa," grotesquely suggesting the image of faces falling like leaves.

57. Cf. the collocation "strashnye gody Ezhovshchiny"/"terrible years of the Ezhovshchina" from "Instead of a Foreword."

58. *Entsiklopediia Brokgauz-Efron*, 62: 201.

59. Lebedev-Kumach, *Kniga pesen*, 10.

60. Brown, *Mayakovsky*, 204.

61. Maiakovskii, *Sobr. soch.*, 1: 317.

62. Ibid.

63. This allusion to Mayakovsky recalls Kornei Chukovskii's 1921 comparison of the two writers ("Akhmatova and Mayakovsky," trans. Pearson, in *Major Soviet Writers*, ed. Brown). Mayakovsky figures as "the poet of the colossal" for whom "words like 'thousand,' 'million,' and 'billion' are commonplace" (p. 44), which, in Chukovskii's view, reflects the cataclysmic times (p. 45). Akhmatova, on the contrary, is the poet of "the microscopic detail" (p. 40), in whose verse "not a single 'million' is to be found" (p. 46). The appearance of the epithet *stomil'onnyi* (one hundred million) in Akhmatova's poetry in 1940 is unprecedented, but not the theme to which it is attached—the fate of the Russian nation. As Chukovskii wrote in 1921, "When the war broke out Akhmatova ... saw only Russia" (p. 46); the same could be said of her response to the revolution. By contrast, Chukovskii calls Mayakovsky an internationalist ("Work is our homeland!") with "no feeling" "for the motherland" (p. 47).

64. Maiakovskii, *Sobr. soch.*, 1: 318.

65. Ibid.	66. Ibid., 361.
67. Ibid.	68. Ibid., 363.
69. Ibid., 362.	70. Ibid., 363.
71. Ibid.	72. Ibid., 362–63.

Chapter 3

1. *Vecher* (*Evening*), of course, was the title of Akhmatova's first book of poems (1912).

2. "Nad mertvoi meduzoi/Smushchenno stoiu" (*SP*, 348)/"Over a dead medusa/I stand confused." The discordant and at first glance baffling image of the "dead medusa" harks back to the portrayal of nature in "At that time," as well as to the following lines from *Right by the Sea*:

И заплывали в бухту медузы—
Словно звезды, упавшие за ночь,
Глубоко под водой голубели.

(*SP*, 324)

And medusas floated into the bay—
Like stars which had fallen overnight,
They showed light blue deep under the water.

The medusas presage the appearance of the poet's muse—"a girl ... with a white pipe." "At that time" confirms the connection between the medusa and the muse when it describes the words of the muse: "a slova—/Kak zvezdy padali sentiabr'skoi noch'iu"/"while her words/Fell like stars in the September night."

3. Vernant, "Aspects mythiques de la mémoire en Grèce"; translation quoted from Eliade, "Mythologies of Memory and Forgetting," 333.

4. Compare Lotman, *Struktura khudozhestvennogo teksta*, 260.

5. Verheul was the first to point out the "central significance . . . of the recurrent motif of literature and literary creation" (*Theme of Time*, 174). His discussion of "Prehistory" (171–76) is the most extensive to date. See also Leiter's treatment of "Prehistory" in her *Akhmatova's Petersburg*, 118–24.

6. Verheul, *Theme of Time*, 174. Although Verheul notes the parallel in a footnote, he does not address its significance.

7. Akhmatova achieves here a synthesis of the Old and New Testament accounts of beginnings, merging the Genesis version with that offered in the Gospel of John: "In the beginning was the Word."

8. Eliade, *Eternal Return*, 57, 59.

9. Compare ibid., 57: "The first act of the ceremony . . . marks a regression into the mythical period before the Creation; all forms are supposed to be confounded in the marine abyss of the beginning."

10. Ibid., 57, 62.

11. Ibid., 69.

12. According to Eliade, "The victory over the waters can only signify the establishment of 'stable forms,' i.e., the Creation" (ibid., 60). For a concise discussion of this aspect of the Genesis account, see Cassuto, *Commentary on the Book of Genesis*, 24–25.

13. These are Pasternak's descriptions of *Nineteen Hundred Five* (*Stikhotvoreniia*, 655–56).

14. Ibid., 247.

15. Akhmatova's high estimation of "Fathers" is evidenced in a poem she dedicated to Pasternak in 1936; entitled "Poet" ("The Poet"), it praises Pasternak's genius by incorporating two striking images from "Fathers" ("Za to, chto dym sravnil s Laokoonom,/Kladbishchenskii vospel chertopolokh" [*SP*, 188]/"Because he compared smoke to Laocoön,/Celebrated the cemetery thistle"; compare Pasternak, *Stikhotvoreniia*, 248–49). Lidiia Chukovskaia's memoirs of Akhmatova attest to Akhmatova's awareness of the affinity of "Prehistory" with "Fathers." In the entry of November 13, 1940, the poet admits to rereading Pasternak of late and subsequently expresses her fondness for "Fathers" (*Zapiski*, 1: 196, 198). Later in the same conversation, to refute someone's claim that she was not a Petersburg poet but a Tsarskoe Selo poet, Akhmatova reads Chukovskaia the first draft of what was to become "Prehistory." Then Akhmatova asks:

"Tell me, isn't it similar to 'Fathers'?"

"No. It has a completely different sound," [Chukovskaia] answered.

"That's what's most important, for there to be a different sound," Anna Andreevna said.

(ibid., 199–200).

Akhmatova's words bespeak a considerable anxiety of influence and reveal the importance of Pasternak's "Fathers" as a stimulus for the writing of "Prehistory."

16. Pasternak, *Stikhotvoreniia*, 248.

17. Ibid., 247–48.

18. Both "Fathers" and "Prehistory" look back to the first chapter of Aleksandr Blok's *Vozmezdie* (*Retribution*, begun in 1910 and unfinished at Blok's death in 1921) and its depiction of the 1870's. Blok portrays Dostoevsky as a habitué not of the underground but of an exclusive Petersburg salon, yet nevertheless the novelist is merely a part of the social canvas of the 1870's. See chapter 1, lines 616–22 and 675–78, in Blok, *Sobr. soch.*, 2: 290–92. Henry Gifford discusses Pasternak's *Nineteen Hundred Five* in the tradition of the Russian narrative poem, including Blok's *Retribution*, but he devotes little attention to "Fathers" (*Pasternak*, 98–110).

19. Pasternak, *Stikhotvoreniia*, 249.

20. Compare Blok's use of the collocation "neslykhannye sobytiia"/ "unheard-of events" in the Foreword to *Retribution* (*Sobr. soch.*, 2: 271).

21. Tiutchev, *Soch.*, 1: 62.

22. As Verheul has observed (*Theme of Time*, 176), the concluding lines of "Prehistory" are echoed in the final sentence (note the structural parallel) of Akhmatova's autobiographical sketch "Korotko o sebe" ("Briefly About Myself"): "Ia schastliva, chto zhila v eti gody i videla sobytiia, kotorym ne bylo ravnykh" (*S*, 1: 47)/"I am fortunate to have lived in these years and seen events which have no equals." The Tiutchev subtext is strongly felt here in the use of the word "schastliva."

23. Akhmatova underscores her generation's conscious selection of its own fate through the motif of the measuring off of time. Compare Ernst Cassirer's comments on the essential mythopoetic unity of measurement and destiny: "Over the Homeric Zeus stands the impersonal power of Moira, and in Germanic mythology the power of destiny, of becoming (*Wurd*), appears at once as the woof of the Norns, the weavers of fate, and as primal law. . . . Here it is also the power of measurement; in the Nordic myth of creation, for example, the world ash tree Yggdrasil is represented as the tree with the right measure, the tree which gives the measure" (Cassirer, *Philosophy of Symbolic Forms*, 1: 116). The connection between destiny and measurement is implicit in the Greek *moira*,

which literally means "lot" or "portion," and is maintained in the Russian *mera* (measure), as well as in its derivative *otmerit'* (to measure off).

24. Akhmatova, *O Pushkine*, 161–62. The same idea is expressed in an even sharper, more paradoxical form in a rough draft version given in the notes to *O Pushkine* (p. 259): "The composition of *The Stone Guest* is similar to that of almost all the novels of Dostoevsky (except *Crime and Punishment*). Everything begins, one wants to say—perhaps somewhat paradoxically, but completely accurately—when everything has ended. In general both Pushkin and Dostoevsky were masters of the *Vorgeschichte*. Inez and the Commander, the love of Juan and Laura, the married life of Doña Anna, Juan's life in Madrid, in exile—all this is barely touched on, but it is touched on in such a way that nothing else is needed. (The same is true of *Mozart and Salieri*.) The novels of Dostoevsky are constructed in the same way. In this lies their tragic richness. And the reader arrives not even in medias res but almost at the curtain's fall [*k shapochnomu razboru*], yet for some reason does not even notice this."

25. So is *Mozart and Salieri*, mentioned in the rough draft. Akhmatova originally envisioned publishing as a separate book of "nonlyric pieces" four texts written in 1940: *The Way of All the Earth*, "Moi molodye ruki" ("My young hands"), the first draft of "Dostoevsky's Russia," and the fragment that ultimately grew into *Poem Without a Hero* (*SP*, 511). The book was to bear the oxymoronic title *Malen'kie poemy* ("Little Narrative Poems"; the *poema* is big by its very nature, as the other acceptable translation—"long poem"—indicates), which pointedly alludes to Pushkin's *Little Tragedies*.

26. The first chapter of Ivanov's study of Dostoevsky is entitled "The Novel-Tragedy"; see Ivanov, *Freedom and the Tragic Life*.

27. Akhmatova, *O Pushkine*, 259.

28. Ibid.

29. Verheul, *Theme of Time*, 172–73. On Dostoevsky and the Church of Vladimir, see Antsiferov, *Peterburg Dostoevskogo*, 18.

30. Verheul, *Theme of Time*, 173.

31. For a guide to Dostoevsky's addresses in Petersburg, see Antsiferov, *Peterburg Dostoevskogo*, 17–23.

32. I am partially indebted here to Antsiferov's discussion of the role of Gorokhovaia in Dostoevsky's work (ibid., 28–29).

33. Akhmatova might well be remembering this descriptive passage from *Unizhennye i oskorblennye* (*The Humiliated and the Insulted*): "The house was small but made of stone, old, two-storied, and painted a dirty yellow. In one of the three windows of the lower floor there protruded a little red coffin—the signboard of an insignificant coffinmaker" (quoted in ibid., 37).

34. For much of his life Dostoevsky himself abided in rooms not much bigger than a coffin, and even at the height of his fame he worked in a small and claustrophobic study. For more on Dostoevsky's spatial preferences, see Grossman, *Dostoevsky*, 502.

35. Ibid., 500.

36. Ibid.

37. On Zosima in *The Brothers Karamazov*, see Linnér, *Starets Zosima*, esp. chap. 4, "The Saints of Reality" (86–111), which is devoted to Zosima's prototypes, including Amvrosii. For another treatment of the relations between Dostoevsky and Amvrosii, see Dunlop's biography of Amvrosii, *Staretz Amvrosy*, 53–81.

38. Dostoevsky, *Pol. sobr. soch.*, 14: 26.

39. Dunlop, *Staretz Amvrosy*, 60.

40. A typical example is the following quotation from the January 1877 issue of Dostoevsky's *Diary of a Writer*: "Unquestionably there is in Russia a life which is in a state of decomposition, and consequently, also a disintegrating family" (quoted in Linnér, *Starets Zosima*, 16).

41. In the first—albeit partial—publication of "Prehistory" (1945), the line reads "Ottsy i deti neponiatny"/"Fathers and children are incomprehensible" (*S*, 1: 415). *The Brothers Karamazov* was at first conceived of as an answer to Turgenev and initially bore the title *Ottsy i deti* (*Fathers and Children*); see Mochulsky, *Dostoevsky*, 537.

42. Kornei Chukovskii was the first to note the resemblance between Akhmatova's rendering of the 1870's and Dostoevsky's *Adolescent*; see his "Chitaia Akhmatovu." His daughter's notes on Akhmatova may well have inspired that observation. According to Chukovskaia, on September 10, 1940, i.e., exactly a week after writing the first draft of "Prehistory," Akhmatova mentioned having recently reread the novel (*Zapiski*, 1: 175). That is, Akhmatova wrote "Prehistory" when she was steeped in Dostoevsky's vision of the 1870's.

43. Mochulsky, *Dostoevsky*, 537.

44. On the reflection of Dostoevsky's life in *The Gambler*, see ibid., 314–21, 324–26; on Dostoevsky and gambling in general, see Frank's *Dostoevsky: The Stir of Liberation*, 258–63, 268–76.

45. Frank describes this incident and its impact on Dostoevsky in *Dostoevsky: The Years of Ordeal*, 49–66.

46. For an analysis of this letter, see ibid., 59–64.

47. Frank discusses both in ibid., 55–57, 87–89.

48. Dostoevsky, *Pol. sobr. soch.*, 21: 134. For a discussion of Dostoevsky's conversion to Russian Orthodoxy and the role of the Russian people in that conversion, see Frank, *Dostoevsky: The Years of Ordeal*, esp. 128–45 but also 87–127.

49. "Prehistory" portrays Dostoevsky's life experiences as symbolically

shaping his art, for the references to penal servitude and the mock execution formally frame the depiction of him at work.

50. The cross likewise symbolizes resurrection and life after death, and its appearance immediately before the cosmogonic act prepares for the emergence of cosmos in the final lines of the text.

51. For a discussion of Dostoevsky's synthesis of realism and idealism, see Jackson, *Dostoevsky's Quest for Form*, 80–81, and likewise the entire chapter "Reality and Its Representation in Art," 71–91.

52. For all its brevity, the description of Staraia Russa is closely linked to that of St. Petersburg. First, the lowly *kanavy* (ditches) of Staraia Russa recall the magnificent *kanaly* (canals) of the capital city. Furthermore, the oxymoronic collocation "pyshnye kanavy"/"luxuriant ditches" in line 23 reiterates the epithet describing St. Petersburg's coffins in line 8—"pyshnye groba"/"luxurious coffins." The city and town segments are also linked by a major structural parallel: both conclude with the speaker's abrupt departure; compare lines 21–22 with lines 26–27.

53. The warning "luchshe ne zagliadyvat'" (line 27)/"it's better not to glance in" echoes the following lines from Akhmatova's 1940 lyric "Londontsam" ("To the Londoners"): "Luchshe zagliadyvat' v okna k Makbetu,/Vmeste s naemnym ubiitsei drozhat'" (*SP*, 209)/"Better to glance in through the windows of Macbeth's house,/To tremble with a hired murderer." The recurrence of the words *okna* (windows), *luchshe* (better), and *zagliadyvat'* (to glance in) in "Prehistory" suggests that the darkened windows of Staraia Russa conceal death, and specifically death by murder.

54. Dostoevsky's narrator parenthetically remarks that the whole town in which Fedor Karamazov lives is "pronizan kanavkami"/"permeated with small ditches" (Dostoevsky, *Pol. sobr. soch.*, 14: 160).

55. The meeting is set by a *kanavka* (small ditch) separating Iliusha Snegirev from the others. Iliusha, referred to six times in the passage as the "mal'chik za kanavkoi"/"boy on the other side of the small ditch," hits Alesha Karamazov with a stone and then bites his finger to avenge his father's public humiliation by Dmitrii Karamazov (ibid., 161–62).

56. The epithet *podgnivshie* (half-rotted) pointedly recalls the following description of the summerhouse in the novel: "No vse uzhe istlelo, pol sgnil, vse polovitsy shatalis', ot dereva pakhlo syrost'iu"/"But everything had already decayed, the floor had rotted, all the planks were loose, the wood smelled musty" (ibid., 96).

57. Smerdiakov mentions that Grigorii accused him of rebelling against his birth and that Ivan Karamazov called him capable of rebelling (ibid., 204–5).

58. Ibid., 353.

59. Ibid., 426.

60. Each of the three motifs is associated with one of the novel's three

generations: the ditches with the children, the summerhouses with the sons as adults, and the dark windows with the generation of the fathers.

61. Pushkin, *Sobr. soch.*, 3: 228, stanza 20.

62. On the guiding role of Optina in Russia's spiritual life, see Kontsevich, *Optina Pustyn'*.

63. Quoted by Zhirmunskii in his commentary, *SP*, 507; he also cites the passage in his *Tvorchestvo Anny Akhmatovoi*, 139–40. Akhmatova's closing words refer to Osip Mandelstam's *Shum vremeni* (*The Noise of Time*, 1925), specifically to the second part of it, entitled "Rebiacheskii imperializm" ("Puerile Imperialism"), which recollects St. Petersburg of the 1890's. "Prehistory" owes much to the "cultural-historical pictures" (Dmitrii Sviatopolk-Mirsky's phrase; see Mandel'shtam, *Sobr. soch.*, 2: 549–51) evoked in *The Noise of Time*, filled as they are with a sense of impending doom. Compare two other sketches of St. Petersburg written by Akhmatova, entitled "Gorod" ("The City") and "Dal'she o gorode" ("More About the City") in Akhmatova, *Sochineniia* (Moscow), 2: 248–50.

64. Semenovskii Square was likewise marked in Akhmatova's memory. In a draft devoted to old Petersburg, Akhmatova recalls the "Semenovskii barracks and Semenovskii Square, where Dostoevsky awaited death," and "the gates from which the members of the People's Will Party were led out to their execution" (*SP*, 507). Only Dostoevsky's death sentence is alluded to in "Prehistory."

65. In "More About the City," Akhmatova recalls St. Petersburg's "kolokol'nyi zvon, zaglushaemyi zvukami goroda"/"ringing of bells, muffled by the sounds of the city" (Akhmatova, *Sochineniia* [Moscow], 2: 249). The sound of ringing bells is recalled in the reference to the bell tower in the second line of "Prehistory"; by 1940, however, the church bells had been removed or silenced.

66. Chukovskii attests to the verisimilitude of Akhmatova's 1870's interior on the basis of his own childhood memories in "Chitaia Akhmatovu," 201.

67. It was published in installments, 1875–77, and first appeared in book form in 1878.

68. The threat to the domestic realm is phonologically expressed in the repetition of the sound combination "k-r." Manifested most saliently in the phrase "*Kareninskoi krasoiu*," it recurs in each of the following lines of the passage ("*koridorakh*," "*kotorymi*," "*kerosinovoiu*," and "*kreslakh*"), subtly disrupting the verbal flow, and it is mirrored, appropriately, in the word "*zerkal*" (mirror). The "k-r" combination recurs in some of the most important words of the text, including "*katorzhanin*"/"convict" and "*krest*"/"cross"; it is also present in the name never voiced but of paramount importance in the Staraia Russa passage: "*Karamazov*."

69. She was born in a town called Bol'shoi Fontan (Big Fountain) on the outskirts of Odessa. See "Korotko o sebe" ("Briefly About Myself"), *S*, 1: 43.

70. Elsewhere Akhmatova recalls how she "was nicknamed 'the wild girl' [*dikaia devochka*], would throw herself from a boat in the open sea, would swim during storms, would tan until her skin peeled, and by all this would shock the provincial young ladies of Sevastopol" (quoted in Zhirmunskii, *Tvorchestvo Anny Akhmatovoi*, 126; also published in Akhmatova, *Sochineniia* [Moscow], 2: 243).

71. Not only is "At that time" set by the sea, the persona is taught to swim in the sea by her muse. In his commentary to *SP*, Zhirmunskii quotes Akhmatova's account of the genesis of *Right by the Sea*, where she underscores its autobiographical basis by linking it with her own childhood: "In it I bid farewell to my Khersones youth, to the 'wild girl' of the beginning of the century, and sensed the iron stride of war" (*SP*, 510–11). Also see Zhirmunskii's discussion of *Right by the Sea* in his *Tvorchestvo Anny Akhmatovoi*, 127–30. Childhood and the sea are also linked in "Esli pleshchetsia lunnaia zhut'"/"If the lunar horror splashes" (dated October 1, 1928): "Vizhu ia skvoz' zelenuiu mut'/I ne detstvo moe i ne more" (*SP*, 185)/"I see through the green murk/Neither my childhood nor the sea."

72. Cirlot, *Dictionary of Symbols*, 230, 268, 356. The recollection of the sea here prepares for the cosmogonic act depicted in the next segment of the text, for water is an essential component of creation myths, as in the Genesis account of the creation; it often figures in those myths as a deluge reducing everything to formlessness (Eliade, *Eternal Return*, 57–60).

73. Among those who have identified the subject of the portrait are Verheul, *Theme of Time*, 175, and Zhirmunskii (*SP*, 507). In her biography of the poet, Amanda Haight erroneously calls Akhmatova's mother "Inna Erazovna" (*Anna Akhmatova*, 7, 13). Chukovskaia records a lovely portrait of Inna Erazmovna drawn by Akhmatova and her childhood friend Valeriia Sergeevna Sreznevskaia. Sreznevskaia is quoted as saying: "'Imagine, Lidiia Korneevna, a small woman with rosy cheeks and an exceptional complexion, light-haired, with exceptional hands.'" And Akhmatova seconds: "'Marvelous little white hands [ruchki]!'" Sreznevskaia then rounds out the portrait drawn in "Prehistory": "'She spoke an extraordinary French, had an eternally falling pince-nez, and didn't know how to do anything, anything at all.'" See the entry for October 13, 1940, Chukovskaia, *Zapiski*, 1: 188. For actual photographs of Inna Erazmovna, see the first two pages of Akhmatova, *Stikhi/Perepiska*. Carl and Ellendea Proffer's interview with Akhmatova's brother Viktor in the same volume contains further information on Inna Erazmovna, including details about her father, her separation from her husband in 1905, and her move to Sakhalin in the late 1920's (ibid., 119, 121–22, 124–25).

74. Pasternak, *Stikhotvoreniia*, 248.

75. Gifford, *Pasternak*, 2.

76. Dobin, *Poeziia Anny Akhmatovoi*, 20. Chukovskaia's entry for October 13, 1940, contains additional details on this subject (*Zapiski*, 1: 188). Compare Viktor Gorenko's comments on his mother's involvement with the People's Will Party in Akhmatova, *Stikhi/Perepiska*, 121.

77. Jackson, *Dostoevsky's Quest for Form*, 47–48. See also chapter 5 as a whole, 40–70.

78. Dostoevsky, *Pol. sobr. soch.*, 13: 92.

79. Ibid., 14: 18.

80. Compare Arkadii Dolgorukii's cherished early memory of his mother holding him up to receive communion in the village church (*The Adolescent*, part I, chapter 5, section 3), ibid., 13: 92.

81. Unlike Dostoevsky's heroes, Akhmatova was not separated at an early age from her mother; the separation came after the revolution, in 1927. Akhmatova mentions her mother's last visit to her in the aforementioned sketch "The City," in Akhmatova, *Sochineniia* (Moscow), 2: 248. After that visit, Inna Erazmovna traveled to Sakhalin to join her son Viktor. Viktor fled to China in 1929, but Inna Erazmovna apparently did not accompany him (Akhmatova, *Stikhi/Perepiska*, 124).

82. Haight, *Anna Akhmatova*, 6–7.

83. Her parents were separated in 1905, and through the gesture of naming the young poet appears to have been symbolically aligning herself with her mother. For more information on Andrei Antonovich, see Haight, *Anna Akhmatova*, 44. Three sentences in the conversation between Sreznevskaia and Akhmatova recorded by Chukovskaia are devoted to him (*Zapiski*, 1: 188), and Akhmatova's tone seems ironic. See also the interview with Viktor Gorenko in Akhmatova, *Stikhi/Perepiska*, 117–21.

84. See Eliade, *Eternal Return*, 73–88.

85. Shklar, "Subversive Genealogies," 148.

86. Ibid., 144, 146.

87. Nedobrovo, "Anna Akhmatova," 63–64 (trans. Myers), 232. The editors of the third volume of Akhmatova's *Sochineniia* have reprinted Nedobrovo's essay in full; see *S*, 3: 473–95 (the passage cited appears on 489).

88. Chukovskaia recorded the poet's praise of the essay at that time: "But Nedobrovo understood my path, my future, guessed and foretold it because he knew me well." See the entry for May 24, 1940, *Zapiski*, 1: 113.

89. Timenchik, "K semioticheskoi interpretatsii 'Poemy bez geroia'," 438.

90. Mandel'shtam, *Sobr. soch.*, 3: 34. Among the others who commented on this topic were Eikhenbaum, *Anna Akhmatova*, 120–32; and

Vinogradov, *O poezii Anny Akhmatovoi*, 451–59. In "Russkaia semanticheskaia poetika kak potentsial'naia kul'turnaia paradigma," Levin et al. begin their discussion of Akhmatova's indebtedness to the nineteenth-century Russian prose tradition with this quotation from Mandelstam, going on to analyze the specific ways in which Akhmatova adapted and transformed narrative conventions in her early work (54–58).

Chapter 4

1. Tsiv'ian, "Zametki k deshifrovke 'Poemy bez geroia'," 256.
2. Pushkin, *Sobr. soch.*, 2: 166. Jeanne van der Eng-Liedmeier notes the ironic Pushkinian tone of the beginning of "Tails" in her article "Poèma bez Geroja," 96.
3. Zhirmunskii, *Tvorchestvo Anny Akhmatovoi*, 26.
4. On this figure and his Mayakovskian characteristics, see Vilenkin, *V sto pervom zerkale*, 263. Eng-Liedmeier gives a somewhat different interpretation of the figure ("Poèma bez Geroja," 81–82). For several other important literary allusions to Mayakovsky in *Poem Without a Hero*, see Nag, "Über Anna Achmatovas 'Deviat'sot trinadtsatyi god'," 77–79.
5. Timenchik, "Neskol'ko primechanii."
6. Timenchik, "Neopublikovannye prozaicheskie zametki Anny Akhmatovoi," 69. The fragment also appears in Akhmatova, *Sochineniia* (Moscow), 2: 222.
7. Akhmatova's collocation "Poet voobshche"/"Poet in general" appears to allude to the words "Poetam/Voobshche."
8. *S*, 2: 108, lines 116–21. The penultimate line has no comma in Struve and Filippov, but the sense requires one. Compare *SP*, 359, and *Sochineniia* (Moscow), 1: 280.
9. Timenchik has shown that the passage cited above contains an allusion to Khlebnikov's 1921 poem "Odinokii litsedei" ("The Lonely Actor") (Timenchik, "Neskol'ko primechanii," 278), where Khlebnikov juxtaposes his own image with that of Akhmatova:

> И пока над Царским Селом
> Лилось пенье и слезы Ахматовой,
> Я, моток волшебницы разматывая,
> Как сонный труп влачился по пустыне,
> Где умирала невозможность:
> Усталый лицедей,
> Шагая на пролом.

> And while over Tsarskoe Selo
> Flowed Akhmatova's singing and tears,
> I, unwinding the skein of the sorceress,

Like a somnolent corpse dragged myself through the desert,
Where impossibility was dying:
The tired actor,
Striding toward the breach.

See Velimir Khlebnikov, *Sobr. soch.*, 2: 307. The fourth line above alludes to Pushkin's 1826 poem "Prorok" ("The Prophet"), conflating its second ("V pustyne mrachnoi ia vlachilsia"/"In the gloomy desert I dragged myself") and twenty-fourth ("Kak trup v pustyne ia lezhal"/"I lay like a corpse in the desert") lines; see Pushkin, *Sobr. soch.*, 2: 82. Just as Theseus killed the Minotaur, Khlebnikov's actor-poet kills a man-eating bull, but the people around him are blind to his feat, a metaphorical reference to the blindness of Khlebnikov's contemporaries to his brilliant innovations. Timenchik notes in the same place that the motif of the untimely death of the poet sounds in Khlebnikov's "Pesn' smushchennogo" ("The Song of the Confused One," 1913), which was dedicated to Akhmatova.

10. The reference is to the protagonists of Lermontov's narrative poem *Demon* (*The Demon*, 1839); Tamara is the epitome of innocence.

11. See Toporov, *Akhmatova i Blok*, 14–21. The phrase in question appears in the first and fourth chapters of "Nineteen Hundred Thirteen," in quotation marks and in italics.

12. The title echoes Mandelstam's "povest' bez fabuly i geroia"/"tale without a plot or a hero" from the following sentence: "Strashno podumat', chto nasha zhizn'—eto povest' bez fabuly i geroia, sdelannaia iz pustoty i stekla, iz goriachego lepeta odnikh otstuplenii, iz peterburgskogo influentsnogo breda" (Mandel'shtam, *Sobr. soch.*, 2: 40)/"It is terrible to think that our life is a tale without a plot or a hero, made of emptiness and glass, of the ardent babble of digressions alone, of the delirium of the Petersburg influenza." Rory Childers and Anna Lisa Crone, among others, have identified this as the source of Akhmatova's title; see their "The Mandel'štam Presence," 77–78, n. 31. In a different vein, Susanne Fusso suggested to me that Akhmatova's title may well be indebted to William Makepeace Thackeray's *Vanity Fair*, which is subtitled *A Novel Without a Hero*.

13. His death is foreshadowed again about two-thirds of the way through the first chapter, immediately after the author's cry "Geroia na avanstsenu!" (*S*, 2: 108, line 139)/"Hero to the proscenium!" which prompts all the shades from 1913 to flee the stage. No hero appears; instead the author is confronted by a black frame, betokening the protagonist's death. The circumstances of his suicide are then foreshadowed, including his farewell speech to his beloved: "*Ia ostavliu tebia zhivoiu,/No ty budesh'* moei *vdovoiu*'" (*S*, 2: 109, lines 153–54)/"*I will leave you alive,/But you will be* my *widow*'." The chapter closes with the protago-

nist's appearance; his suicide is prefigured even more emphatically in the image of a "struika krovi"/"little stream of blood" (*S*, 2: 110, lines 219–20) flowing down his cheeks. Chapters 2 and 3 are loaded with references to the impending denouement: for example, the protagonist is called "Tot, s ulybkoi zhertvy vechernei" (*S*, 2: 115, line 340)/"He with the smile of the victim in the evening sacrifice."

14. Zhirmunskii, *Tvorchestvo Anny Akhmatovoi*, 157; see also Timenchik, "Akhmatova i Pushkin. Zametki k teme. III."

15. She calls him a "dragunskii kornet so stikhami/I s bessmylennoi smert'iu v grudi" (*S*, 2: 120, lines 429–30)/"cornet of the dragoons with poems/And a meaningless death in his breast."

16. See *S*, 2: 117–18. "V Letnem tonko pela fliugarka" (line 358)/"In the Summer Garden a weather vane sang thinly" foreshadows war through its allusion to Pushkin's "Tale of the Golden Cockerel" ("Skazka o zolotom petushke"), while "Veter rval so steny afishi" (line 364)/"The wind tore posters from the wall" foretells the revolution by mimicking the powerful, capricious wind of revolution in Blok's long poem *Dvenadtsat'* (*The Twelve*).

17. On the merging of the images of Kniazev and Mandelstam in *Poem Without a Hero*, see Haight, *Anna Akhmatova*, 148–59.

18. On the multiple allusions to Mandelstam's poetry in the First Dedication, see Childers and Crone, "The Mandel'štam Presence," 57–59 and 63–66.

19. A street in Moscow, Prechistenka was renamed Kropotkinskaia after the revolution in honor of Prince Petr Alekseevich Kropotkin (1842–1921), the Russian scientist and revolutionary.

20. Nadezhda Mandel'shtam, *Vtoraia kniga*, 488, translated by Max Hayward as *Hope Abandoned*, 435.

21. When the actual moment of the protagonist's suicide is dramatized in chapter 4, Mandelstam's words are not repeated, which serves to underscore their singularity.

22. This line recalls the different circumstances of Pushkin's death through an allusion to the poem Lermontov wrote to commemorate it—"Smert' poeta" ("The Death of a Poet," 1837), namely to the lines: "Ne vynesla dusha Poeta/Pozora melochnykh obid"/"The Poet's soul could not endure/The shame of petty wrongs." See Lermontov, *Sobr. soch.*, 1: 21.

23. Osip Mandel'shtam, *Sobr. soch.*, 1: 202.

24. Nadezhda Mandel'shtam, *Vospominaniia*, 36–41, 91–94, 165–70, translated by Max Hayward as *Hope Against Hope*, 33–38, 85–88, 157–62.

25. Mandel'shtam, *Sobr. soch.*, 1: 162. Compare the beginning of the first numbered poem of *Requiem*: "Uvodili tebia na rassvete" (*S*, 1: 363)/"They led you away at dawn." It is no wonder that Mandelstam thought

the poem was dedicated to him; in fact, it commemorates the arrest of Nikolai Punin (*S*, 2: 181). For a translation and interpretation of Mandelstam's poem see Gregory Freidin, *Coat of Many Colors*, 233–35.

26. Although images of torture (for instance, "krovavye kosti v kolese"/ "bloody bones in the wheel") figure prominently in the poem, the perpetrators of the torture are not imaged, making it less objectionable than the Stalin poem in the eyes of the authorities. According to Nadezhda Mandelstam, "The 'Wolf' cycle did not bode any particular troubles: camp at the very worst"; as for the Stalin poem, however, "No one doubted that he would pay for [it] with his life" (Nadezhda Mandel'shtam, *Vospominaniia*, 16; compare Hayward's translation, *Hope Against Hope*, 12).

27. *S*, 3: 502. The same six-line stanza, with a few small changes, is printed as the twelfth stanza of "Tails" in Akhmatova, *Ia—golos vash*, 248.

28. Eng-Liedmeier gives a somewhat different interpretation of *reshka* ("Poèma bez Geroja," 96).

29. Long before this poem's publication in the USSR, Viktor Zhirmunskii identified it as the source of the epigraph (*SP*, 517–18). He cites only the lines relating to Akhmatova, which she called "the best thing that has been said about my poetry" (*SP*, 518). The text was first published in the West in Kliuev, *Sochineniia*, 2: 258–61, and first appeared in the USSR in *Den' poezii, 1981* (Moscow, 1981), 188–90.

30. Kliuev, *Sochineniia*, 2: 258.

31. Filippov, "Nikolai Kliuev. Materialy dlia biografii," in Kliuev, *Sochineniia*, 1: 150–51.

32. Konstantin Azadovskii, *Nikolai Kliuev. Put' poeta*, 317–20. For a brief account in English of Kliuev's life and work, see John Glad, "Klyuev, Nikolai Alekseevich," in *Handbook of Russian Literature*, ed. Terras, 227–28.

33. Kliuev, *Sochineniia*, 2: 259. Zhirmunskii cites these lines accurately in his commentary (*SP*, 518), but Chernykh quotes the *Den' poezii, 1981* publication (p. 189), which erroneously replaces the second line's "Oblozhennyi" with "Obózhzhennyi"/"scorched." See Akhmatova, *Sochineniia* (Moscow), 1: 448.

34. *SP*, 370. In the Struve and Filippov edition of *Poem Without a Hero*, this line reads: "V pechnoi trube voet veter, i v etom voe mozhno ugadat' sleduiushchie strofy" (*S*, 2: 122) / "The wind howls in the stovepipe, and in this howl can be divined the following stanzas." Struve and Filippov accepted the other version of the sentence but learned of it too late to emend the text; they did, however, append a note to volume 2 correcting the sentence (*S*, 2: 604).

35. In his critique of Akhmatova's Petersburg tale, the editor invokes

none of the ideological criteria of Socialist Realism (compare Bulgakov's portrayal of the response to the Master's novel in *The Master and Margarita*). On the whole, his incomprehension sooner typifies the average reader's, and his words echo the readers' complaints adduced in the work's prefatory prose: see "Iz pis'ma k N"/"From a Letter to N" and "Instead of a Foreword" (*S*, 2: 97–100). Nevertheless, the phrasing of his final question—"k chemu nam *segodnia* eti . . ."/"what good to us *today* are these . . ." (emphasis added)—recalls the claim that Akhmatova's poetry was out of step with the times, a criticism repeatedly voiced in the 1920's and 1930's.

36. On the place and significance of this hymn in the Orthodox liturgy, see Wellesz, *History of Byzantine Music and Hymnography*, 138–39.

37. For example, "Muzykal'nyi iashchik gremel" (*S*, 2: 123, line 21)/ "The music box roared," from stanza IV; stanza V's "I otboia ot muzyki net" (line 27)/"And there's no end to the music"; the author heard from afar the "voi" "adskoi arlekinady" (*S*, 2: 123–24, lines 32–33)/"howl" "of the hellish harlequinade," in stanza VI.

38. These stanzas constitute the thorniest textological problem in *Poem Without a Hero*. I reproduce the version of them given in *S* (2: 124–25), which incorporates the last changes made by Akhmatova; for the work's publication history, see *S*, 2: 357–64. In 1987 Elisabeth von Erdmann-Pandžić published a superb critical edition of *Poem Without a Hero* ('*Poèma bez geroja*' *von Anna A. Achmatova*); she takes as her basic text Struve and Filippov's edition but gives all variants published over the years, including the version printed in *Sochineniia* (Moscow), 1: 273–300. Since the appearance of her book, a new version of the text has been published by Chernykh in *Ia—golos vash*, 231–54; Chernykh not only incorporates lines omitted by Akhmatova directly into "Tails" (the same is true of Jeanne Rude's edition of the work; compare Akhmatova, *Poème sans héros*), he includes an additional stanza (numbered XII, p. 248) published elsewhere as a rough draft from "Tails" (see *S*, 3: 502, and 3: 624, n. 225). *Ia—golos vash* lacks a critical apparatus, and nowhere are these changes explained or justified.

39. Although Western publications of the *poema* show no comma here, the sense of the first two lines requires one. When the stanza was first published in Russia, the line was equipped with a comma (see *Sochineniia* [Moscow], 1: 292), and subsequent Soviet editions follow suit.

40. In contrast to Struve and Filippov, Haight ("Anna Akhmatova's *Poema bez geroya*, 491), Rude (*Poème sans héros*, 111), and Zhirmunskii (*SP*, 372) omit this stanza entirely from the body of the *poema*. Zhirmunskii publishes it in a special appendix of strophes excluded from the text of *Poem Without a Hero* (*SP*, 380), citing an authorized typewritten copy of the *poema* belonging to Tat'iana Tsiv'ian, where the stanza appears

(numbered V-a) in the section "Primechaniia redaktora" ("Editor's Notes") as one not included in "Tails." In *Sochineniia* (Moscow), the stanza is reinstated in "Tails" as the eleventh stanza (1: 292); *Ia—golos vash* follows suit. The Hemschemeyer-Reeder bilingual edition of the *poema* follows Zhirmunskii both in printing this stanza separately from the *poema* and in his explanation of it, without noting the placement of this stanza in Struve and Filippov. See *Complete Poems of Anna Akhmatova*, trans. Hemschemeyer, ed. Reeder, 2: 474, 780.

41. Rude, *Poème sans héros*, 111. Haight's edition of the text glosses the "Seventh" as a reference to Shostakovich's Seventh (Leningrad) Symphony ("Anna Akhmatova's *Poema bez geroya*," 490, n. 23; compare Struve and Filippov's commentary, *S*, 2: 387), so that the words "my 'Seventh'" would evidently refer to an analogue of Shostakovich's symphony in Akhmatova's own work. A parallel between Akhmatova's "Seventh" and Shostakovich's does operate in *Poem Without a Hero*, for one variant of the end of the "Epilogue" depicts the evacuation of the composer and his "Seventh" from Leningrad. The fates of these two works are antithetical: the composer takes his "Seventh" to safety, but Akhmatova is unable to protect hers.

42. Nadezhda Mandelstam claims that "some copies" of this edition survived when they were carried off by the printers. See her *Vtoraia kniga*, 422, translated by Max Hayward as *Hope Abandoned*, 375.

43. The title "Odd" survives as the heading of one part of "The Seventh Book." In Akhmatova's poetry proper, the ill-fated seventh book is recalled in one of the Tashkent poems: "A ia dopisyvaiu 'Nechet'" (*SP*, 219)/"And I am finishing writing *Odd*."

44. A version of the elegy was finally published in 1989, in Akhmatova, *Ia—golos vash*, 297–98.

45. Chukovskaia, "Polumertvaia i nemaia," 435.

46. Ibid.

47. The same number of years—thirty—is featured in the last quatrain of Akhmatova's poem "Prolog" ("Prologue"), "Ne liroiu vliublennogo"/ "Not with the lyre of one in love," which dates from the mid-1950's:

> Я не искала прибыли,
> Я славы не ждала,
> Я под крылом у гибели
> Все тридцать лет жила.
>
> (*S*, 3: 77)

> I did not seek profit,
> And did not expect glory,
> I lived under death's wing
> For thirty full years.

Chernykh published the poem in *Ia—golos vash* without a title and with a slightly different first line: "Ne s liroiu vliublennogo" (p. 279).

48. Akhmatova, *Ia—golos vash*, 297.

49. The elegy's last lines envision the persona breaking silence at some time in the future to conquer death: "No ia ego kogda-nibud' narushu,/ Chtob smert' pozvat' k pozornomu stolbu"/"But sometime I will break it/ To summon death to the pillory" (ibid., 298).

50. Ibid.

51. Ibid., 297. Compare the reference to Socrates' fate in the poem "Zashchitnikam Stalina" ("To the Defenders of Stalin") published in the same volume (282):

> Это те, что кричали:«Варраву
> Отпусти нам для праздника», те,
> Что велели Сократу отраву
> Пить в тюремной глухой тесноте.
>
> Им бы этот же вылить напиток
> В их невинно клевещущий рот,
> Этим милым любителям пыток,
> Знатокам в производстве сирот.

> They are the ones who shouted: "For the holiday
> Release to us Barabbas," the ones
> Who ordered Socrates to drink
> Poison in the prison's muffled closeness.
>
> That drink should be poured into their
> Innocently slandering mouths,
> Those dear lovers of torture,
> Experts in the production of orphans.

52. In another version, the second line reads: "Voiny, smerti, rozhden-iia"/"Wars, deaths, births." The last element of the series smacks of the absurd, for it in no way motivates the poet's silence. Chukovskaia pinpointed the enigma of the line: "But isn't it strange that because of deaths and births—after all, some people die in all decades, others are born!—the poet cannot write? War did not hinder Akhmatova's writing, either. Her wartime poems, published a multitude of times, are well-known to everyone" ("Polumertvaia i nemaia," 433). In the same article, Chukovskaia publishes a corrected version of the line: "Pytki, ssylki i smerti . . ."/ "Tortures, exiles, and deaths . . ." (432, 434).

53. Ibid.

54. Naturally, the number of lines omitted from "Tails" and marked with ellipses varies from redaction to redaction—from one and a half stan-

zas to three full stanzas. On the omitted stanzas, see also Chukovskaia, *Zapiski*, 2: 364.

55. Compare the more direct treatment of the poet's silencing in the lyric "Vse ushli i nikto ne vernulsia"/"Everyone left and no one returned," written at the end of the 1940's in the aftermath of the August 14, 1946, decree:

> Наградили меня немотою,
> На весь мир окаянно кляня,
> Обкормили меня клеветою,
> Опоили отравой меня.
>
> (S, 3: 73)

> They rewarded me with muteness,
> Cursing me damningly to the whole world,
> They fed me with slander,
> Gave me poison to drink.

As in the ninth stanza of "Tails," the theme of silencing looms large, but here the poet herself, not her "Seventh," is the victim.

56. A variant ending of the tenth stanza attested by Chukovskaia confirms the causal relationship between the poet's silence and the "Pytki, ssylki, i kazni"/"Tortures, exiles, and executions": "Pet' ia/V etom uzhase ne mogu"/"Sing/In this horror I cannot."

57. Chukovskaia, "Polumertvaia i nemaia," 430.

58. Pushkin omitted twenty-three full stanzas, plus a total of twenty-two lines from three other strophes. In some versions of *Poem Without a Hero*, two and one-half stanzas are omitted from "Tails."

59. Iurii Tynianov, "O kompozitsii *Evgeniia Onegina*," in *Poetika*, 59–60.

60. Pushkin's defense was partially incorporated into the foreword to the publication of the last chapter of *Eugene Onegin* in 1832. See Pushkin, *Sobr. soch.*, 6: 482.

61. The paragraph is published together with several other notes under the title "Oproverzhenie na kritiki" ("A Refutation of Critiques"); see ibid., 306.

62. M. L. Gofman has pointed out how that "confession" is belied by the drafts of *Eugene Onegin*: "Pushkin in some instances did replace one strophe with another, and 'corrected' and 'fused' [stanzas] very often" ("Propushchennye strofy," 10).

63. Although the phrase "did not want" apparently describes instances when the author for personal reasons decided to withhold certain stanzas from publication, "could not" is a patent reference to censorship. Compare Gofman's glosses of these phrases, ibid., 2. Gofman notes that both phrases had until then (1922) been narrowly construed as alluding to "the

impossibility of printing [the stanzas—S.A.] because of censorship [tsen-zurnye usloviia]" (ibid., 1).

64. Ibid., 9–10.

65. Lotman, *Kommentarii*, 306. Just twelve lines of the stanza are extant, which prompted Gofman to categorize it with the unfinished strophes ("Propushchennye strofy," 10).

66. Lotman, *Kommentarii*, 306.

67. The translation is by Nabokov, Pushkin, *Eugene Onegin*, 3: 58.

68. Ryleev is best known for his *Dumy* (*Meditations*, 1821–23), a series of poems on historical subjects, which Pushkin evaluated as follows in a letter to Ryleev: "What shall I say about your 'Dumy'? They all contain moments of poetry: the closing lines of 'Peter in Ostrogozhsk' are extraordinarily original. But in general they are weak both in invention and form. They are all in the same style. The description of the place of action, the hero's monologue, and the didactic element are points common to them all (*loci topici*). There is nothing national or Russian about them, apart from the names—except for 'Ivan Susanin,' the first *duma* in which I begin to have an inkling of the real talent you possess" (quoted in O'Meara, *K. F. Ryleev*, 184).

69. Lotman, *Kommentarii*, 306. Nabokov, too, felt censorship's imprint on this stanza, but in a different way: he wonders if the final two lines were not omitted by Grot—the first to publish them—because of censorship (*Eugene Onegin*, trans. Nabokov, 3: 58). Such a hypothesis, however, does not explain the loss of these lines: Grot could have omitted them, but he would not have destroyed them. I suspect that for Pushkin the stanza was unfinishable; the two missing lines testify to the intensity of his grief for Ryleev and the other executed Decembrists. In any case, the absence of the lines does have semantic implications, for the stanza's truncation mirrors the untimely cessation of Ryleev's life.

70. Akhmatova, *O Pushkine*, 157.

71. Timenchik, "Printsipy tsitirovaniia u Akhmatovoi v sopostavlenii s Blokom." According to Timenchik, Akhmatova is simultaneously alluding to Viazemskii's well-known account of how one of Pushkin's first listeners reacted to the line: "Someone said: 'We don't feel sorry at all! . . . Because you yourself made Lensky more humorous than attractive. In the portrait you have drawn of him, there are traits and shades of caricature'" (quoted in Timenchik, "Printsipy tsitirovaniia," 127).

72. Lotman, *Kommentarii*, 306.

73. The line serves as an epigraph to "Instead of a Foreword" (*S*, 2: 99).

74. For the complex history of this line, see Lotman, *Kommentarii*, 372–73.

75. On Gumilev's arrest and execution, see Struve, "N. S. Gumilev. Zhizn' i lichnost'," in Gumilev, *Sobr. soch.*, 1: xxxvi–xlii.

76. Rude was to the best of my knowledge the first to associate these lines with Mayakovsky; see Rude, *Poème sans héros*, 32–33.

77. On Mayakovsky's posthumous fate, see Brown, *Mayakovsky*, 369–70.

78. Maiakovskii, *Sobr. soch.*, 6: 176.

79. The circumstances of the cycle's writing are inscribed, obliquely to be sure, in the cycle itself. See my article "'Bol'shim Maiakovskim putem,'" 260–63.

80. The positioning of Fate on the threshold recalls the setting of the young poet's *gibel'* (violent death) at the end of Part One. As for Akhmatova's sense of the imminence of her death, compare the lines already quoted from the poem "Prologue": "Ia pod krylom u gibeli/Vse tridtsat' let zhila" (*S*, 3: 76)/"I lived under death's wing/For thirty full years."

81. For an introduction to the role of *Macbeth* in Akhmatova's poetry, see Timenchik, "Akhmatova's *Macbeth*." The theme of ineradicable guilt is first introduced indirectly in the quotation from Akhmatova's "Novogodniaia ballada" ("New Year's Ballad," 1923) at the beginning of chapter 1: "I vino, kak otrava, zhzhet" (line 8)/"And the wine burns like poison"; this recalls the line immediately preceding it—"Otchego moi pal'tsy slovno v krovi"/"Why are my fingers as if bloodied"—which is printed in the first of the author's notes to the text (*S*, 2: 133). This unappeased guilt, whose source is later termed a "davnii grekh" (line 45)/"sin of long ago," was in fact the main impetus to the writing of "Nineteen Hundred Thirteen."

82. Chukovskaia, "Polumertvaia i nemaia," 434. The comma in the penultimate line is missing there, but it appears in Chukovskaia, *Zapiski*, 2: 516. Compare *S*, 3: 116, which has a dash instead of a comma. In "Polumertvaia i nemaia," Chukovskaia prints with no omissions five stanzas from "Tails," numbered VIII, IX, X ("Vrag pytal"/"The enemy tortured"), Xa, and Xb. The same stanzas are appended to her memoirs of Akhmatova, but with the addition of the thirteenth stanza and the omission of all Roman numerals; what is published in Struve and Filippov as stanza XI ("I osobenno, esli"/"And especially if") was omitted entirely when Akhmatova dictated the strophes to her. See Chukovskaia, *Zapiski*, 2: 364, 516–17. The two omitted stanzas (Chukovskaia's Xa and Xb) are numbered X and XI in *S*, 3: 116.

83. Nadezhda Mandelstam defines this word in her *Vospominaniia*, 313; the translation is taken, with a few small changes, from Haight, *Anna Akhmatova*, 153: "Permission was given to reside no closer than one hundred and five versts from the capitals, and all the places the railway reached in this zone were absolutely packed with people who had been in the camps and in exile. Local residents called the men 'one-hundred-versters,' and the women they called more precisely 'one-hundred-and-fivers.' This word reminded them of the martyr Paraskeva-Piatnitsa [*piatnitsa* means

"Friday," from the word *piat'* (five)] as well as of the one hundred and fifth verst. I told Anna Andreevna of this word, and it found its way into the *poema.*"

84. *Golubye* (blue) is a simple adjective; *posinelye* (dark blue) is a participle, which literally means "which had turned dark blue."

85. On *The Trojan Women* in Akhmatova's poetry, see Tsiv'ian, "Antichnye geroini—zerkala Akhmatovoi, 106–9; and Milivoe Jovanovich, "K razboru 'chuzhikh golosov'," 174, 178.

86. *Agamemnon*, trans. Morshead, in *Seven Famous Greek Plays*, ed. Oates and O'Neill, 90.

87. The lyric in question is "Vse uzhli, i nikto ne vernulsia"/"Everyone left, and no one returned."

88. As in the framing texts of *Requiem* and the ninth stanza of "Tails," Akhmatova foregrounds the detail of the women's mouths: "Posinelye stisnuv guby"/"Having pressed shut our dark blue lips." The closed mouths of these women recall the mouth of Akhmatova's "Seventh," stopped with earth, as well as the poet's own forced silence in the omitted lines of the tenth and twelfth stanzas.

89. Childers and Crone convincingly argue that the passage from the "Epilogue" contains several salient references to Mandelstam's death and works, but they contend that the "double" described by Akhmatova is Mandelstam ("The Mandel'štam Presence," 71–73), an interpretation that leaves many details unexplained, such as the accusatory "Za tebia ia zaplatila"/"For you I paid."

90. This destruction is proclaimed at the beginning of the prose remarks prefacing the "Epilogue": "Gorod stoit v razvalinakh" (*S*, 2: 129)/"The city is in ruins."

91. The latter echoes the initial line of a poem from the late 1940's, "Vse ushli i nikto ne vernulsia" (*S*, 3: 72)/"Everyone left and no one returned."

Chapter 5

1. The specifics were first brought to light by Haight, *Anna Akhmatova*, 140–42, 168–72. Sir Isaiah Berlin describes his encounters with Akhmatova and lists the poems dedicated, in his view, by Akhmatova to him, in "Meetings with Russian Writers in 1945 and 1956," *Personal Impressions*, 189–208.

2. On the resolution and its aftermath, see Haight, *Anna Akhmatova*, 143–47, 159–63.

3. In addition to the sources cited above, Lidiia Chukovskaia treats the "nonmeeting" of 1956 in the second volume of her memoirs of Akhmatova; Chukovskaia, *Zapiski*, 2: 170–71.

4. For a history of the cycle's publication and a discussion of the re-

lationship between the various drafts and redactions, see the fine doctoral dissertation of Marcia Rose Satin, "Akhmatova's 'Shipovnik tsvetet,'" 4–21.

5. See Zhirmunskii's discussion of the cycle's publication history, *SP*, 489.

6. Meilakh and Toporov identify the epigraph as Fet's translation in their "Akhmatova i Dante," 44. In the original, Aeneas's utterance reads "invitus, regina, tuo de litore cessi"/"unwillingly, O queen, I parted from thy shores" (Virgil, vol. 1, *Eclogues, Georgics, Aeneid 1–6*, and vol. 2, *Aeneid 7–12, The Minor Poems* [Loeb Classical Library edition], 1: 538–39, line 460.

7. See Book VI, lines 458–60; Virgil, 1: 536–39. Aeneas is simply reiterating what he told Dido on the eve of his departure from Carthage in Bk. IV: "Italiam non sponte sequor" (line 361)/"Not of free will do I follow Italy!" (Virgil, 1: 420–21).

8. Eliot, "What Is a Classic?" in *On Poetry and Poets*, 64. Eliot's reading of this encounter between Aeneas and Dido is compelling: "It is complex in meaning and economical in expression, for it not only tells us about the attitude of Dido—still more important is what it tells us about the attitude of Aeneas. Dido's behaviour appears almost as a projection of Aeneas's own conscience: this, we feel, is the way in which Aeneas's conscience would *expect* Dido to behave to him. The point, it seems to me, is not that Dido is unforgiving . . . : what matters most is, that Aeneas does not forgive himself—and this, significantly, in spite of the fact of which he is well aware, that all that he has done has been in compliance with destiny" (63–64). Aeneas may not forgive himself in this scene, but he never again speaks of Dido in the course of the *Aeneid*, consigning her memory to oblivion.

9. Virgil, 1: 539.

10. Erlich, *Russian Formalism*, 224. Coined by Boris Eikhenbaum, the term was also used by Iurii Tynianov in his *Problema stikhotvornogo iazyka*. Erlich gives one example: "Thus the triple repetition of the rounded *u* (oo) in the first line of Pushkin's poem *Ruslan i Liudmila* ('*U* lukomor'ia *du*b zelenyi') is cited by Tynianov as a 'case of phonetic gesture'; one ought to add that what is suggested here are not specific or unequivocal gestures" (224).

11. Akhmatova was very interested in the role of Dido's sister Anna in the *Aeneid*; at one point she planned to use as an epigraph to "Don't be afraid" Dido's exclamation from the beginning of Book IV: "Anna soror!" (Akhmatova, *Sochineniia* [Moscow], 1: 428–29). Used as an epigraph, the phrase not only addresses Dido's sister Anna, it reaches across the centuries to address Anna Akhmatova, as if proclaiming the similarity in their fates.

12. Virgil, 2: 106–7.

13. Ibid.

14. Meilakh and Toporov, "Akhmatova i Dante," 44.

15. Dante, *Divine Comedy*, trans. Singleton, *Inferno*, 1: 6.

16. Ibid., 7.

17. The events evoked in *The Sweetbrier Blooms* take place in a Leningrad devastated by war and by a long siege. Hence the description of the city in the ninth poem of the cycle: "I gorod, smertno obessilen,/Byl Troi v etot chas drevnei" (*SP*, 241)/"And the city, mortally weakened,/Was at that hour more ancient than Troy."

18. For a different interpretation of the allusion to Dante, see Meilakh and Toporov, "Akhmatova i Dante," 45–46.

19. Dante, *Inferno*, 1: 7.

20. Singleton notes that "silenzio" can refer to both space and time (*Inferno*, 2: 14), an ambiguity highly relevant to *The Sweetbrier Blooms*: not only does Akhmatova write after a long period of silence, but a great distance separates her from her addressee.

21. The fourth, fifth, sixth, eighth, ninth, and tenth poems all date from 1956; both the prefatory poem and the first numbered text were written in 1961; the eleventh and twelfth date from 1962, and the thirteenth from 1964. The seventh text alone is undated, but it was not written before 1956.

22. Dante, *Inferno*, 1: 7.

23. See *S*, 3: 532, for the publication history of this poem.

24. The last line's metaphoric expression of ruin recalls a similar metaphor in the seventh text of *The Sweetbrier Blooms*: "I vstretit' ia byla gotova/Moei sud'by deviatyi val" (*SP*, 241)/"And I was ready to meet/ The ninth wave of my fate." The "ninth wave," according to nautical superstition, is fatal to the sailor.

25. Cupid is "donisque furentem incendat reginam atque ossibus implicet ignem" (Book I, lines 659–60)/"by his gifts [to] kindle the queen to madness and send the flame into her very marrow" (Virgil, 1: 286–87).

26. The speaker's refusal to name the gift outright contrasts with the treatment of the same topos in the third dedication of *Poem Without a Hero*; there the speaker does not hesitate to call the visitor's gift by name: "No ne pervuiu vetv' sireni,/Ne kol'tso, ne sladost' molenii—/On pogibel' mne prineset" (*S*, 2: 103)/"But not the first branch of lilac,/Not a ring, not the sweetness of prayers—/It is perdition he will bring to me."

27. The participle *sozhzhennaia* denotes that which has been totally destroyed by fire, like the English "burned up."

28. Mandel'shtam, *Sobr. soch.*, 1: 167. See Satin, "Akhmatova's 'Shipovnik tsvetet'," 220. Satin notes that in Mandelstam's poetry smoke is associated with ritualistic sacrifice (221).

29. Satin was the first to point out the indebtedness of "The Burned

Notebook" to "The Burned Letter" (ibid., 230–31), but she does not address the significance of this. Sonia Ketchian briefly mentions Pushkin's text in her discussion of the theme of fire in *The Sweetbrier Blooms*; see her *Poetry of Anna Akhmatova*, 30.

30. Pushkin, *Sobr. soch.*, 2: 7.

31. Compare also the use of the word *khotela* in Pushkin and Akhmatova.

32. The same flight is portrayed from a different perspective in the cycle's eighth poem (dated August 18, 1956), which describes the persona's house as "tot navsegda opustoshennyi dom,/Otkuda uneslas' stikhov sozhzhennykh staia" (*SP*, 241)/"that forever devastated house,/From which the flock of burned verses flew away." The collocation "stikhov sozhzhennykh staia"/"flock of burned verses" recalls Akhmatova's use of avian metaphors to image poetry and creative inspiration in the early lyrics, as in the title of her third book of poems, *White Flock* (1917). That phrase derives from the lyric "Ia ne znaiu, ty zhiv ili umer" (1915)/"I do not know if you are living or dead": "I stikhov moikh belaia staia" (*SP*, 119)/"And the white flock of my poems." As for the epithet *belyi* (white), compare the use of the compound *belosnezhnyi* (snow-white) in the poem "Tvorchestvo" ("Creative Work," 1936): "I prosto prodiktovannye strochki/Lozhatsia v belosnezhnuiu tetrad'" (*SP*, 210)/"And the simply dictated lines/Settle in the snow-white notebook."

33. The precise dating of the play's burning is given in Chernykh's commentary to Anna Akhmatova, *Sochineniia* (Moscow), 1: 430. Compare Haight, who writes that Akhmatova burned the play "during her first month back" from Tashkent (*Anna Akhmatova*, 137).

34. It is not known exactly what manuscripts perished in the 1930's and in 1949; in 1944, the main loss was the play *Enūma elish*; Roman Timenchik told me in June 1989 that some prose written in Tashkent was also destroyed at that time. Little is known about the prose, but the play has been described in detail by Nadezhda Mandelstam, who heard Akhmatova read it in Tashkent. It treated the predicament of the writer during Stalin's rule in a grotesque style reminiscent of Kafka and Gogol. The heroine, a poet, is arrested in the middle of the night, tried—she does not know for what—and convicted by a "writers' tribunal"; then "she is immediately locked up in the slammer" [tut zhe upriatvaiut v katalazhku] (translation mine), where "for the first time she feels free." According to Mandelstam, "All the commonplaces of official literature and ideology were reproduced in it in fantastically concentrated form and with deadly accuracy." See Nadezhda Mandel'shtam, *Vtoraia kniga*, 397–401; the English translation except where noted is Hayward's, *Hope Abandoned*, 352–56. *Enūma elish* proved to be almost prophetic of what was to happen to Akhmatova in August 1946, but Akhmatova insisted that it simply reflected her own per-

secution and that of other writers in the 1920's and 1930's (*Vtoraia kniga,* 402; *Hope Abandoned,* 357).

35. Chukovskaia, *Zapiski,* 1: 10. The third sentence attributed to Akhmatova is particularly resonant. Autumn for Akhmatova was always the season of loss, and in the later poetry its tragic nature is even more pronounced. The 1943 poem "Tri oseni" ("Three Autumns") is typical in this regard. Autumnal imagery pervades *The Sweetbrier Blooms,* from the sixth poem's reference to autumn as a harbinger of the foreigner's ruinous visit, to the eighth poem's "Po oseni tragicheskoi stupaia" (*SP,* 241)/"Crossing the tragic autumn," to the tenth poem's grim autumnal landscape.

36. The folklike shift in theme from the first pair of lines to the second is anticipated in the first line's *uzornaia skatert'* ("patterned tablecloth"), which may be read as a metaphor for the poetic text: both text and cloth involve weaving, and patterning implies rhythm, design.

37. The same notion is expressed elsewhere in the cycle as well. To give but one example, the persona's condition in "In a Shattered Mirror"—"I zakruzhilas' golova,/Kak nad pylaiushcheiu bezdnoi" (*SP,* 241)/"And my head spun round,/As if over a flaming abyss"—harks back to the notebook's plight in the opening lines of "The Burned Notebook": "I pod toboiu ugol'ki kostra"/"And beneath you are the embers of the fire."

38. See Book IV, lines 612–29, Virgil, 1: 436–39.

39. The miraculous survival of the poems recalls Woland's words to Margarita in Bulgakov's *The Master and Margarita*: "Rukopisi ne goriat"/ "Manuscripts do not burn." Akhmatova's treatment of the burning of poems in *The Sweetbrier Blooms* was surely influenced by Bulgakov's novel, which Akhmatova read in manuscript in Tashkent. In the early 1930's Bulgakov had in a fit of despair burned the drafts of what was to become *The Master and Margarita,* an event he later incorporated into the novel in the story of the Master's burning the manuscript of his novel in a stove. The manuscript is later recovered through the good graces of the devil. Paradoxically, Bulgakov's reader holds the Master's book in hand throughout. Much the same paradox operates in *The Sweetbrier Blooms.* Akhmatova's close friend the actress Faina Georgievna Ranevskaia recollects in her memoirs Akhmatova's ecstatic response to Bulgakov's novel when she first read it: "In Tashkent I often stayed overnight with [Akhmatova], and I would lie on the floor listening to Bulgakov's *Master and Margarita.* . . . She would read aloud, repeating: 'Faina, this is brilliant; he is a genius'" (from a letter by Ranevskaia to Margarita Aliger, quoted in Aliger's memoirs of Akhmatova, "V poslednii raz," 332–33).

40. Meilakh and Toporov, "Akhmatova i Dante," 53.

41. Compare the related image from the 1959 lyric "Poet" ("The Poet"), which describes the poet's labors: "A posle podslushat' u lesa,/U

sosen, molchal'nits na vid" (*SP*, 203)/"And afterward to overhear from the forest,/From the pines, so taciturn by appearance."

42. Mandel'shtam, *Sobr. soch.*, 1: 167.

43. Keats borrowed the story from the *Decameron* and adhered closely to Boccaccio's narrative. The story is the fifth one told on the fourth day—the day devoted to unhappy tales of love.

44. Keats, *Complete Poetical Works*, 115–16 (stanzas xxxiii–xxxix).

45. Ibid., 117 (stanza lii).

46. Lines 5–10 from the eighth poem of the cycle conjure up the persona's realm in terms recalling the world of the dead evoked in *Requiem*:

> Мы встретились с тобой в невероятный год,
> Когда уже иссякли мира силы,
> Всё было в трауре, всё никло от невзгод,
> И были свежи лишь могилы.
> Без фонарей как смоль был черен невский вал,
> Глухая ночь вокруг стеной стояла...
>
> (*SP*, 241)

> You and I met in that unbelievable year,
> When the world's strength had already been exhausted,
> All was in mourning, all languished from adversity,
> And only the graves were fresh.
> Without lanterns the Neva embankment was pitch-black,
> Blind night was all around like a wall . . .

These dirgelike lines evoke an utterly debilitated, moribund world where death reigns supreme. One word deviates from the rhetoric of privation—"svezhi"/"fresh"—yet oxymoronically it, too, characterizes death: "I byli svezhi lish' mogily"/"And only the graves were fresh." Compare the oxymoronic beginning of *Requiem*'s "Introduction": "Eto bylo, kogda uly-balsia/Tol'ko mertvyi, spokoistviiu rad" (*S*, 1: 362)/"This was when only the dead smiled,/Glad for the tranquillity." While the Leningrad of *Requiem* is peopled by the dead, in *The Sweetbrier Blooms* the city is eerily unpopulated, reflecting its state after the devastating siege during World War II in which 600,000 inhabitants perished. The end of the passage is dominated by images of darkness and confinement ("nevskii val"/"the Neva embankment"; "Glukhaia noch'," literally, "the dead of night"; "vokrug stenoi stoiala"/"was all around like a wall") which together are suggestive of a grave.

47. Keats, *Complete Poetical Works*, 112 (stanza xiii).

48. Virgil, 1: 265–67.

49. Ibid., 397–99.   50. Ibid., 427.

51. Ibid., 433.   52. Ibid., 538–39.

53. Dante, *Divine Comedy*, trans. Singleton, *Purgatorio*, 1: 328–29.

54. Meilakh and Toporov, "Akhmatova i Dante," 48.
55. Ibid., 48–49.
56. Dante, *Purgatorio*, 1: 334–35.
57. Ibid., 340–41.
58. Akhmatova, *Stikhotvoreniia. 1909–1960*, 266.
59. Keats, *Complete Poetical Works*, 117–18, stanzas li–liii, lix.
60. Sobolewski, "Keats' 'Isabella, or The Pot of Basil'."
61. Pushkin, *Sobr. soch.*, 4: 121.
62. The translation is Johnston's in Pushkin, *Eugene Onegin*, 181.
63. Pushkin, *Sobr. soch.*, 4: 121; trans. Johnston, *Eugene Onegin*, 181.
64. Pushkin, *Sobr. soch.*, 4: 122; trans. Johnston, *Eugene Onegin*, 182.
65. Akhmatova knew the drafts of *Eugene Onegin* well, and in the variants of stanza 7, chapter 7, the phrase "tsvetet shipovnik"/"the sweetbrier blooms" occurs three times. See Nabokov's commentary on the drafts, *Eugene Onegin*, 3: 77–78.
66. Akhmatova made several amendments to the essay in 1957 before its publication in 1958 (*O Pushkine*, 234). In 1958–59, Akhmatova composed a series of other additions to the essay that were never incorporated into the essay proper; they are published in *O Pushkine*, 161–71.
67. The translation is Nabokov's; see his *Eugene Onegin*, 3: 80.
68. Akhmatova, *O Pushkine*, 107.

Chapter 6

1. The elegy appears in both *SP* (331–32) and *S* (1: 312–13) as the fourth Northern Elegy, but according to the internal chronology of the cycle outlined by Zhirmunskii (*SP*, 506–7), the work stands sixth in the cycle. Chernykh prints the first six elegies in the order suggested by Zhirmunskii in Akhmatova, *Sochineniia* (Moscow), 1: 253–58, as well as in *Ia—golos vash*, 214–19.
2. On Akhmatova's relationship with Garshin, see Haight, *Anna Akhmatova*, 127, 136–37, and Mandel'shtam, *Vtoraia kniga*, 502–3 (translated by Max Hayward as *Hope Abandoned*, 449–50). Garshin's name appears frequently in Chukovskaia's first volume of memoirs; her second volume contains a guide to Garshin in Akhmatova's poetry (*Zapiski*, 2: 549–51).
3. That role has been compellingly defined by Levin et al. in "Russkaia semanticheskaia poetika": "In Akhmatova's semantic system, *memory-faithfulness*, which is opposed to *oblivion-betrayal*, takes on the meaning of a source of positive, constructive value. The preservation of memories is the pledge of the uninterruptedness and continuity of life, and it becomes the confirmation of the reality of existence. Life appears in the form of the totality of memories, consciously selected. . . . In opposition to this, obliv-

ion is a betrayal of life, its interruption and destruction" (p. 51). The notion of memory as a moral imperative, as a means of preserving integrity by maintaining continuity with the past, is of paramount importance in the sixth elegy.

4. Compare Akhmatova's use of the word *epokha* in the 1940 lyric "Kogda pogrebaiut epokhu" (*SP*, 208)/"When an epoch is buried," as well as in the opening lines of "Menia, kak reku" (*Sochineniia* [Moscow], 1: 256)/"I, like a river," the fifth Northern Elegy.

5. A useful point of comparison is Akhmatova's early study of memory, "Kak belyi kamen' v glubine kolodtsa" (1916; *SP*, 124–25)/"Like a white stone in the depths of a well," which compares memory to the depths of a well, with a secondary comparison to the depths of the speaker's eyes. The committing of an object to memory is conceived of as an interiorization protecting the object and the emotions associated with it from the vicissitudes of time.

6. The phrase "khoromy pamiati"/"mansion of memory" is used by the poet in her late prose reminiscences (Akhmatova, *Sochineniia* [Moscow], 2: 242). "Terema [pamiati]"/"tower chambers [of memory]" appears in the 1921 lyric "Bezhetsk" (*SP*, 150), in which a personified Memory casts open her door to the persona, who refuses to enter. "Podval pamiati" (*SP*, 196) ("The Cellar of Memory," 1940) conceives of remembering as a descent into a hostile domain, a descent that threatens the persona's sanity.

7. Saint Augustine, *Confessions*, 214–16, 224.

8. Compare "Like a white stone in the depths of a well," which characterizes one of the persona's recollections in the same oxymoronic terms: "Ono vesel'e i ono stradan'e" (*SP*, 124)/"It is gaiety and it is suffering."

9. As for the table from which the inkspot has not been wiped, compare the metaphor "table of memory" from Shakespeare's *Hamlet*, where table is meant in the sense of tablet:

> Remember thee?
> Ay, thou poor ghost, while memory holds a seat
> In this distracted globe. Remember thee?
> Yea, from the table of my memory
> I'll wipe away all trivial fond records
>
> (I. v. 95–99).

10. In her book *Literature and Negation*, Maire Jannus Kurrik defines the connotations of affirmation and negation in a way that directly bears on the relation between the first and second epochs in Akhmatova's elegy: "Affirmation . . . 'draws together' or makes the symbol. It is integration, coherence, accord" (p. 1). By contrast, "negation, taken as the antonym of symbolic, is a 'tearing apart,' a sundering, separating, dividing, alienation,

dissociating. It is linked to the dispersed, the dismembered, the disparate" (p. 1). The transition from the first to the second epochs is in fact a shift from unity and coherence to alienation and disintegration.

11. Frye, *Anatomy of Criticism*, 213.

12. It also sees the onset of physical discomfort (in contrast to the first epoch's bliss), as reflected in the sensitivity to heat and cold: "Gde kholodno zimoi, a letom zharko"/"Where it's cold in winter and hot in summer." Compare the sensitization of the corporeal surface accompanying the biblical fall ("they knew that they were naked," Gen. 3: 7), as well as the physical discomfort to which Adam and Eve are condemned ("In the sweat of thy face shalt thou eat bread," Gen. 3: 19).

13. The fall from the first epoch is subtly measured in the echo of the fourth line's telo (body) in the verb *istlevat'* (to disintegrate). There is an untranslatable play on words in line 14: literally *plamennyi* means "flaming," and *istlevat'* designates both "moldering" and "smoldering."

14. According to Zhirmunskii (*SP*, 479), the poem was first published in *Zvezda*, no. 3–4 (1940): 75.

15. Akhmatova makes a similar allusion to multiple deaths in her poem to Pasternak, first published in the same issue of *Zvezda* as "Kogda chelovek umiraet": "eto znachit, on/. . . . ./Opiat' prishel s kakikh-to pokhoron" (emphasis added; *SP*, 188)/"this means that he/. . . . ./Has *once again* come from some funeral."

16. Not only does the word *portrety* (portraits) stand at the end of the verse line in both, the octet's "izmeniaiutsia" is echoed in the elegy's "*is-*podtishka *meniaiutsia.*"

17. To use Saint Augustine's terms, the portraits are images of that "visible object," which has "vanish[ed] from sight but not from the memory," images which are "retained within us" (Saint Augustine, *Confessions,* 225).

18. This reading is later confirmed in the reference to "those who died" in line 40: "Chto tekh, kto umer, my by ne uznali"/"That we wouldn't recognize those who died."

19. See, for instance, Deut. 21: 6; Psa. 26: 6, 73: 13; Matt. 27: 24–25.

20. Compare Chukovskaia's perceptive comments on "Memories have three epochs" (*Zapiski*, 2: 118–19):

> I love it, but it is a merciless piece—it may be the most despair-inducing poem in all of Russian poetry. Not grief, not sorrow, not tragedy—but courageous cruelty. With these lines the poet takes away from man his last dignity—not just love, but the memory of love; not just the loved ones, but the very memory of them. . . . It is "with soap" that is insulting here. . . . Tiutchev speaks about the death of grief in a much more elevated way. . . .

At least without this washing of hands with soap and without the communal apartment neighbor. Without the refined cruelty.

Chukovskaia is referring to Tiutchev's lyric "Est' v moem stradal'cheskom zastoe"/"There is in my unending state of suffering," and specifically to two lines that appear to have inspired Akhmatova's picture of the second epoch of memories: "Minuvshee ne veet legkoi ten'iu,/A pod zemlei, kak trup, lezhit ono." (Tiutchev, *Soch.*, 1: 171.)/"The past does not waft like a light shade,/But lies like a corpse underground." In her reply to Chukovskaia, Akhmatova affects incomprehension: "I don't know why this elegy is such a frightening thing [*strashilishche*] for you. . . . Nobody ever told me that. It's an elegy like any other" (*Zapiski*, 2: 119).

21. Just as *slezinka* (a single tear) harks back to the first epoch's *slezy* (tears), the verb *striakhivaiut* (brush away) alliteratively recalls the first epoch's *struiatsia* (are streaming). Compare this line from "Tri oseni" ("Three Autumns"), a lyric that is closely related on several levels to the sixth Northern Elegy and its three epochs: "Striakhnuv vtoropiakh mimoletnye slezy" (*SP*, 228)/"Having hastily brushed off [their] fleeting tears." Akhmatova's "beglaia slezinka" distantly echoes the lines from *Eugene Onegin* describing the encounter of a young woman with Lensky's tombstone (chapter 6, stanza 41): "Glazami *beglymi* chitaet/Prostuiu nadpis'— i *sleza*/Tumanit nezhnye glaza" (emphasis added; Pushkin, *Sobr. soch.*, 4: 116). Nabokov gives this translation: "with skimming eyes she reads/the simple scripture—and a tear/dims her soft eyes (*Eugene Onegin*, 1: 246).

22. *The Old Testament of the Jerusalem Bible*, ed. Alexander Jones (Garden City, N.Y.: Doubleday, 1966), 735. With reference to the sigh, compare the bookish idiom *ispustit' poslednii vzdokh*, a euphemism for "to die."

23. Pushkin, *Sobr. soch.*, 3: 256.

24. The root of this verb, -men-, also figures in the verb *smeniaet* (replaces) in line 20.

25. Compare the fourth line of "Vse ushli i nikto ne vernulsia"/"Everyone left and no one returned," written in the late 1940's, describing the addressee's backward glance at the poet "Chtob uvidet' vse nebo v krovi" (*S*, 3: 72)/"In order to see the whole sky suffused with blood." In Akhmatova's early lyrics the same motif appears in connection with World War I, in these lines, for instance, from the third of the *Epicheskie motivy* (*Epic Motifs*), which is dated 1914–16:

Когда я вышла, ослепил меня
Прозрачный отблеск на вещах и лицах,
Как будто лепестки лежали
Тех желто-розовых, некрупных роз.

(*SP*, 326)

When I came out, I was blinded
By the transparent reflection on things and faces,
As if everywhere lay the petals
Of those yellowish-pink small roses.

Akhmatova is alluding here to Blok's line "Krovavyi otsvet v litsakh est'"/
"There is a bloody reflection in faces," from the poem "Rozhdennye v
goda glukhie" ("Those born in the stagnant years," Blok, *Sobr. soch.*, 2:
236). The opening quatrain of Blok's poem concludes with the lines
"My—deti strashnykh let Rossii—/Zabyt' ne v silakh nichego."/"We—
the children of Russia's terrible years—/Have not the power to forget anything." Akhmatova's sixth Northern Elegy polemicizes with Blok, showing
that the people of Russia's truly terrible years do not have the power to
remember anything.

26. On this aspect of Akhmatova's poetics, see Meilakh, "Ob imenakh
A. A. Akhmatovoi; I: Anna," 39–40.

27. The line is from the last strophe of *Eugene Onegin*, in Pushkin, *Sobr.
soch.*, 4: 162.

28. Mandel'shtam, *Sobr. soch.*, 1: 240.

29. The theme of forgetting runs throughout Akhmatova's poetry. In a
1914 lyric, for example, the persona proclaims her own forgetfulness:
"Stala zabyvchivei vsekh zabyvchivykh" (*SP*, 88)/"I have become more
forgetful than all of the forgetful." Compare Akhmatova's self-
characterization in her poem commemorating the death of Mikhail Bulgakov: "Mne . . . /Vse poteriavshei, vsekh zabyvshei" (*SP*, 289)/"Me . . .
/Who has lost everything, forgotten everyone."

30. Rohde, *Psyche*, 253.

31. Saint Augustine, *Confessions*, 225–26.

32. The spatial indices of the third epoch's return hint that the house
visited is actually identical to the isolated house of the second epoch. The
adverbs *tuda* ("Bezhim tuda"/"We run there") and *tam* ("Tam vse drugoe"/"Everything is different there") both point to the isolated house. The
subsequent negation of the first of them ("My ne tuda popali"/"We've
landed in the wrong place") follows the scene of nonrecognition and can
be read as a rationalization of the failure to remember. The rhythmical
scheme of lines 32–34 realizes the sharpness of the break with the past in
a striking violation of the metrical pattern of the poem. Each line is broken
by a caesura in the middle of a foot, with the rest of the line showing a
markedly trochaic, not iambic, rhythm.

33. Compare the concluding lines of "V zazerkal'e" ("Through the
Looking Glass," 1963), from the cycle *Polnochnye stikhi* (*Midnight
Verses*): "My v adskom kruge,/A mozhet, eto i ne my" (*SP*, 248)/"We are
in an infernal circle,/But perhaps this isn't even us."

34. The irreconcilability of the past and the present is expressed in somewhat different terms at the beginning of the fifth Northern Elegy (Akhmatova, *Sochineniia* [Moscow], 1: 256):

> Меня, как реку,
> Суровая эпоха повернула.
> Мне подменили жизнь. В другое русло,
> Мимо другого, потекла она,
> И я своих не знаю берегов.

> I, like a river,
> Have been turned by the harsh epoch.
> They switched lives on me. Into a different bed,
> Past another, it has flowed,
> And I do not recognize my banks.

As in "Memories have three epochs," alienation is conveyed through the motif of nonrecognition, but here it characterizes the attitude toward the present life, not the past. The third line above quotes Mandelstam's *Egyptian Stamp*: "Ia ne znaiu zhizni: mne podmenili ee eshche togda, kogda ia uznal khrust mysh'iaka na zubakh u chernovolosoi frantsuzskoi liubovnitsy, mladshei sestry nashei gordoi Anny" (Mandel'shtam, *Sobr. soch.*, 2: 34)/"I do not know life: they switched it on me at the time I came to know the crunch of arsenic on the teeth of the dark-haired French lover, the younger sister of our proud Anna."

35. I am indebted to Victor Erlich for this idea.

36. Potts, *Elegiac Mode*, 39.

37. What is even more deeply suppressed in the elegy is the difference to Akhmatova. Garshin's betrayal of her is alluded to most directly in the lines "A te, s kem nam razluku Bog poslal,/Prekrasno oboshlis' bez nas"/ "And those from whom God separated us/Have managed beautifully without us."

38. Curtius, *European Literature and the Latin Middle Ages*, 195, 198. For an extensive examination of the *locus amoenus* topos and its role in the Western literary imagination, see Giamatti, *Earthly Paradise*.

39. In several of the later lyrics, the "green garden" finds its antithesis in the ominous image of the *chernyi sad* (black garden). The beginning of the fourth Northern Elegy (written in Tashkent in March 1942) is a good example (Akhmatova, *Sochineniia* [Moscow], 1: 256):

> Так вот он—тот осенний пейзаж,
> Которого я так всю жизнь боялась:
> И небо—как пылающая бездна,
> И звуки города—как с того света
> Услышанные, чуждые навеки,
> Как будто все, с чем я внутри себя

Всю жизнь боролась, получило жизнь
Отдельную и воплотилось в эти
Слепые стены, в этот черный сад...

So here it is—that autumnal landscape
Which I so feared all my life:
And the sky is like a flaming abyss,
And the sounds of the city are as if heard,
Alien forever, from the other world.
As if everything I struggled with inside me
All my life obtained a separate
Life, and was incarnated in these
Blind walls, in this black garden . . .

The black garden bespeaks suffering and death, as does the likening of the sky to a "pylaiushchaia bezdna"/"flaming abyss." The latter image is the antithesis of the protective *svod* (vault) of the sky or the overspreading trees in the *locus amoenus*.

40. See Tsiv'ian, "Zametki k deshifrovke 'Poemy bez geroia'," 272.

41. On the allusions to Pushkin's Tsarskoe Selo poems within the digression, see Timenchik, "Akhmatova i Pushkin: Zametki k teme," 43–44.

42. Akhmatova's Tsarskoe Selo poems also draw heavily on other poets' treatments of Tsarskoe Selo. On this aspect of Akhmatova's poems, as well as on their indebtedness to Pushkin, see ibid., 32–55. See also Slinina, "Pushkinskie motivy v tsarskosel'skikh stikhakh Anny Akhmatovoi," 129–39.

43. According to Innokentii Annenskii, it was in Tsarskoe Selo, "in this park chiefly of 'recollections'," that there was "to develop for the first time in Pushkin's soul a penchant for the poetic form of recollections" ("Pushkin i Tsarskoe Selo," *Knigi otrazhenii*, 309).

44. Pushkin, *Sobr. soch.*, 2: 192.

45. Ibid.

46. Ibid. Note Akhmatova's allusion to Pushkin's "predchuvstvuia bedy" in the 1911 Tsarskoe Selo lyric "Sad" ("Garden"): "Zdes' moi pokoi naveki vziat/Predchuvstviem bedy" (*SP*, 49)/"Here my repose is forever seized/By a presentiment of woe."

47. Boris Eikhenbaum wrote about the persona of the early lyrics, "We gradually find out her past . . . know the places where she lived and is living (the south, Kiev, Tsarskoe Selo, Petersburg), we know, finally, her house, her rooms" (*Anna Akhmatova*, 127).

48. See *SP*, 117. The "white house" first figures in the poem "Tvoi belyi dom i tikhii sad ostavliu" ("I shall leave your white house and quiet garden," 1913).

49. Akhmatova's high regard for "The Prodigal Son" has been noted by

many memoirists. My source is Nadezhda Mandel'shtam, *Vtoraia kniga*, 47, translated by Max Hayward as *Hope Abandoned*, 38.

50. Gumilev, *Sobr. soch.*, 1: 196.

51. Ibid., 199. The return to the former house also figures prominently in Gumilev's triptych "Vozvrashchenie Odisseia" ("The Return of Odysseus," 1910); see ibid., 137–42.

52. Ibid., 2: 48–49.

53. Ibid., 49. Akhmatova used the first of these lines as an epigraph to her "Tsarskosel'skaia oda" ("Tsarskoe Selo Ode," 1961), which conjures up a racy picture of Tsarskoe Selo in the 1900's. See *SP*, 262–63.

54. Zhirmunskii identifies it as a house owned by E. I. Shukhardina and located at the corner of Shirokaia (Broad) Street and Bezymiannyi (Nameless) Lane (*SP*, 479), and cites the following passage from Akhmatova's memoirs: "Along one side of that lane there were no houses, but starting (from Shukhardina's houses) there stretched a very decrepit, unpainted board fence" (*SP*, 492). On Gumilev's courtship of Anna Gorenko, see Haight, *Anna Akhmatova*, 8–9.

55. Akhmatova, *Sochineniia* (Moscow), 2: 241.

56. *SP*, 195. Zhirmunskii identifies the house as Shukhardina's (*SP*, 479). When this text was first published, the initial line read "Piatnadtsatiletnie ruki"/"Fifteen-year-old hands" (*SP*, 479).

57. *SP*, 479. Reprinted in Akhmatova, *Sochineniia* (Moscow), 2: 242.

58. Akhmatova, *Sochineniia* (Moscow), 2: 241.

59. Ibid.

60. Ibid., 240–41. Both wallpaper and the color yellow are foregrounded in the sketch, linking Shukhardina's house with the interior pictured in "Prehistory."

61. *SP*, 401. The poem in question is "Pust' golosa organa snova grianut" ("Let the organ's voices thunder out anew"). The stanza in which this line appears was removed from the poem when it was printed in *The Flight of Time*; see *SP*, 170, 401. The original version of the poem is given in *S*, 1: 205–6.

62. The third Northern Elegy, "V tom dome bylo ochen' strashno zhit'" ("It was very frightening to live in that house," 1921), is also important in this connection. As Omry Ronen has written, in it "the fears of 1921 are projected to the peaceful pre-1914 family house to become, in retrospect, a shared premonition of terror and death." See "A Beam upon the Axe," 165.

63. Compare these lines from the unfinished "little narrative poem" "My young hands": "Kto znaet, kak tikho v dome,/Kuda ne vernulsia syn" (*SP*, 195)/"Who knows how quiet it is in a house/To which the son has not returned."

64. I am grateful to Stephanie Sandler for calling this allusion to my attention.

65. Pushkin, *Sobr. soch.*, 4: 113.

66. This translation is based on those of both Nabokov (*Eugene Onegin*, 1: 242) and Johnston (*Eugene Onegin*, 170), to whom the brilliant last line entirely belongs. Nabokov's commentary on the passage is worth citing. While what precedes it recycles the conventional tropes of the romantic elegy, "the rich and original metaphor of the deserted house, closed inner shutters, whitened windowpanes, departed female owner (the soul being feminine in Russian), with which XXXII ends is Pushkin's own contribution, a sample as it were of what *he* can do" (*Eugene Onegin*, 3: 53).

67. The epithet *opustelyi* recurs in the fourth poem of the 1940 cycle *V sorokovom godu* (*In 1940*), "Uzh ia l' ne znala bessonnitsy"/"Have I not known insomnia," in the lines "Vkhozhu v doma opustelye,/V nedavnii chei-to uiut" (*SP*, 209)/"I walk into deserted houses,/Into someone's recent coziness." The Russian *uiut*, which is perfectly rendered by the German *gemütlichkeit*, is everything that makes a house a home.

68. Bachelard, *Poetics of Space*, 4.

69. Ibid., xxxvii.

70. Akhmatova's use of the word "mrak"/"darkness" here recalls its presence in Pushkin's Tsarskoe Selo poems. Among her posthumously published notes on Pushkin is one entitled "O smelosti vyrazheniia" ("On Boldness of Expression"), which contains the comment: "Istinnaia smelost' samogo Pushkina: 'Velikolepnyi mrak . . .' i 'sumrak vash sviashchennyi'."/"The true boldness of Pushkin himself: 'The magnificent darkness . . .' and 'your sacred dusk'." Both phrases describe the gardens of Tsarskoe Selo: the first is from "V nachale zhizni shkolu pomniu ia" ("I remember a school at the beginning of my life") and the second is from "Memories in Tsarskoe Selo" (1829). See Gershtein and Vatsuro, "Zametki A. A. Akhmatovoi o Pushkine," 32–33.

71. The source is the first chapter of *Vozmezdie* (*Retribution*), which describes the nineteenth century as *zheleznyi* (iron) and *zhestokii* (cruel). As for the twentieth century, Blok predicts: "Dvadtsatyi vek . . . Eshche bezdomnei,/Eshche strashnee zhizni mgla."/"The twentieth century . . . More homeless still,/More terrible still is the gloom of life" (*Sobr. soch.*, 2: 276–77).

72. Vitalii Vilenkin writes that the last note he saw in Akhmatova's archives about revising *Poem Without a Hero* was dated April 19, 1965 (*V sto pervom zerkale*, 213), that is, less than a year before her death.

Bibliography

Editions and Translations of Anna Akhmatova's Work

"Avtobiograficheskaia proza." *Literaturnoe obozrenie* 5 (1989): 3–17.
The Complete Poems of Anna Akhmatova. Translated by Judith Hemsche-
  meyer and edited with an introduction by Roberta Reeder. 2 vols. Som-
  erville, Mass.: Zephyr Press, 1990.
Ia—golos vash. . . . Edited by V. A. Chernykh with an introduction by Da-
  vid Samoilov. Moscow: Izdatel'stvo "Knizhnaia palata," 1989.
"Nashi publikatsii." Edited and with an afterword and commentary by
  Mikhail Meilakh. *Smena* 5 (Mar. 1989): 18.
"Neizdannye stranitsy iz "Vospominanii o Mandel'shtame." In *Sochinen-
  iia* (Paris), 3: 128–32.
O Pushkine: Stat'i i zametki. Edited and with an afterword by E. G. Ger-
  shtein. Leningrad: Sovetskii pisatel', 1977.
Poem Without a Hero. Translated and annotated by Carl Proffer. In *Se-
  lected Poems*, ed. Arndt.
Poème sans héros. Edited and with a commentary by Jeanne Rude. Paris:
  Seghers, 1970.
Requiem. Translated by Robin Kimball. In *Selected Poems*, ed. Arndt.
Selected Poems. Edited and translated by Walter Arndt. Ann Arbor, Mich.:
  Ardis, 1976.
Sochineniia. 3 vols. Vols. 1 and 2 edited by G. P. Struve and B. A. Filippov.
  Munich: Inter-Language Literary Associates. Vol. 1, 2d ed., 1967; vol.
  2, 1968. Vol. 3, edited by G. P. Struve, N. A. Struve, and B. A. Filippov.
  Paris: YMCA-Press, 1983.
Sochineniia. 2 vols. Vol. 1 edited by V. A. Chernykh with an introduction
  by Mikhail Dudin. Vol. 2 edited by E. G. Gershtein, L. A. Mandrykina,
  V. A. Chernykh, and N. N. Glen. Moscow: Khudozhestvennaia litera-
  tura, 1986.
Stikhi/Perepiska/Vospominaniia/Ikonografiia. Compiled by Ellendea Prof-
  fer. Ann Arbor, Mich.: Ardis, 1977.

Stikhotvoreniia. 1909–1960. Moscow: Khudozhestvennaia literatura, 1961.

Stikhotvoreniia i poemy. Biblioteka poeta. Bol'shaia seriia. Edited by V. M. Zhirmunskii with an introduction by A. A. Surkov. 2d ed. Leningrad: Sovetskii pisatel', 1976.

"Tale Without a Hero" and Twenty-Two Poems by Anna Akhmatova. Edited by Jeanne van der Eng-Liedmeier and Kees Verheul. Dutch Studies in Russian Literature, 3. The Hague: Mouton, 1973.

Other Works

Aeschylus. *Agamemnon.* Translated by E. D. A. Morshead. In *Seven Greek Plays*, edited by Whitney J. Oates and Eugene O'Neill, Jr., 48–116. New York: Modern Library, 1950.

Aliger, Margarita. "V poslednii raz." In Margarita Aliger, *Tropinka vo rzhi: O poezii i o poetakh*, 331–98. Moscow: Sovetskii pisatel', 1980.

Amert, Susan. "'Bol'shim Maiakovskim putem': Akhmatova and the *kazennyi gimn.*" In *The Speech of Unknown Eyes: Akhmatova's Readers on Her Poetry*, edited by Wendy Rosslyn, 257–65. Nottingham, Eng.: Astra Press, 1989.

Annenkov, Iurii. *Dnevnik moikh vstrech. Tsikl tragedii.* Vol. 1. New York: Inter-Language Literary Associates, 1966.

Annenskii, Innokentii. *Knigi otrazhenii.* Edited by N. T. Ashimbaeva, I. I. Podol'skaia, and A. V. Fedorov. Moscow: Nauka, 1979.

———. *Stikhotvoreniia i tragedii.* Biblioteka poeta. Bol'shaia seriia. Edited and with an introduction by A. V. Fedorov. 2d ed. Leningrad: Sovetskii pisatel', 1959.

Anrep, Boris. "O chernom kol'tse." With notes and additional commentary by G. P. Struve. In *Sochineniia* (Paris), 3: 439–65.

Antsiferov, N. P. *Dusha Peterburga.* Petersburg: Brokgauz-Efron, 1922. Reprint. Paris: YMCA-Press, 1978.

———. *Peterburg Dostoevskogo.* Petersburg: Brokgauz-Efron, 1923.

Arnheim, Rudolf. *Art and Visual Perception.* New Version. Berkeley: University of California Press, 1974.

Augustine, Saint. *Confessions.* Translated and with an introduction by R. S. Pine-Coffin. London: Penguin Books, 1961.

Azadovskii, K. M. "Menia nazval 'kitezhankoi': Anna Akhmatova i Nikolai Kliuev." *Literaturnoe obozrenie* 5 (1989): 66–71.

———. *Nikolai Kliuev. Put' poeta.* Leningrad: Sovetskii pisatel', 1990.

Babaev, E. "Pushkinskie stranitsy Anny Akhmatovoi." *Novyi mir* 1 (Jan. 1987): 153–66.

Bachelard, Gaston. *The Poetics of Space.* Translated by Maria Jolas, with a foreword by Etienne Gilson. Boston: Beacon Press, 1969.

Bakhtin, M. M. *The Dialogic Imagination: Four Essays.* Edited by Michael Holquist. Translated by Caryl Emerson and Michael Holquist. Austin: University of Texas Press, 1981.

———. *Estetika slovesnogo tvorchestva.* Moscow: Iskusstvo, 1979.

———. *Voprosy literatury i estetiki.* Moscow: Khudozhestvennaia literatura, 1975.

Baran, Genrikh. "Pis'ma A. A. Akhmatovoi k N. I. Khardzhievu." *Russian Literature* 7/8 (1974): 5–17.

Baratynskii, E. A. *Polnoe sobranie sochinenii.* Biblioteka poeta. Bol'shaia seriia. Edited and with an introduction by E. N. Kupreianova. Leningrad: Sovetskii pisatel', 1957.

Barfield, Owen. *Poetic Diction: A Study in Meaning.* Foreword by Howard Nemerov and afterword by the author. Middletown, Conn.: Wesleyan University Press, 1973.

Barthes, Roland. *Fragments d'un discours amoureux.* Paris: Éditions du Seuil, 1977.

Baudelaire, Charles. *The Flowers of Evil.* Edited by Marthiel and Jackson Matthews. New York: New Directions, 1958.

Benveniste, Emile. *Problems in General Linguistics.* Translated by Mary Elizabeth Meek. Coral Gables: University of Florida Press, 1971.

Berlin, Sir Isaiah. *Personal Impressions.* New York: Viking Press, 1980.

———. "Vstrechi s russkimi pisateliami: 1945 i 1956." *Slavica Hierosolymitana* 5–6 (1981): 593–641.

Blok, A. A. *Sobranie sochineniia.* 6 vols. Edited by M. A. Dudin, V. N. Orlov, and A. A. Surkov. Leningrad: Khudozhestvennaia literatura, 1980–83.

Bloom, Harold. *The Anxiety of Influence.* London: Oxford University Press, 1973.

———. *Poetry and Repression.* New Haven, Conn.: Yale University Press, 1976.

Bogomolova, N. A. "'Takim ia vizhu oblik vash i vzgliad'." *Literaturnoe obozrenie* 5 (1989): 37–43.

Briusov, V. Ia. *Izbrannye sochineniia.* Moscow: Khudozhestvennaia literatura, 1980.

Brodsky, Joseph. Introduction to *Poems,* by Anna Akhmatova. Translated by Lyn Coffin. New York: Norton, 1983.

———. *Less Than One: Selected Essays.* New York: Farrar, Straus, Giroux, 1986.

Brown, Edward J. *Mayakovsky: A Poet in the Revolution.* Princeton, N.J.: Princeton University Press, 1973.

Budyko, Iu. I. "Ia poslal tebe chernuiu rozu v bokale...." *Russkaia literatura* 4 (1984): 217–21.

———. "Istoriia odnogo posviashcheniia." *Russkaia literatura* 1 (1984): 235–38.

Cameron, Sharon. *Lyric Time: Dickinson and the Limits of Genre.* Baltimore, Md.: Johns Hopkins University Press, 1979; paperback ed., 1981.

Cassirer, Ernst. *Language and Myth.* Translated and with an introduction by Susanne K. Langer. New York: Harper and Brothers, 1946.

———. *The Philosophy of Symbolic Forms.* 3 vols. Translated by Ralph Manheim. New Haven, Conn.: Yale University Press, 1955; paperback ed., n.d.

Cassuto, U. *A Commentary on the Book of Genesis.* Translated by Israel Abrahams. Jerusalem: Magnes Press, 1961; reprint ed., 1978.

Childers, Rory, and Anna Lisa Crone. "The Mandel'štam Presence in the Dedications of *Poèma bez geroja.*" *Russian Literature* 15, no. 1 (1984): 51–84.

Chukovskaia, Lidiia. "Polumertvaia i nemaia." *Kontinent* 7 (1976): 430–36.

———. *Zapiski ob Anne Akhmatovoi.* 2 vols. Vol. 1, 2d ed. Paris: YMCA-Press, 1984. Vol. 2, Paris: YMCA-Press, 1980.

Chukovskii, Kornei. "Akhmatova i Maiakovskii." *Dom iskusstv* 1 (1920): 23–42. (Translated by John Pearson in *Major Soviet Writers: Essays in Criticism,* edited by Edward J. Brown, 33–53. London: Oxford University Press, 1973.) Reprinted in *Voprosy literatury* 1 (1988): 177–205.

———. "Anna Akhmatova." In Kornei Chukovskii, *Sobranie sochinenii v shesti tomakh,* vol. 5, 725–55. Moscow: Khudozhestvennaia literatura, 1967.

———. "Chitaia Akhmatovu." *Moskva* 5 (1964): 200–203.

———. "Chukovskii ob Akhmatovoi. Po arkhivnym materialam." Edited and annotated by Elena Chukovskaia. *Novyi mir* 3 (Mar. 1987): 227–39.

Cirlot, J. E. *A Dictionary of Symbols.* Translated by Jack Sage. New York: Philosophical Library, 1962.

Clark, Katerina. *The Soviet Novel: History as Ritual.* Chicago: University of Chicago Press, 1981.

Crone, Anna Lisa. "Anna Akhmatova and the Imitation of Annenskij." *Wiener Slawistischen Almanach* 7 (1981): 81–93.

———. "Blok as Don Juan in Akhmatova's 'Poema bez geroia." *Russian Language Journal* 35, nos. 121–22 (1981): 145–62.

———. "Three Sources for Akhmatova's 'Ne strashchai menia groznoi sud'boi'." *Russian Language Journal* 31, no. 109 (1977): 147–55.

Curtius, Ernst Robert. *European Literature and the Late Middle Ages.* Translated by Willard R. Trask. Princeton, N.J.: Princeton University Press, 1973.

Dal', Vladimir. *Tolkovyi slovar' zhivago velikorusskago iazyka.* 4 vols. 2d ed. St. Petersburg: Vol'f, 1881.

Dante Alighieri. *The Divine Comedy.* Translated and with a commentary by Charles S. Singleton. *Inferno.* 2 vols. *Purgatorio.* 2 vols. *Paradiso.* 2 vols. Princeton, N.J.: Princeton University Press, 1977.

Dedulin, Sergei, and Gabriel' Superfin, eds. *Akhmatovskii sbornik. I.* Paris: Institut d'études slaves, 1989.

Den' poezii. Moscow, 1980.

Deschartes, O. "Etre et Mémoire selon Vyatcheslav Ivanov." *Oxford Slavonic Papers* 7 (1957): 83–98.

Dobin, E. S. *Poeziia Anny Akhmatovoi.* Leningrad: Sovetskii pisatel', 1968.

Dostoevskii, F. M. *Polnoe sobranie sochinenii.* 30 vols. Leningrad: Nauka, 1972–83.

Driver, Sam. "Acmeism." *Slavic and East European Journal* 12, no. 2 (1968): 141–56.

———. *Anna Akhmatova.* New York: Twayne, 1972.

———. "Axmatova's 'Poèma bez geroja' and Blok's 'Vozmezdie'." In *Aleksandr Blok Centennial Conference,* edited by W. N. Vickery and B. Sagatov, 89–99. Columbus, Ohio: Slavica, 1984.

———. "Directions in Akhmatova's Poetry Since the Early Period." *Russian Language Journal,* Supplementary Issue: *Toward a Definition of Acmeism* (Spring 1975): 84–91.

Dunlop, John B. *Staretz Amvrosy: Model for Dostoevsky's Staretz Zossima.* Belmont, Mass.: Nordland, 1972.

Eikhenbaum, B. M. *Anna Akhmatova: Opyt analiza.* Petersburg, 1923. Reprint. Paris: Lev, 1980.

Eliade, Mircea. *The Myth of the Eternal Return.* Translated by Willard R. Trask. 2d ed. Princeton, N.J.: Princeton University Press, 1974.

———. "Mythologies of Memory and Forgetting." *History of Religions* 2 (Winter 1963): 329–44.

Eliot, T. S. *The Complete Poems and Plays, 1909–1950.* New York: Harcourt, Brace and World, 1971.

———. *On Poetry and Poets.* New York: Farrar, Straus, Giroux, 1943.

Elliot, Robert C. *The Literary Persona.* Chicago: University of Chicago Press, 1982.

Emerson, Caryl. *Boris Godunov: Transpositions of a Russian Theme.* Bloomington: Indiana University Press, 1986.

Eng-Liedmeier, Jeanne van der. "'Poem without a Hero'." In Anna Akhmatova, *Tale Without a Hero and Twenty-Two Poems by Anna Akhmatova,* edited by Jeanne van der Eng-Liedmeier and Kees Verheul, 63–114. The Hague: Mouton, 1973.

———. "Reception as a Theme in Akhmatova's Early Poetry." In *Dutch Contributions to the Eighth International Congress of Slavists,* edited by Jan M. Meijer, 205–31. Amsterdam: John Benjamins, 1979.

————. "Reception as a Theme in Akhmatova's Later Poetry." *Russian Literature* 15 (1984): 360–94.

Entsiklopediia Brokgauz-Efron. 86 vols. St. Petersburg, 1890–1907.

Epictetus. *The Discourses as Reported by Arrian, the Manual, and Fragments*. 2 vols. Translated by W. A. Oldfather. Loeb Classical Library. Cambridge, Mass.: Harvard University Press, 1966–67.

Erdmann-Pandžić, Elisabeth von. *'Poèma bez geroja' von Anna A. Achmatova: Variantenedition und Interpretation von Symbolstrukturen*. Bausteine zur Geschichte der Literatur bei den Slaven. Vol. 25. Cologne: Böhlau Verlag, 1987.

Erlich, Victor. *The Double Image: Concepts of the Poet in Slavic Literatures*. Baltimore, Md.: Johns Hopkins University Press, 1964.

————. *Russian Formalism*. 3d ed. The Hague: Mouton, 1969.

————, ed. *Twentieth-Century Russian Literary Criticism*. New Haven, Conn.: Yale University Press, 1975.

Etkind, Efim. "Die Unsterblichkeit des Gedächtnisses: Anna Achmatovas Poem 'Requiem'." *Die Welt der Slaven* 29, no. 2 (1984): 360–94.

————. *Materiia stikha*. Bibliothèque russe de l'Institut d'études slaves. Vol. 48. Paris: Institut d'études slaves, 1978.

Faryno, Jerzy. "Kod Akhmatovoi." *Russian Literature* 7/8 (1974): 83–102.

————. "'Tainy remesla' Akhmatovoi." *Wiener Slawistischer Almanach* 5 (1980): 17–81.

Feder, Lillian. *Ancient Myth in Modern Poetry*. Princeton, N.J.: Princeton University Press, 1971.

Fernandez, James W. "Reflections on Looking into Mirrors." *Semiotica* 30 (1980): 27–39.

Filippov, B. P. "Poema bez geroia." In *Sochineniia* (Munich), 2: 53–92.

————. "Zametki ob Anne Akhmatovoi." In *Sochineniia* (Paris), 3: 5–16.

Fleishman, Lazar'. *Boris Pasternak v dvadtsatye gody*. Munich: Wilhelm Fink, n.d.

————. *Boris Pasternak v tridtsatye gody*. Jerusalem: Magnes Press, 1984.

Frank, Joseph. *Dostoevsky: The Stir of Liberation, 1860–1865*. Princeton, N.J.: Princeton University Press, 1986.

————. *Dostoevsky: The Years of Ordeal, 1850–1859*. Princeton, N.J.: Princeton University Press, 1983.

Frank, Viktor. "Beg vremeni." In *Sochineniia* (Munich), 2: 39–53.

Freidin, Gregory. *A Coat of Many Colors: Osip Mandelstam and His Mythologies of Self-Presentation*. Berkeley: University of California Press, 1987.

Freud, Sigmund. "Mourning and Melancholia." In Sigmund Freud, *Collected Papers*, vol. 4, edited by Joan Riviere, 152–70. New York, London: Hogarth Press and the Institute of Psycho-Analysis, 1925.

Frye, Northrop. *Anatomy of Criticism*. Princeton, N.J.: Princeton University Press, 1957; paperback ed., 1973.

Gasparov, M. L. "Stikh Akhmatovoi: chetyre ego etapa." *Literaturnoe obozrenie* 5 (1989): 26–28.

Genette, Gérard. *Narrative Discourse: An Essay in Method*. Translated by Jane E. Lewin with a foreword by Jonathan Culler. Ithaca, N.Y.: Cornell University Press, 1980.

Gershtein, E. G. "Memuary i fakty." In Anna Akhmatova, *Stikhi/Perepiska/Vospominaniia/Ikonografiia*, compiled by Ellendea Proffer, 103–14. Ann Arbor, Mich.: Ardis, 1977.

———. "Neizdannye zametki Anny Akhmatovoi o Pushkine." *Voprosy literatury* 1 (1970): 158–206.

Gershtein, E. G., and V. E. Vatsuro. "Zametki A. A. Akhmatovoi o Pushkine." *Vremennik Pushkinskoi komissii, 1970*, 30–44. Leningrad: Akademiia Nauk SSSR, 1972.

Giamatti, A. Bartlett. *The Earthly Paradise and the Renaissance Epic*. Princeton, N.J.: Princeton University Press, 1966; paperback ed., 1969.

Gifford, Henry. *Pasternak: A Critical Study*. Cambridge: Cambridge University Press, 1977.

Ginzburg, Lidiia. *O lirike*. 2d ed. Leningrad: Sovetskii pisatel', 1974.

———. *O starom i o novom: Stat'i i ocherki*. Leningrad: Sovetskii pisatel', 1982.

Gofman, M. L. "Propushchennye strofy *Evgeniia Onegina*." *Pushkin i ego sovremenniki. Materialy i issledovaniia*, 33–35 (1922): 1–344.

Goldman, Howard. "Anna Akhmatova's Hamlet: The Immortality of Personality and the Discontinuity of Time." *Slavic and East European Journal* 22, no. 4 (1980): 484–93.

Gollerbakh, E. *Gorod muz*. 2d ed. Leningrad, 1930. Reprint. Paris: Lev, 1980.

Griakalova, N. Iu. "Fol'klornye traditsii v poezii Anny Akhmatovoi." *Russkaia literatura* 1 (1982): 47–64.

Grossman, Leonid. "Anna Akhmatova." In Leonid Grossman, *Mastera slova*, 301–11. Moscow: Sovremennye problemy, 1928.

———. *Dostoevsky: A Biography*. Translated by Mary Mackler. Indianapolis: Bobbs-Merrill, 1975.

Gumilev, N. S. *Sobranie sochinenii*. 4 vols. Edited by G. P. Struve and B. A. Filippov. Washington, D.C.: Victor Kamkin, 1962–68.

Haight, Amanda. *Anna Akhmatova: A Poetic Pilgrimage*. New York: Oxford University Press, 1976.

———. "Anna Akhmatova's *Poema bez geroya*." *Slavonic and East European Review* 45 (1967): 474–96.

Hollander, John, ed. *Modern Poetry: Essays in Criticism*. London: Oxford University Press, 1968.

Holquist, Michael. *Dostoevsky and the Novel*. Princeton, N.J.: Princeton University Press, 1977.

Hošek, Chaviva, and Patricia Parker, eds. *Lyric Poetry: Beyond New Criticism*. Ithaca, N.Y.: Cornell University Press, 1985.

Il'ina, Nataliia. "Anna Akhmatova v poslednie gody ee zhizni." *Oktiabr'* 2 (Feb. 1977): 107–43.

———. "Plody prosveshcheniia, ili Vlast' t'my." *Ogonek* 22 (May 1990): 6–8.

Ivanov, Viacheslav. *Freedom and the Tragic Life: A Study in Dostoevsky*. Translated by Norman Cameron. New York: Noonday Press. Paperback ed., 1971.

———. *Po zvezdam*. St. Petersburg, 1909. Reprint ed., Letchworth, Eng.: Bradda Books, 1971.

Ivanov, Viacheslav, and M. O. Gershenzon. *Perepiska iz dvukh uglov*. Petersburg: "Alkonost," 1921. Translated by Marc Raeff in *Russian Intellectual History*, edited by Marc Raeff, 372–401. New York: Harcourt, Brace, and World, 1966.

Ivanov, Viacheslav Vsevolodovich. "Problema imennogo stilia v russkoi poezii XX veka." *Slavica Hierosolymitana* 5–6 (1981): 277–87.

Jackson, Robert Louis. *Dostoevsky's Quest for Form: A Study of His Philosophy of Art*. 2d ed. Bloomington, Ind.: Physsardt Publishers, 1978.

Jakobson, Roman. "The Prose of the Poet Pasternak." Translated by John Rignall and Angela Livingstone. In *Pasternak: Modern Judgements*, edited by Donald Davie and Angela Livingstone, 135–51. Nashville: Aurora Publishers, 1970.

———. *Puškin and His Sculptural Myth*. Translated and edited by John Burbank. The Hague: Mouton, 1975.

Jovanovich, Milivoe. "K razboru 'chuzhikh golosov' v *Rekvieme* Akhmatovoi." *Russian Literature* 15 (1984): 169–81.

Karlinsky, Simon. *Marina Tsvetaeva*. Cambridge: Cambridge University Press, 1986.

———. *Marina Tsvetaeva: Her Life and Art*. Berkeley: University of California Press, 1966.

Keats, John. *Complete Poetical Works and Letters*. Cambridge Edition. Edited by Horace E. Scudder. Boston: Houghton Mifflin, 1899.

Kermode, Frank. *The Sense of an Ending*. London: Oxford University Press, 1966.

Ketchian, Sonia. "The Genre of Podrazhanie and Anna Achmatova." *Russian Literature* 15 (1984): 151–68.

———. *The Poetry of Anna Akhmatova: A Conquest of Time and Space*. Slavistische Beiträge, vol. 196. Munich: Otto Sagner, 1986.

Khlebnikov, Velimir. *Sobranie sochinenii*. 5 vols. Edited and with an introduction by Vladimir Markov. Revised reprint of *Sobrannye proizvedeniia* (Moscow, 1928–33). Munich: Wilhelm Fink, 1968.

Khodasevich, V. F. *O Pushkine*. Berlin: Petropolis, 1937.

Kliuev, Nikolai. *Sochineniia*. 2 vols. Edited by G. P. Struve and B. A. Filippov. Munich: A. Neimanis, 1969.

Kontsevich, I. M. *Optina Pustyn' i eia vremia*. Jordanville, N.Y.: Holy Trinity Monastery, 1970.

Koor, M. "Materialy k bibliografii A. A. Akhmatovoi (1911–1917)." *Trudy po russkoi i slavianskoi filologii* 11 (Tartu, 1968): 279–94.

Kristeva, Julia. *Desire in Language: A Semiotic Approach to Literature and Art*. Edited by Leon S. Roudiez; translated by Thomas Gora, Alice Jardine, and Leon S. Roudiez. New York: Columbia University Press, 1980.

Krook, Dorothea. *Elements of Tragedy*. New Haven, Conn.: Yale University Press, 1969.

Kurrik, Maire Jaanus. *Literature and Negation*. New York: Columbia University Press, 1979.

Kuzmin, Mikhail. Introduction to *Vecher*, by Anna Akhmatova. In *Sochineniia* (Munich), 2: 471–73. (First appeared in St. Petersburg, 1912.)

———. "O prekrasnoi iasnosti." *Apollon* 4 (Jan. 1910): 5–10.

Lebedev-Kumach, Vasilii. *Kniga pesen*. Moscow: Khudozhestvennaia literatura, 1938.

———. *Pesni i stikhotvoreniia*. Moscow: Khudozhestvennaia literatura, 1960.

Leiter, Sharon. *Akhmatova's Petersburg*. Philadelphia: University of Pennsylvania Press, 1983.

Lermontov, Mikhail. *Sobranie sochinenii*. 4 vols. Moscow: Khudozhestvennaia literatura, 1983–84.

Levin, Iu. I., D. M. Segal, R. D. Timenchik, V. N. Toporov, and T. V. Tsiv'ian. "Russkaia semanticheskaia poetika kak potentsial'naia kul'turnaia paradigma." *Russian Literature* 7/8 (1974): 47–82.

Likhachev, D. S. "Akhmatova i Gogol'." In D. S. Likhachev, *Literatura-realnost'-literatura*, 155–60. Leningrad: Sovetskii pisatel', 1984.

Linnér, Sven. *Starets Zosima in* The Brothers Karamazov: *A Study in the Mimesis of Virtue*. Stockholm: Almqvist & Wiksell, 1975.

Loseff, Lev. *On the Beneficence of Censorship: Aesopian Language in Modern Russian Literature*. Arbeiten und Texte zur Slavistik, 31. Munich: Otto Sagner, 1984.

Lotman, Iu. M. *Aleksandr Sergeevich Pushkin. Biografiia pisatelia*. Leningrad: Prosveshchenie, 1982.

———. *Analiz poeticheskogo teksta*. Leningrad: Prosveshchenie, 1972.

———. *Roman A. S. Pushkina "Evgenii Onegin": Kommentarii*. Leningrad: Prosveshchenie, 1980.

———. *Struktura khudozhestvennogo teksta*. Moscow, 1970. Reprint ed., Providence, R.I.: Brown University Press, 1971.

———. "Tekst i struktura auditorii." *Trudy po znakovym sistemam* 9 (Tartu, 1977): 55–61.

Lozinskii, Mikhail, trans. *Bozhestvennaia komediia*, by Dante Alighieri. Moscow: Moskovskii rabochii, 1986.

Lukács, Georg. *The Theory of the Novel*. Translated by Anna Bostock. Cambridge, Mass.: MIT Press, 1971.

Luknitskaia, Vera. *Pered toboi zemlia*. Leningrad: Lenizdat, 1988.

Maiakovskii, Vladimir. *Sobranie sochinenii*. 12 vols. Moscow: Pravda, 1978.

Makogonenko, G. P. ". . . Iz tret'ei epokhi vospominanii." *Druzhba narodov* 3 (1987): 232–40.

———. "O sbornike Anny Akhmatovoi 'Nechet'." *Voprosy literatury* 2 (1986): 170–90.

Mandel'shtam, Nadezhda. *Mozart and Salieri*. Translated by Robert A. McLean. Ann Arbor, Mich.: Ardis, 1973.

———. *Vospominaniia*. New York, 1970. Translated by Max Hayward as *Hope Against Hope*. New York: Atheneum, 1970.

———. *Vtoraia kniga*. Paris: YMCA-Press, 1978. Translated by Max Hayward as *Hope Abandoned*. London: Collins & Harvill, 1974.

Mandel'shtam, Osip. *The Noise of Time: The Prose of Mandelstam*. Translated and with an introduction by Clarence Brown. San Francisco: North Point Press, 1986.

———. *Sobranie sochinenii*. 3 vols. Edited by G. P. Struve and B. A. Filippov. New York: Inter-Language Literary Associates, 1969–71.

Mandrykina, L. A. "Iz rukopisnogo naslediia A. A. Akhmatovoi." *Neva* 6 (1979): 196–99.

———. "Nenapisannaia kniga: 'Listki iz dnevnika' A. A. Akhmatovoi." In *Knigi. Arkhivy. Avtografy*, edited by A. S. Myl'nikov et al., 57–76. Moscow: Kniga, 1973.

Meilakh, M. B. "Ob imenakh A. A. Akhmatovoi. I: Anna." *Russian Literature* 10/11 (1975): 33–57.

———. Review of *The Theme of Time in the Poetry of Anna Akhmatova*, by Kees Verheul. *Russian Literature* 7/8 (1974): 203–13.

Meilakh, M. B., and V. N. Toporov. "Akhmatova i Dante." *International Journal of Slavic Linguistics and Poetics* 15 (1972): 29–75.

Mickiewicz, Denis, ed. *Toward a Definition of Acmeism*. *Russian Language Journal*, supplementary issue (Spring 1975).

Mochul'skii, Konstantin. *Dostoevsky: His Life and Works*. Translated by Michael A. Minihan. Princeton, N.J.: Princeton University Press, 1967.

———. "Poeticheskoe tvorchestvo Anny Akhmatovoi." *Russkaia mysl'* 3–4 (Sofia, 1921): 185–201.

Mukařovský, Jan. *The Word and Verbal Art*. Translated and edited by John Burbank and Peter Steiner, with a foreword by René Wellek. New Haven, Conn.: Yale University Press, 1977.

Nag, Martin. "Über Anna Achmatovas 'Deviat'sot trinadtsatyi god'." *Scando-Slavica* 13 (1967): 77–82.

Naiman, Anatolii. *Rasskazy o Anne Akhmatovoi*. Moscow: Khudozhestvennaia literatura, 1989.

Nedobrovo, N. V. "Anna Akhmatova." *Russkaia mysl'* 7 (1915): sec. 2, 50–68. Reprinted in Akhmatova, *Sochineniia* (Paris), 3: 473–95. Translated by Alan Myers in *Russian Literature Triquarterly* 9 (Spring 1974): 221–36.

Nekrasov, N. A. *Sobranie stikhotvorenii*. Edited by K. I. Chukovskii with an introduction by A. M. Egolina. 2 vols. Leningrad: Sovetskii pisatel', 1949.

Nilus, Sergei Aleksandrovich. *Sila Bozhiia i Nemoshch' Chelovecheskaia: Optinskii Starets Feodosii*. Platina, Calif.: St. Herman of Alaska Brotherhood, 1976.

O'Meara, Patrick. *K. F. Ryleev: A Political Biography of the Decembrist Poet*. Princeton, N.J.: Princeton University Press, 1984.

Pamiati A. A. Akhmatovoi. Paris: YMCA-Press, 1974.

Pasternak, Boris. *Stikhotvoreniia i poemy*. Biblioteka poeta. Bol'shaia seriia. Edited, compiled, and annotated by L. A. Ozerov, with an introduction by A. D. Siniavskii. 2d ed. Moscow and Leningrad: Sovetskii pisatel', 1965.

Pavlovskii, A. I. *Anna Akhmatova. Ocherk tvorchestva*. Leningrad: Lenizdat, 1966.

———. "Bulgakov i Akhmatova." *Russkaia literatura* 4 (1988): 3–17.

Peirce, Charles Sanders. "The Icon, Index, and Symbol." In *Collected Papers of Charles Sanders Peirce*, edited by Charles Hartshorne and Paul Weiss, vol. 2, 156–73. Cambridge, Mass.: Harvard University Press, 1932.

Potts, Abbie Findlay. *The Elegiac Mode*. Ithaca, N.Y.: Cornell University Press, 1967.

Praz, Mario. *The Romantic Agony*. Translated by Angus Davidson. 2d ed. London: Oxford University Press, 1970.

Princeton Encyclopedia of Poetry and Poetics. Enlarged ed. (1974). S. v. "Elegy," by Stephen F. Fogle.

Pushkin, A. S. *Eugene Onegin*. Translated by Charles Johnston with an introduction by John Bayley. Harmondsworth, Eng.: Penguin Books, 1979.

———. *Eugene Onegin*. Translated and with a commentary by Vladimir Nabokov. 4 vols. Princeton, N.J.: Princeton University Press, 1964.

—————. *Sobranie sochinenii.* 10 vols. Moscow: Khudozhestvennaia literatura, 1974–78.

Rannit, Aleksis. "Anna Akhmatova Considered in a Context of Art Nouveau." In *Sochineniia* (Munich), 2: 5–39.

Rice, Tamara Talbot. *A Concise History of Russian Art.* New York: Praeger, 1963.

Rohde, Erwin. *Psyche: The Cult of Souls and Belief in Immortality Among the Greeks.* Translated by W. B. Hillis. New York: Harcourt, Brace, 1925.

Ronen, Omry. "A Beam upon the Axe: Some Antecedents of Osip Mandel'štam's 'Umyvalsja noč'ju na dvore. . . .'" *Slavica Hierosolymitana* 1 (1977): 158–76.

—————. *An Approach to Mandel'štam.* Jerusalem: Magnes Press, 1983.

—————. "The Dry River and the Black Ice: Anamnesis and Amnesia in Mandel'štam's 'Ja slovo pozabyl, čto ja xotel skazat'. . . .'" *Slavica Hierosolymitana* 1 (1977): 177–84.

—————. "K istorii akmeisticheskikh tekstov: Opushchennye strofy i podtekst." *Slavica Hierosolymitana* 3 (1978): 68–74.

—————. "Leksicheskii povtor, podtekst i smysl v poetike Osipa Mandel'shtama." In *Slavic Poetics: Essays in Honor of Kiril Taranovsky*, edited by Roman Jakobson et al., 367–87. The Hague: Mouton, 1973.

—————. "Mandel'štam's 'Kaščej'." In *Studies Presented to Professor Roman Jakobson by His Students*, edited by Charles Gribble, 252–64. Cambridge, Mass.: Slavica Publishers, 1968.

Roskina, Nataliia. *Chetyre glavy. Iz literaturnykh vospominanii.* Paris: YMCA-Press, 1980.

Rosslyn, Wendy. "Boris Anrep and the Poems of Anna Akhmatova." *Modern Language Review* 74 (1979): 884–96.

—————. *The Prince, the Fool and the Nunnery: The Religious Theme in the Early Poetry of Anna Akhmatova.* Amersham, Eng.: Avebury, 1984.

—————. "Theatre, Theatricality and Akhmatova's *Poema bez geroya.*" *Essays in Poetics* 13, no. 1 (1988): 89–108.

—————, ed. *The Speech of Unknown Eyes: Akhmatova's Readers on Her Poetry.* Nottingham, Eng.: Astra Press, 1989.

Rude, Jeanne. *Anna Akhmatova.* Poètes d'aujourd'hui, 179. Paris: Seghers, 1968.

Sandler, Stephanie. *Distant Pleasures: Alexander Pushkin and the Writing of Exile.* Stanford, Calif.: Stanford University Press, 1989.

Satin, Marcia Rose. "Akhmatova's 'Shipovnik tsvetet': A Study of Creative Method." Ph.D. dissertation, University of Pennsylvania, 1978.

Saulenko, L. L. "Pushkinskaia traditsiia v 'Poeme bez geroia' Anny Akhmatovoi." *Voprosy russkoi literatury* 2 (L'vov, 1980): 42–50.

Scherr, Barry. *Russian Poetry: Meter, Rhythm, and Rhyme.* Berkeley: University of California Press, 1986.

Segal, Dmitrii. "Literatura kak okhrannaia gramota." *Slavica Hierosolymitana* 5–6 (1981): 151–244.

Shcheglov, Iu. K. "Iz nabliudenii nad poeticheskim mirom Akhmatovoi ('Serdtse b'etsia rovno, merno . . .')." *Russian Literature* 11 (1982): 49–90.

Shklar, Judith N. "Subversive Genealogies." In *Myth, Symbol, and Culture,* edited by Clifford Geertz, 129–54. New York: Norton, 1971.

Singer, Irving. "Erotic Transformations in the Legend of Dido and Aeneas." *Modern Language Notes* 90 (1975): 767–83.

Siniavskii, Andrei. "Pasternak's Poetry." Translated by Elizabeth Henderson. In *Pasternak: A Collection of Critical Essays,* edited by Victor Erlich, 68–109. Englewood Cliffs, N.J.: Prentice-Hall, 1978.

———. "Raskovannyi golos (K 75-letiiu A. Akhmatovoi)." *Novyi mir* 6 (June 1974): 176.

Slinina, E. V. "Pushkinskie motivy v tsarskosel'skikh stikhakh Anny Akhmatovoi." In *Pushkinskii sbornik,* edited by E. V. Slinina, 129–39. Pskov: Gosudarstvennyi pedagogicheskii institut, 1973.

Smirnov, I. P. "K izucheniiu simvoliki Anny Akhmatovoi (Rannee tvorchestvo)." In *Poetika i stilistika russkoi literatury: Pamiati akademika V. V. Vinogradova,* edited by M. P. Alekseev et al., 279–87. Leningrad: Nauka, 1971.

———. "Prichinno-sledstvennye struktury poeticheskikh proizvedenii." In *Issledovaniia po poetike i stilistike,* edited by V. V. Vinogradov, 212–47. Leningrad: Nauka, 1972.

Smith, Barbara Herrnstein. *Poetic Closure: A Study of How Poems End.* Chicago: University of Chicago Press, 1968.

Smith, Eric. *By Mourning Tongues: Studies in English Elegy.* Ipswich: Boydell Press, 1977.

Sobolewski, John. "Keats' 'Isabella, or The Pot of Basil' and Other Intertexts for Axmatova's 'Šipovnik cvetet'." Photocopy.

Sreznevskaia, V. S. "Iz vospominanii V. S. Sreznevskoi." In Nikolai Gumilev, *Neizdannoe i nesobrannoe,* edited by Michael Basker and Sheelagh Duffin Graham, 157–68. Paris: YMCA-Press, 1986.

Stankiewicz, Edward. "Centripetal and Centrifugal Structures in Poetry." *Semiotica* 38, no. 3–4 (1982): 217–42.

———. "Problems in Emotive Language." In *Approaches to Semiotics,* edited by Thomas A. Sebeok, Alfred S. Hayes, and Mary C. Bateson, 239–64. The Hague: Mouton, 1964.

Starobinski, Jean. "The Inside and the Outside." *Hudson Review* 28 (Autumn 1975): 333–51.

Striedter, Jurij. "Poetic Genre and the Sense of History in Pushkin." *New Literary History* 8, no. 2 (Winter 1977): 295–310.

Struve, Gleb. "Akhmatova i Boris Anrep." In *Sochineniia* (Paris), 3: 428–38.

———. "Akhmatova i Nikolai Nedobrovo." In *Sochineniia* (Paris), 3: 371–418.

———. "K istorii russkoi literatury 1910-kh godov. Pis'ma N. V. Nedobrovo k B. V. Anrepu." *Slavica Hierosolymitana* 5–6 (1981): 425–66.

———. "N. S. Gumilev: Zhizn' i lichnost'." In N. S. Gumilev, *Sobranie sochinenii*, 4 vols. Edited by G. P. Struve and B. A. Filippov, 1: vii–lvi. Washington, D.C.: Victor Kamkin, 1962–68.

———. *Russian Literature Under Lenin and Stalin.* Norman: University of Oklahoma Press, 1971.

Struve, Nikita. "Vosem' chasov s Annoi Akhmatovoi." In *Sochineniia* (Munich), 2: 325–46.

Superfin, G. G., and R. D. Timenchik, eds. "Pis'ma Anny Akhmatovoi k V. Ia. Briusovu." *Zapiski otdela rukopisei vsesoiuznoi biblioteki imeni V. I. Lenina* 33 (Moscow, 1972): 272–79.

Taranovsky, Kiril. *Essays on Mandel'štam.* Cambridge, Mass.: Harvard University Press, 1976.

———. "O vzaimootnoshenii stikhotvornogo ritma i tematiki." In *American Contributions to the Fifth International Congress of Slavists*, vol. 1, Linguistic Contributions, 287–322. Slavistic Printings and Reprintings, no. 46. The Hague: Mouton, 1963.

———. "Zametka k stat'e M. B. Meilakha i V. N. Toporova 'Akhmatova i Dante'." *International Journal of Slavic Linguistics and Poetics* 16 (1973): 177–78.

———. "Zhizn' daiushchii golos: Zametka o Pasternake i Akhmatovoi." In *Voz'mi na radost': To Honour Jeanne van der Eng-Liedmeier*, edited by V. J. Amsenga et al., 149–56. Amsterdam: Slavic Seminar, 1980.

Terras, Victor, ed. *Handbook of Russian Literature.* New Haven, Conn.: Yale University Press, 1985.

———. *A Karamazov Companion.* Madison: University of Wisconsin Press, 1981.

Timasheff, N. S. *Religion in Soviet Russia, 1917–1942.* New York: Sheed & Ward, 1942. Reprint. Westport, Conn.: Greenwood Press, 1979.

Timenchik, R. D. "Akhmatova i Pushkin (Razbor stikhotvoreniia 'Smuglyi otrok brodil po alleiam')." In *Pushkinskii sbornik*, 124–31. Uchenye zapiski latviiskogo gosudarstvennogo universiteta, 106. Riga: Latviiskii gosudarstvennyi universitet, 1968.

———. "Akhmatova i Pushkin: Zametki k teme." In *Pushkinskii sbornik*, vol. 2, 32–55. Uchenye zapiski latviiskogo gosudarstvennogo universiteta, 215. Riga: Latviiskii gosudarstvennyi universitet, 1974.

———. "Akhmatova i Pushkin: Zametki k teme. III: 'Nevidimykh zvon kopyt'." In *Pushkin i russkaia literatura*, edited by I. I. Brunenietse et al., 119–33. Riga: Latviiskii gosudarstvennyi universitet, 1986.

———. "Akhmatova's Macbeth." Translated by Howard Goldman. *Slavic and East European Journal* 24, no. 4 (1980): 362–68.

———. "Avtometaopisanie u Akhmatovoi." *Russian Literature* 10/11 (1975): 213–26.

———. "K analizu 'Poemy bez geroia'." In *Materialy XXII studencheskoi konferentsii*, 121–23. Tartu: Tartuskii gosudarstvennyi universitet, 1967.

———. "Khram Premudrosti Boga: Stikhotvorenie Anny Akhmatovoi 'Shiroko raspakhnuty vorota'." *Slavica Hierosolymitana* 5–6 (1981): 297–317.

———. "K semioticheskoi interpretatsii 'Poemy bez geroia'." *Trudy po znakovym sistemam* 6 (Tartu, 1973): 438–42.

———. "Neopublikovannye prozaicheskie zametki Anny Akhmatovoi." *Izvestiia AN SSSR. Seriia literatury i iazyka* 43 (1984): 65–76.

———. "Neskol'ko primechanii k stat'e T. Tsiv'ian." *Trudy po znakovym sistemam* 5 (Tartu, 1971): 278–80.

———. "Otryvok iz perevoda *Makbeta*." *Literaturnoe obozrenie* 5 (1989): 18–21.

———. "Printsipy tsitirovaniia u Akhmatovoi v sopostavlenii s Blokom." In *Tezisy I Vsesoiuznoi (III) konferentsii "Tvorchestvo A. A. Bloka i russkaia kul'tura XX veka,"* edited by Z. G. Mints, 124–27. Tartu: Tartuskii gosudarstvennyi universitet, 1975.

———. "Rizhskii epizod v 'Poeme bez geroia' Anny Akhmatovoi." *Daugava* 80 (Feb. 1984): 113–21.

———. "Tekst v tekste u akmeistov." *Trudy po znakovym sistemam* 14 (Tartu, 1977): 65–75.

———. "Zametki ob akmeizme: I." *Russian Literature* 7/8 (1974): 23–46.

———. "Zametki ob akmeizme: II." *Russian Literature* 5 (1977): 281–300.

———. "Zametki ob akmeisme: III." *Russian Literature* 9 (1981): 175–90.

Timenchik, R. D., and A. V. Lavrov. "Materialy A. A. Akhmatovoi v rukopisnom otdele Pushkinskogo doma." In *Ezhegodnik rukopisnogo otdela Pushkinskogo doma, 1974*, ed. M. P. Alekseev et al., 53–82. Leningrad: Nauka, 1976.

Timenchik, R. D., V. N. Toporov, and T. V. Tsiv'ian. "Akhmatova i Kuzmin." *Russian Literature* 6 (1978): 213–305.

———. "Sny Bloka i 'Peterburgskii tekst' nachala XX veka." In *Tezisy I Vsesoiuznoi (III) konferentsii " Tvorchestvo A. A. Bloka i russkaia kul'-*

tura XX veka," edited by Z. G. Mints, 129–35. Tartu: Tartuskii gosu-darstvennyi universitet, 1975.

Tiutchev, F. I. *Sochineniia*. 2 vols. Moscow: Pravda, 1980.

Toporov, V. N. *Akhmatova i Blok*. Modern Russian Literature and Culture, 5. Berkeley, Calif.: Berkeley Slavic Studies, 1981.

———. "K otzvukam zapadnoevropeiskoi poezii u Akhmatovoi." In *Slavic Poetics: Essays in Honor of Kiril Taranovsky*, edited by Roman Jakobson et al., 467–75. The Hague: Mouton, 1973.

———. "K otzvukam zapadnoevropeiskoi poezii v Akhmatovoi (T. S. Eliot)." *International Journal of Slavic Linguistics and Poetics* 16 (1973): 157–76.

Toporov, V. N., and T. V. Tsiv'ian. "O nervalianskom podtekste v russkom akmeizme: Akhmatova i Mandel'shtam." *Russian Literature* 15 (1984): 29–50.

Tsekh poetov. Vol. 1. Berlin, 1922. Reprint ed., Ann Arbor, Mich.: Ardis, 1978.

Tsiv'ian, T. V. "Akhmatova i muzyka." *Russian Literature* 10/11 (1975): 173–212.

———. "Antichnye geroini—zerkala Akhmatovoi." *Russian Literature* 7/8 (1974): 103–19.

———. "Materialy k poetike Anny Akhmatovoi." *Trudy po znakovym sistemam* 3 (Tartu, 1967): 180–208.

———. "Zametki k deshifrovke 'Poemy bez geroia'." *Trudy po znakovym sistemam* 5 (Tartu, 1971): 255–80.

Tsvetaeva, Marina. "Poety s istoriei i poety bez istorii." Translated from the Serbo-Croatian by O. Kutasova. In Marina Tsvetaeva, *Sochineniia*. Vol. 2, 424–57. Moscow, 1980.

Tynianov, Iurii. *Arkhaisty i novatory*. Leningrad, 1929. Reprint ed., Munich: Wilhelm Fink, 1967.

———. *Poetika. Istoriia literatury. Kino*. Moscow: Nauka, 1977.

———. *Problema stikhotvornogo iazyka*. Leningrad, 1924. Reprint ed., The Hague: Mouton, 1963.

Uspensky, Boris. *A Poetics of Composition: The Structure of the Artistic Text*. Translated by Valentina Zavarin and Susan Wittig. Berkeley: University of California Press, 1973.

Vance, Eugene. "Roland and the Poetics of Memory." In *Textual Strategies: Perspectives in Post-Structural Criticism*, edited and with an introduction by J. V. Harari, 374–403. Ithaca, N.Y.: Cornell University Press, 1979.

Varnedoe, J. T. K. Introduction to *Modern Portraits: The Self and Others*. New York: Columbia University and the Wildenstein Gallery, 1976.

Venclova, Tomas. *Neustoichivoe ravnovesie: Vosem' russkikh poetiches-*

kikh tekstov. Yale Russian and East European Publications, 9. New Haven, Conn.: Yale Center for International and Area Studies, 1986.

Verheul, Kees. "Public Themes in the Poetry of Anna Akhmatova." *Russian Literature* 1 (1971): 73–112.

——. *The Theme of Time in the Poetry of Anna Akhmatova.* The Hague: Mouton, 1971.

Vernant, Jean Pierre. "Aspects mythiques de la mémoire en Grèce." *Journal de Psychologie* 56 (1959): 1–29.

——. *Mythe et pensée chez les grecs: Études de psychologie historique.* Paris: François Maspero, 1965.

Vilenkin, V. Ia. *V sto pervom zerkale.* Moscow: Sovetskii pisatel', 1987.

Vinogradov, V. V. *O poezii Anny Akhmatovoi (Stilisticheskie nabroski).* Leningrad, 1925. Reprinted in his *Poetika russkoi literatury,* 346–59. Moscow: Nauka, 1976.

Virgil. Vol. 1. *Eclogues, Georgics, Aeneid 1–6.* Loeb Classical Library. Translated by Rushton Fairclough. Rev. ed. Cambridge, Mass.: Harvard University Press, 1978. Vol. 2. *Aeneid 7–12. The Minor Poems.* Cambridge, Mass.: Harvard University Press, 1969.

Voogd-Stojanova, T. "Tsezura i slovorazdely v poeme A. Akhmatovoi *Rekviem.*" In *Dutch Contributions to the Seventh International Congress of Slavists,* edited by André Van Holk, 317–33. The Hague: Mouton, 1973.

Wellesz, Egon. *A History of Byzantine Music and Hymnography.* Oxford: Oxford University Press, 1949.

Woodward, James B. "Semantic Parallelism in the Verse of Akhmatova." *Slavic and East European Journal* 15, no. 4 (1971): 455–65.

Zhirmunskii, V. M. "Anna Akhmatova i Aleksandr Blok." *Russkaia literatura* 3 (Leningrad, 1970): 57–82.

——. *Bairon i Pushkin: Pushkin i zapadnye literatury.* Leningrad: Nauka, 1978.

——. *Tvorchestvo Anny Akhmatovoi.* Leningrad: Nauka, 1973.

——. *Voprosy teorii literatury. Stat'i 1916–1926.* Leningrad: Academia, 1928.

Index

In this index an "f" after a number indicates a separate reference on the next page, and an "ff" indicates separate references on the next two pages. A continuous discussion over two or more pages is indicated by a span of page numbers, e.g., "pp. 57–58." *Passim* is used for a cluster of references in close but not consecutive sequence.

Library of Congress Cataloging-in-Publication Data

Amert, Susan.
    In a shattered mirror / the later poetry of Anna
Akhmatova / Susan Amert.
       p.   cm.
    Includes bibliographical references and index.
    ISBN 0–8047–1982–9:
    1. Akhmatova, Anna Andreevna, 1889–1966—
Criticism and interpretation.   I. Title.
PG3476.A324Z535 1992
891.71'42—dc20

                             91–29985
                               CIP